Washington's
Wilderness Areas

THE COMPLETE GUIDE

TEXT BY
KAI HUSCHKE

PHOTOGRAPHY BY
CHARLES GURCHE

WESTCLIFFE PUBLISHERS
westcliffepublishers.com

We arrive in the outdoors unannounced,
and yet Mother Nature accepts us with
grace. Whether or not she tests our personal
limits, we are all equals in her presence.
The outdoors, especially nature that has been
beyond man's gross manipulation, is the
place I feel the most civilized, allowing
me to gain the clearest understanding
of my capacities and responsibilities as a
human being. I owe Mother Nature for
her teachings, but I owe my parents for
the introduction. To my father, who is still
within a physical distance to grasp, danke schön;
and to my mother, who is still nurturing
me with her energy from beyond, grazie.

Cascade below Mount Rainier, Mount Rainier National Park

4

ISBN: 1-56579-441-9
TEXT: Kai Huschke, © 2003. All rights reserved.
PHOTOGRAPHY: Charles Gurche, © 2003. All rights reserved.
MAP ILLUSTRATIONS: Rebecca Finkel, © 2003. All rights reserved.

EDITOR: Martha Ripley Gray
DESIGN AND PRODUCTION: Rebecca Finkel, F + P Graphic Design, Inc.; Ft. Collins, CO
PRODUCTION MANAGER: Craig Keyzer

PUBLISHED BY: Westcliffe Publishers, Inc.
P.O. Box 1261
Englewood, Colorado 80150
westcliffepublishers.com

PRINTED IN CHINA THROUGH: World Print, Ltd.

LIBRARY OF CONGRESS CATALOGING-IN-PUBLICATION DATA:
Huschke, Kai.
Washington's wilderness areas : the complete guide /
text by Kai Huschke; photography by Charles Gurche.
p. cm.
Includes bibliographical references (p.) and index.
ISBN 1-56579-441-9
1. Wilderness areas — Washington (State) —
Guidebooks. 2. Hiking — Washington (State) — Guidebooks.
3. Washington (State) — Guidebooks. I. Title.
QH76.5.W2H87 2003
917.97—dc21   2003041146

For more information about other fine books and calendars from Westcliffe Publishers, please contact your local bookstore, call us at 1-800-523-3692, write for our free color catalog, or visit us on the Web at westcliffepublishers.com.

PLEASE NOTE:
Risk is always a factor in backcountry and high-mountain travel. Many of the activities described in this book can be dangerous, especially when weather is adverse or unpredictable, and when unforeseen events or conditions create a hazardous situation. The author has done his best to provide the reader with accurate information about backcountry travel, as well as to point out some of its potential hazards. It is the responsibility of the users of this guide to learn the necessary skills for safe backcountry travel, and to exercise caution in potentially hazardous areas, especially on glaciers and avalanche-prone terrain. The author and publisher disclaim any liability for injury or other damage caused by backcountry traveling, or performing any other activity described in this book.

COVER: *Mount Rainier and Summit Lake from Clearwater Wilderness*
OPPOSITE: *Windy Ridge, Mount St. Helens National Volcanic Monument*

Table of Contents

Acknowledgments

THIS BOOK WOULD NOT EXIST if not for the existence of the
following places: Alpine Lakes, Boulder River, Buckhorn,
Clearwater, Colonel Bob, Glacier Peak, Glacier View, Goat
Rocks, Henry M. Jackson, Indian Heaven, Juniper Dunes,
Lake Chelan–Sawtooth, Mount Adams, Mount Baker,
Mount Rainier, Mount Skokomish, Mount St. Helens,
Noisy-Diobsud, Norse Peak, North Cascades, Olympic,
Pasayten, Salmo-Priest, San Juan, Tatoosh, The Brothers,
Trapper Creek, Washington Islands, Wenaha-Tucannon,
William O. Douglas, and Wonder Mountain. Thank you
for the hospitality and wisdom.

This book could not bear my name or take its
finished form if not for the dedicated stewardship of
Martha Ripley Gray. Deserving credit is also due Charles
Gurche; Linda Doyle and Jenna Browning at Westcliffe
Publishers; and the creative work of Rebecca Finkel. I am
also grateful for the efforts and kindness of Stacy Hanson
at Green Trails Maps.

Finally, this book did not arrive to receive the efforts
it has from the above-mentioned people by emanating solely
from my efforts. To my *amorosa,* Laura, my father, my sister
and brothers, and friends who helped encourage me, or at
the very least goaded me into completing this project, thank
you. I toast everyone, and shout my gratitude from all the
splendid wild places I have been, and those still to come.

Pelton Peak near Cascade Pass, Stephen T. Mather Wilderness

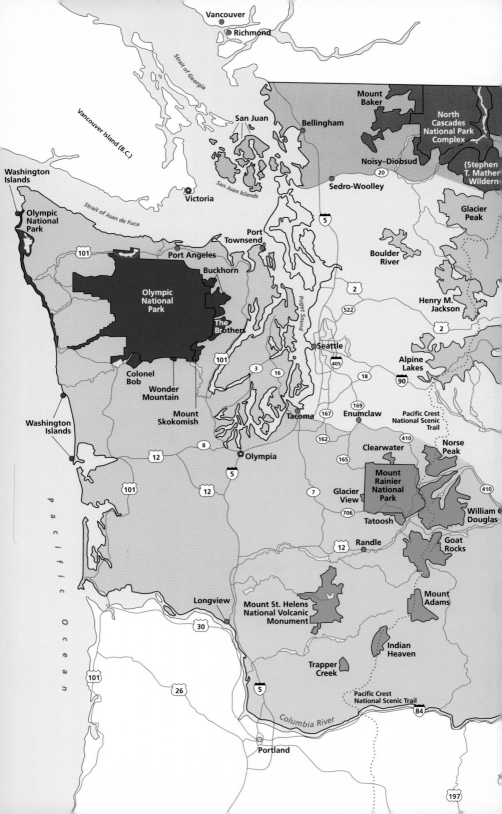

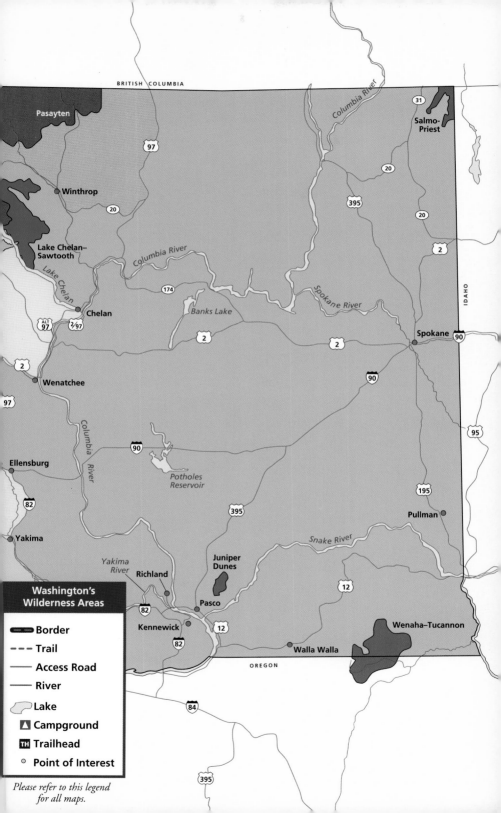

BRITISH COLUMBIA

Pasayten

Salmo-
Priest

31

97

20

Winthrop

20

395

20

Lake Chelan–
Sawtooth

2

Columbia River

Lake Chelan

174

Banks Lake

Spokane River

Spokane

90

IDAHO

ALT
97

2/97

Chelan

2

2

2

Wenatchee

90

97

95

Ellensburg

Columbia River

90

Potholes
Reservoir

195

82

395

Pullman

Yakima

Snake River

Yakima River

Juniper
Dunes

Richland

12

Pasco

Wenaha–Tucannon

82

Kennewick

12

82

Walla Walla

OREGON

84

395

Washington's
Wilderness Areas

▬▬▬▬ **Border**

----- **Trail**

——— **Access Road**

——— **River**

🗢 **Lake**

▲ **Campground**

TH **Trailhead**

○ **Point of Interest**

Please refer to this legend
for all maps.

The Wilderness Act, 1964

The Definition of Wilderness

"A wilderness, in contrast with those areas where man and his own works dominate the landscape, is hereby recognized as an area where the earth and its community of life are untrammeled by man, where man himself is a visitor who does not remain. An area of wilderness is further defined to mean in this Act an area of undeveloped Federal land retaining its primeval character and influence, without permanent improvements or human habitation, which is protected and managed so as to preserve its natural conditions and which (1) generally appears to have been affected primarily by the forces of nature, with the imprint of man's work substantially unnoticeable; (2) has outstanding opportunities for solitude or a primitive and unconfined type of recreation; (3) has at least five thousand acres of land or is of sufficient size as to make practicable its preservation and use in an unimpaired condition; and (4) may also contain ecological, geological, or other features of scientific, educational, scenic, or historical value."

View of Mount Adams from Goat Rocks Wilderness

Preface

ON ONE OF THE TRIPS taken to photograph for this book, my family and I hiked to a remote beach on the Olympic coast. The August afternoon was crystal clear. As we walked through a rainforest, the light passing through the canopy lit mossy places with an emerald glow. We felt miniature beneath the immense cedar, hemlock, and fir.

In a few miles, the trail emptied out to a broad beach, hemmed in with cliffs at either end. Out in the blue ocean, silhouetted sea stacks knifed into the horizon. Waves crashed on the shoreline, reflecting a glint of sunlight each time they curled. The wet, gravel-covered beach also reflected the dazzling sunbeams with hundreds of brilliant sparkles.

After settling into our campsite, we began to explore and discovered a community of campers like ourselves. The beach was a small meeting ground, and people were greeting one another, sharing their excitement about this place. Others just passed by with a smile and hello. One couple I met took my picture, which I received in the mail a couple weeks later.

No doubt, this wilderness coast summoned us, and then enriched us with its powerful presence. But it really doesn't matter where you are. The power may come from a star-filled desert sky, from the alpenglow on a high peak, or from the whisper of an aspen grove. And so we return to natural places, again and again.

Trying to translate the energy of wild places into a photograph is another story. How can a two-dimensional image reveal the true soul of the land? Well, of course, it can't. But at times, an image can spark something inside us, remind us of our connection to the land, and help us to remember what is at stake in its preservation. I have tried hard to communicate as best I can the inspiration that can be found in these wild places.

We are lucky in the Northwest. There is quite a good amount of wilderness, and other roadless lands may someday join the system. It has been quite a task to try and record these wild areas with bulky 4x5 camera equipment. I have actually only scratched the surface, which is good to know. It has been a great opportunity, and I have learned much along the way. Kai and I hope you may use this guide for a wondrous and passion-filled experience in these wild places.

—CHARLES GURCHE

Tide pools at twilight, Olympic National Park

Introduction

EVERY ONE OF US HAS SOME KNOWLEDGE of the natural world, and that collection of data molds our individual perceptions, influencing the types of relationships we have with nature. This knowledge is realized in experience, or more likely through many experiences that we then relive in actions, thoughts, and memories throughout our lives.

We select nature journeys, as I did on a backpacking trip to Buckskin Lake in the Pasayten Wilderness. Edging along a rough, narrow trail beneath Buckskin Ridge, I became so dazzled by the mountain vistas that I had to consciously keep my balance in check so as not to slide down the steep slope for hundreds of feet.

On another morning, after the coastal haze had dissolved into the sky and ocean, I walked in and around secluded coves and by treasure mounds of severely weathered driftwood beached on the shore. Entranced by the shapes these forest castaways had become, I lingered for over an hour in what seemed like a minute. Finally I made my way to the tide pools and jettylike collection of rocks that make up Strawberry Point along the Olympic coast.

At other times, the journeys select us. I once reached the summit of Colonel Bob just as the sun was spreading thick and red, beyond the lowland cloud cover, into the valleys and drainages as far I could see. I felt lucky being up so high alongside the Olympic Mountains to the northwest, until I realized that I was only up there on a day hike, light was fading by the minute, and I had failed to bring a headlamp. I ran down the east side of Colonel Bob into the dusk-filled Moonshine Flats below, and onward to the crest of the Quinault Ridge. Dusk was doing an excellent impression of dark as I tried to quickly reach the dry creek bed of Ziegler. I knew that I had to get to Ziegler Creek, where the trail would be easier to follow, if I wanted to have even the slightest chance of reaching the trailhead, still miles away.

When I arrived at the creek, darkness was in full force; nothing was visible except the grayish-black underside of the marine cloud layer settled above the treetops, which I focused on, neck craned and mouth agape. I even lost the trail three or four times and was forced to get down on my hands and knees to feel the difference between the trail and the forest floor.

Shortly before midnight, after falling off the trail twice, but having developed a pretty good technique of hiking by feel—sweeping the trail with my feet and tapping at the edges with my hiking poles—I arrived at the trailhead. I was amazed at how quickly the direness of the situation disappeared, just like the sun had hours before, and all because I felt safe in the sanctuary of an inanimate object, my camper van.

$\sim$

In his essay "The Etiquette of Freedom," poet and essayist Gary Snyder challenges conventionally accepted perspectives on the word "wild." Snyder challenges himself to imagine nature's definitions of the word, then compares these with cultural definitions as documented in the *Oxford English Dictionary (OED)*. "Wild" animals, according to the *OED*, are "not tame, undomesticated, unruly," Snyder notes; from nature's perspective, wild animals are "free agents, each with its own endowments,

Tarn, Pasayten Wilderness

living within natural systems." "Wild" land, per the *OED,* is "uninhabited, uncultivated"; for nature, a wildland is "a place where the original and potential vegetation and fauna are intact and in full interaction and the landforms are entirely the result of nonhuman forces." In the *OED,* "wild" behavior is "violent"; nature would parse this as "fiercely resisting any oppression." Such redefinitions can be instructive and put both hands deeper into the truth.

We must accept the offerings and hardships, both tangible and intangible, of Mother Nature whenever we choose to be a part of her world. Human beings are merely an element of nature, of wildness, as we interact with the systems of the wilderness areas we fleetingly visit.

Whatever journeys you select, and whatever journeys select you, I truly hope that *Washington's Wilderness Areas* in words and photographs will help you to enjoy the vast and diverse marvels these wilderness areas contain. Still, it's the experience and wisdom that each of us takes with us to these fabulous places in Washington that will truly define the levels of enjoyment and understanding that are earned while a guest in the wilderness.

Wilderness in Washington

THE WEEKEND IS APPROACHING. The month is August. The snowpack was light this past winter in the Olympics and the Cascades, but above normal in the Selkirk Mountains. The Skyline Ridge Trail in Olympic National Park has been cleared, giving hikers easier access to the spectacular high-line journey through heather and huckleberry parklands above the North Fork Quinault and Queets River valleys.

Farther to the east and north, wildflowers such as aster, cinquefoil, lupine, monkeyflower, paintbrush, and red columbine are peaking on the slopes of Tatoosh Ridge; in Bird Creek Meadows adjacent to the Mount Adams Wilderness; and in Horseshoe Basin in the Pasayten Wilderness. The weather outlook for the next three days, statewide, calls for sun-filled skies and above-average temperatures. People are deciding. Hikers, backpackers, kayakers, equestrians, birdwatchers, and climbers in cities like Seattle, Spokane, Kennewick, and Walla Walla, and in towns like Forks, Okanogan, Dusty, Chewelah, and Sunnyside—all are choosing where this weekend's adventure will take them.

Tents, motorboats, mobile homes, canoes, climbing gear, backpacks, and bicycles see action on the weekends, when most people of Washington recreate, venturing out into the so-called great outdoors. Most people like their outdoor excursions to mimic their everyday outings when it comes to convenience. They like ease in getting there, ease in being there, and ease in returning home early Sunday afternoon to beat the mad reverse exodus they were immersed in on Friday evening.

These "most people" also demand a certain level of aesthetics for the efforts of convenience. From Hurricane Ridge, Mount Olympus is close enough that you can cup your hands together to seemingly contain this magnificent, compact collection of glaciated peaks. Heather Meadows, just north of Mount Baker Ski Resort, is one of the grandest subalpine/alpine settings in all of Washington. With an easy drive to Paradise Lodge on the south side of Mount Rainier, and a walk of a half mile along an asphalt pathway, visitors can hope to feel the energy of Washington's tallest mountain (14,410 feet). Fight the traffic getting there, fight the traffic while there, and fight the traffic going home. Nature nicely packaged, presented, used, and returned, all in less than 48 hours.

The state of Washington, of course, has many choices for recreation destinations. There are county parks, state parks, national parks, wildlife refuges, beaches, national monuments, national recreation areas, national forests, land under the Bureau of Land Management, and wilderness areas, the topic of this guidebook. Washington currently has 30 federally designated wilderness areas (I have added to these the exceptional Mount St. Helens National Volcanic Monument). The majority are managed by the U.S. Forest Service. Three of the wilderness areas are managed by the National Park Service, two by the U.S. Fish and Wildlife Service, and one, Juniper Dunes, by the Bureau of Land Management. Washington is third (behind Alaska and California) in the amount of land under wilderness protection, at approximately 4.3 million acres, or almost 10 percent of the state's total acreage.

Several major geographic features define Washington, east to west: the Columbia River, Columbia Basin, Cascade Range (including six Cascade volcanoes), Puget Sound, and Olympic Peninsula. This short list hints at the incredible amount of diversity within the state—edged by coastal tide pools and capped by glaciated peaks—and within Washington's wilderness areas.

Not all the hikes listed in this book are strenuous, long-distance epics, but all of them will require effort, the pleasurable kind that hiking and backpacking provide. And you will find that you are just like the perplexed people mentioned earlier, trying to choose where in the state to travel to when trying to decide upon which wilderness area to discover.

The climate and life zones are quite varied. Rialto Beach is at sea level, while Desolation Peak in the North Cascades rises to 6,102 feet. Also varied is the geography: an abundance of lakes adorns The Enchantments in the Alpine Lakes Wilderness, while sand dunes and western juniper trees characterize the Juniper Dunes Wilderness. You can take short hikes to spectacular places like Minotaur Lake in the Henry M. Jackson Wilderness, or the miniature, subalpine parkland on Mount Ellinor in the Mount Skokomish Wilderness. You can also undertake long, multiday hikes like the Boundary Trail in the Pasayten Wilderness, or Skyline Ridge in Olympic National Park. In essence, you will have many choices for hikes after choosing which wilderness area to visit.

The wilderness areas are grouped into regions: Olympic Peninsula, North Cascades, Central Cascades, South Cascades, and Eastern Washington. The Olympic Peninsula region contains the most diversity, ranging from coastal grassland to rainforest and from subalpine to glacial. It also contains the only two wilderness areas closed to human visitation, San Juan and Washington Islands. The North Cascades region boasts the most spectacular peaks of Washington's Cascade Range, as well as the rolling, open world of the Pasayten highlands in the eastern Pasayten Wilderness.

Lakes, mountains, and creeks crowd the Central Cascades region. The Southern Cascades region is the domain of the major Cascade volcanoes Mounts Rainier, Adams, and St. Helens. East of the tall, rust-colored peaks on the eastern half of the William O. Douglas Wilderness begins the massive geographic indentation of the Columbia Basin. On its outer edges lie the east Cascade mountains of the Lake Chelan–Sawtooth Wilderness, the start of the Rockies in the Selkirk Mountains at the northeastern corner of the state, and the Blue Mountains that straddle the Oregon border in the southeastern corner.

The wilderness areas of Washington owe their existence to a collective philosophy that recognized and advocated nature for nature's sake. This perspective has been influential in Washington at least since the formation of Mount Rainier National Park in 1899. The state's first wilderness areas in Glacier Peak and Goat Rocks were designated in 1964, and a windfall of 24 wilderness designations passed in 1984. Conservation has fostered the growth of outdoor recreation, but a central dilemma remains: how to both allow and restrict human access at the same time. Obvious restrictions include the cessation of logging, mining, and grazing within wilderness areas. Obvious "allowables" are hiking, backpacking, and horseback riding. But these rules alone do not preserve nature.

The San Juan and Washington Islands Wilderness Areas exist for the sake of the flora and fauna that inhabit these islands, islets, reefs, rocks, and waters—and do not allow direct human intrusion. But the other 28 wilderness areas in Washington have been established for human consumption, if only sensory. Popularity is, however, usually an indication that we are getting too much of a good thing. Wilderness areas with high numbers of visitors, such as Alpine Lakes, Mount Rainier National Park, and Olympic National Park, are susceptible to damage in the form of overused trails, trashed campsites, vandalized parking areas, and noise pollution, to name a few. The Wilderness Act of 1964 was put in place to protect against such impacts.

We are a society influenced by visual appeal, and I am sure the pictures by Charlie Gurche in this book will convince nearly everyone who sees them to visit every wilderness area in the state. I would encourage that undertaking. There are times when doing so is the best way to achieve understanding: settling into camp up high at Bear Pass and watching the crater on Mount St. Helens swallow the last bit of the day's sunlight; counting the different wildflower species while enjoying a handful of huckle-berries on a hillside en route to the top of Green Mountain in the Glacier Peak Wilderness; or any number of other ineffable experiences in the wilderness.

Those people mentioned earlier who want "instant" nature gratification may have misguided methods or ideas, but they should still be commended for their efforts to venture beyond their front lawns and steering wheels and into some form of nature. I believe that conservation of current wilderness areas and establishment of future ones in Washington require people to visit these wild places. Visitors become supporters of the wilderness and can work to establish viable human guidelines for protection (as in the Wilderness Act) that will ultimately allow the more appropriate curator, Nature, to protect herself. It is all possible when done with respect: respect for the lakes, creeks, meadows, trails, campsites, and each other.

So don't delay; pack it up and head on out. The wilderness areas of Washington are expecting you!

Lupine meadow, Mount Rainier National Park

Washington's Life Zones

STAND AT 1,000 FEET IN ELEVATION in Juniper Dunes and you'll see rye grass, balsamroot, and western juniper trees. Stand at 1,000 feet on the Olympic Peninsula and you might be surrounded by western red cedar, giant ferns, and salmonberry. Timberline on Mount Rainier won't be the same as timberline on Mount Adams. The wilderness areas of Washington range from sea level to 14,410 feet, which contributes substantially to the variability between the different life zones. Other influences are wind, precipitation, soil moisture retention, geography, latitude, and location. What is location? In Washington, that means where a wilderness area lies in relation to two major mountain ranges, which dramatically affect the weather you can expect.

Weather moves predominantly from west to east in Washington, originating out of the North Pacific (in winter, some cold fronts also move south from Canada). These movements are neither steady nor equitable in their distribution of rain and snow over Washington. The first obstacle, or weather interrupter, is the Olympic Mountains. The west side of these mountains receives 140 inches of precipitation a year, more than twice the amount that the east side receives (60 inches). Yet the dry, dunelike environment of the San Juan Islands receives an extremely low amount of precipitation for the region, just 26 inches. The islands provide an environment amenable to the growth of Rocky Mountain juniper trees, a species normally found much farther to the east and south. This effect is called being in the "rain shadow," which is the identical effect caused by the state's second major weather interrupter, the Cascade Range.

The western slope of Washington's Cascades receives some 100 inches of precipitation a year—far more than the eastern slopes and beyond, where precipitation averages closer to 40 inches. (An exception is the Salmo-Priest Wilderness, in the Rockies of far northeastern Washington, which sees on average over 50 inches of precipitation.) Precipitation in the Wenaha-Tucannon Wilderness east of the divide is registered at just 32 inches.

In the following rough outline, please note that these life zones are not in reality as neatly separated by elevation levels but in fact mixed and overlapping. Also, you'll find that the tree mix will vary from wilderness area to wilderness area. What holds true is that the forests of Washington, and of the greater Northwest, are coniferous dominant, not hardwood. Not for nothing is Washington called the Evergreen State. Other trees worth mentioning besides those that are climax dominant are Alaska yellow cedar, aspen, noble fir, Pacific yew, western larch, and western red cedar.

Animal and plant life is accordingly diverse and plentiful, with everything from starfish and seals to flying ants and grizzly bears, mussels to heather, salmon to Dolly Varden trout, Sitka spruce to whitebark pine. There is great variability, variety, and complexity to each of the life zones. They have been presented here merely to provide the most basic introduction to the different life zones, or "neighborhoods," you will find when venturing in Washington's wilderness areas.

Oceanside Intertidal Zone: Sea Level

This zone has four distinct levels: spray, high, middle, and low. When the tide is low or even negative, the most interesting to explore of the exposed tide pools are in the middle and low zones. Sea creatures to observe in the various zones include anemone, California mussel, finger limpet, gooseneck barnacle, ochre sea star, purple shore crab, sea urchin, and starfish.

Humid Transition Zone: Sea Level to 1,500 Feet

Needing a high amount of moisture, Sitka spruce is climax dominant along the coastal lowlands. Moving higher, the Pacific Northwest rainforest consists of sun-loving Douglas fir and the more shade-tolerant western hemlock. Streamside broadleaf trees include bigleaf maple, alder, cottonwood, and dogwood. Understory consists of fern, moss, salal, and salmonberry.

Canadian Zone: 1,500 to 4,500 Feet

The west side of the Cascades is dominated by western hemlock, western red cedar, and Pacific silver fir. On the east side of the Cascades you'll find lodgepole pine, Douglas fir, and Engelmann spruce. The understory consists of evergreen shrubs and huckleberry.

Hudsonian Zone: 4,500 Feet to Timberline

The west side is dominated by mountain hemlock and subalpine fir, the east side by subalpine fir and whitebark pine.

Arctic-Alpine Zone: Above Timberline

In this zone, stunted trees are outnumbered by blankets of heather, wildflowers, and patches of huckleberry. Beyond this plant life zone, the world is left primarily to snowfields, glaciers, and rock.

Arid Transition Zone: 100 to 6,000 Feet, East Slope of the Cascade Divide

This variable, widespread zone occurs in the driest areas of the state. It is sometimes called the Ponderosa Pine Zone for the dominant tree species in woodland sites. Understory consists of Oregon grape, sagebrush, snowberry, and wild currant.

Hiking in Washington

OLYMPIC NATIONAL PARK IS PERHAPS the most diverse wilderness area in Washington. Coastal hikes, rainforest strolls, subalpine wildflower meadows to lunch in, and glacier climbs are all possible within one place. The park is an example of the range of environments you can venture into in wilderness areas all across Washington. It is also thrilling to think about and discover that Washington has an amazing diversity in its wilderness areas. As each wilderness area has a particular geography, elevation range, flora and fauna, weather, and water availability, so each requires different preparations and expectations.

Start by finding out about conditions—trails, campsites, weather, road access, and permits, among others—in advance. The best people to contact are backcountry rangers and trail crew personnel. If they are unavailable, front-desk personnel should have fairly up-to-date information supplied by the backcountry rangers. Second, don't set out without informing a friend or family member of your plans: where you are going, who is going with you, and how long you plan to be away. The keys to any great wilderness adventure are knowing current conditions and taking a general knowledge of safe and proper hiking with you. The information below will help to enhance the quality of your visits into Washington's wilderness.

Passes and Permits

All the wilderness areas, with the exception of the national parks, island wilderness areas (no public access), and Juniper Dunes, are located within national forests and require a Northwest Forest Pass, which allows you to park a vehicle at trailheads. Every ranger district sells the pass, which can be bought per day or annually. The majority of the money goes back to the district in which the pass is purchased, to be used for trail and trailhead facility maintenance. Mount Rainier and Olympic National Parks have separate entry fees. Most trailheads will have either a sign-in sheet or a permit requirement. Additional backcountry camping permits are required for the following areas: Mount Rainier National Park, North Cascades National Park Complex, Mount Margaret Backcountry in Mount St. Helens National Volcanic Monument, The Enchantments in Alpine Lakes Wilderness, and Olympic National Park. Each area has slightly different rules for obtaining a permit, so be sure to contact the corresponding ranger districts or information centers for details (see Appendix C, p. 246).

Leave No Trace

These are principles to respect when in wilderness areas or anywhere out in nature. This code is meant to enhance both your own personal enjoyment and that of others, today and in future generations. I have freely organized and presented here what I think are the most crucial points of the Leave No Trace outdoor ethics; please also see the full discussion at www.lnt.org.

Old-growth Sitka spruce, Hoh Rain Forest, Olympic National Park

Plan ahead and prepare
- Be versed in and aware of any special regulations for the area you want to visit (permits, closures, dog allowances, etc.).
- Avoid "peak" visitation times, and travel in small groups.

Use Care on Trails and at Campsites
- Stay on designated trails even during wet periods, when it is tempting to walk around the muddy sections onto the ground cover or through the bushes. Also, don't cut corners; hiking isn't a race.
- Camp in designated sites or in sites that have obviously been used before.
- Camp at least 200 feet from water sources (lakes, ponds, rivers, streams, etc.).
- Wash yourself and dishes at least 200 feet from a water source, preferably with a biodegradable soap. Another good habit to develop is to strain and scatter dishwater.
- If possible, avoid building fires. If fires are permitted and fire rings are available, use them.
- If you carry it in, carry it out. Trash, macro and micro, needs to be taken out. Some might even suggest packing out solid waste, but using pit toilets or proper disposal methods ("cat hole": 6 to 8 inches deep, buried and covered, and at least 200 feet from a water source) will suffice. Toilet paper and hygiene products should be packed out.
- Basically avoid or minimize the impact to trails, campsites, historic sites, and any protected areas with which you come in contact.

Respect Wildlife and Other Visitors
- Simply look; don't touch or make contact with any wildlife.
- Be prepared to be friendly. Smile, say "hello," and be courteous to other hikers and backpackers. They are in the wilderness for the same reasons you are: beauty, serenity, and escape. Don't spoil your own outing or another's by improper behavior to other people, wildlife, or the environment.

Dogs and Horses

The national parks—Mount Rainier, Olympic, and North Cascades—plus Mount St. Helens National Volcanic Monument and The Enchantments in Alpine Lakes, do not allow dogs. The parks also have a restricted number of trails that horses are allowed on. Dogs are allowed in other wilderness and recreation areas. If you bring dogs, make sure to bury their feces the same way you would your own; keep dogs under control by leash or voice command; keep them on the trail; do not allow them to chase wild birds or animals; and keep them quiet and at a distance from others who do not want them nearby. Besides the companionship and sense of security a dog can bring, especially for female backpackers and hikers, dogs seem to smile at being in the wilderness, just like people.

Most equestrians are responsible trail users who respect the rules of tying or picketing horses at least 200 feet away from any water source; feeding horses only

Yellow fawn lilies blanket Heather Pass, Stephen T. Mather Wilderness

processed feeds; and keeping horses from overgrazing areas around horse camps. If you should come across horses on the trail, make sure to make your presence known by speaking. This will obviously alert the rider, but it will also cue the horse that there is a human nearby and not some wild animal. Make sure to give the right-of-way to the rider.

If you are hiking along a slope, step off the trail downhill. The first thing this does is to remove you from the horse's path, which requires a wide berth. Second, if the horse does get spooked, it will veer away from the hiker, moving uphill, which will allow the rider to gain control easier than if the horse heads downhill, picking up speed with each stride. We all like the wilderness, including dogs and horses, so be prepared to share.

Drinking Water

You have a few choices with drinking water. The easiest solution is to pack in water from a reliable source. For a day hike this is feasible, but for an overnight or multiday hike this is unrealistic. Instead, you will need to find water sources, such as rivers, streams, lakes, springs, or snowfields. Unless you know with absolute certainty a water source is uncontaminated or are fond of intestinal pain and discomfort, go ahead and drink the water straight (untreated); otherwise I suggest treating the water by boiling, filtering, or using tablets to make it potable.

Weather

With so much variability in geography and elevation, Washington's wilderness areas can be hiked year-round. However, nearly every wilderness area is subject to four seasons; this can translate into heavy snowpacks for many of the high-country areas. Typically the snows melt off in the lower elevations and east of the Cascade divide first. Trails can be accessible by early or mid-June. West of the divide in the higher elevations, trails normally don't become snow-free until the middle of July. Of course these times vary depending on snowpack levels and the weather mix (precipitation and temperature) during spring and early summer. Normally, from mid-July to the beginning of October, the weather is ideal, with warm temperatures and little rainfall. However, snowfall in September and even in August is possible at higher elevations. Pack accordingly and contact the regional ranger district for both trail conditions and the local weather forecast before heading out.

Hazards

Since it largely results from a lack of proper fitness or knowledge, most backcountry harm is self-inflicted. Muscle soreness, sprained ankles, scratches, dehydration, bruises, blisters, hypothermia, and good old fatigue represent the majority of the hazards you can expect when exploring the wilderness. Horseflies, ticks, and mosquitoes are the only creatures that might do any attacking. Encounters with wild animals are very rare and shouldn't preoccupy people or prevent them from hiking. Basically, use common sense.

Some natural hazards do require a measure of caution: tidal movements along the Olympic coast, creek and river fords during high water, rockfall on steep switch-back slopes, down trees across the trails, and the obstacles of glacier travel, for which an ice ax and other mountaineering equipment can be necessary. Another hazard to avoid is getting lost. Make sure to carry the Ten Essentials listed on p. 31, and don't forget your map and compass.

Equipment

This subject is more about personal preferences than definites. But some equipment basics should be considered carefully, such as footwear, clothing, and packs. I believe comfort is number one, followed by durability.

- If your footwear doesn't fit properly, hiking can be a nightmare. Also, if the footwear isn't rugged enough for rocky and rough trails, the chances for turned ankles and blisters increases dramatically. Look for both low-top and high-top hiking footwear.
- Choose socks with a wool/synthetic blend, which hold their shape over multiple days, dry quickly, add warmth whether dry or wet, and are far more comfortable than cotton or synthetic socks.

Mount Baker at sunset, Mount Baker Wilderness

Full moon above blasted forest, Mount St. Helens National Volcanic Monument

- Choose clothes that will breathe, dry quickly, and provide warmth. Stay away from 100 percent cotton clothing. Also, loose, comfortably fitting pants, shorts, and tops will make hiking more enjoyable.

- Choose a backpack that fits your body type. This will require visiting an outdoor retailer and having an expert fit you. If you plan on spending time in the wilderness, it is worth the effort and extra money for a quality pack, plus it will last longer than an inexpensive one.

- A final thing I can recommend is hiking with a stick or, better yet, hiking or ski poles. The poles keep your arms active, help support the extra weight of a backpack, and help to brace your body in the event of a slip or trip when hiking. Also, your legs and body will be thankful for the help.

Key Rules and Regulations for Wilderness Areas

- Maximum party size is 12, although smaller groups are recommended.
- Maximum length of camping at any one site is generally 14 days.
- No motorized vehicles or equipment, or other mechanical means of transportation including bicycles and hang gliders, are allowed.
- Firearms are not allowed in national parks. Where allowed, restrictions on where and when they can be discharged apply.
- Collecting cultural artifacts or disturbing archaeological or pictograph sites is prohibited.

Ten Essentials

1. Maps/Trail Information: Take this book or make a photocopy of the map and trail information for the selected hike from this book. You could also carry the corresponding Green Trails or USGS map(s) for greater detail. Keep maps and trail information from the elements by securing them in a plastic bag or sleeve.

2. Compass: Learn how to use one, and make sure the declination is set for the area you are in.

3. Flashlight/Headlamp: Either will work when artificial light is needed. A headlamp is more convenient because it allows your hands to be free. Be sure to pack an extra bulb and batteries. Another tip: Reverse the batteries inside the flashlight/headlamp so if the on/off switch is accidentally bumped, the batteries won't be drained.

4. Extra Food: Carry an extra day's worth of food. High protein/energy bars will suffice.

5. Extra Clothing: This includes items to help you warm up and others to keep you dry. These will be useful both for day hikes and for those times when you are inevitably caught in the wilderness for longer than you expected.

6. Sunglasses: These come in handy if you expect to travel across snow. If you plan on extensive snow travel, then glacier glasses are the recommended eyewear to pack.

7. First-Aid Kit: Either purchase a good prepackaged kit or build one. Having first-aid training will be extremely helpful in situations where more serious injuries occur.

8. Knife: A multi-tool is preferred. Take the old, faithful pocket knife or a more versatile multi-tool.

9. Matches/Lighter: Take both. Carry waterproof matches, waterproof striker, and lighter in a waterproof container.

10. Fire Starter: These include candles, solid chemical fuels, or compressed wood chip balls.

How to Use This Guide

THIS BOOK IS MEANT AS AN INTRODUCTION to the wilderness areas of Washington, including three vast national parks and one nonwilderness area with wildland attributes, the Mount St. Helens National Volcanic Monument. I've included descriptions of hikes in 27 of these 31 areas. Those without trail descriptions are the San Juan and Washington Islands, which have almost no access; and Wonder Mountain and Juniper Dunes, which are only accessible by cross-country travel. Large areas like Alpine Lakes, Pasayten, and Glacier Peak have multiple hikes listed, whereas smaller areas like Colonel Bob, Indian Heaven, and Boulder River have descriptions for only one hike. Hikes were chosen to give as wide as possible a representation of the features of each area, as well as a variety of commitment levels (day hike, destination, loop, multiday backpack). The hikes are in essence suggested itineraries for visiting a wilderness area in Washington.

Along with a variety of hiking distances and challenges, you'll find statistics for each hike: distance, elevation range, total elevation gain, difficulty, and corresponding Green Trails Maps or USGS maps. The trail information is comprehensive enough to indicate steep sections, water crossings, campsites, noteworthy features, and mileage points along the trail. I have tried to give a basic representation of what to expect both with regard to both physical challenge and, to a degree, scenic quality.

The maps in this book have been created with all the necessary information to access and complete each hike. For greater detail on each hike, or for additional information, the corresponding Green Trails Maps or USGS maps are listed as well. I chose to primarily reference Green Trails Maps, because of their compact size, ease of reading, numerous listed geographical features, clean representation of vegetated zones, and inclusion of distances from marked points. Green Trails Maps and USGS maps are available at most ranger districts, outdoor stores, and map or travel stores.

Hikes are rated by difficulty: Easy, Moderate, or Strenuous. I have tried to assign ratings to each hike based upon the "average" hiker. Still, it is inevitable that some hikes will be underrated and some overrated. I did not list the number of hours it will take to complete a hike because of the varying pace of each hiker. If you hike enough in a variety of terrain, you learn how much time will be needed for a moderate 7-mile hike.

Distance in the mountains is a difficult thing to measure. Rockslides, down trees, creek crossings, exposed tree roots, snow travel, and trail reroutings make it impossible to gauge exact distances. So the distances given for the hikes reflect my best attempt to be accurate utilizing maps, guidebooks, and my internal gauge, which I believe has been well tuned from thousands of miles of hiking in the mountains. There will be discrepancies between this book, Green Trails Maps and USGS maps, other guidebooks, and you, with respect to trail length. However, the distances listed in this book should be within one- to three-tenths of a mile of the "actual" distance. Mileage is usually total miles up to that point in the hike. A good rule to follow when hiking is to go at a pace that can be sustained comfortably for the entire day, even if you have only set off for a 5-mile hike.

Arnica, lupine, and aster, Mount Rainier National Park

For each wilderness area, you'll find information on geographic and human history, current geography, plant and wildlife varieties, vitals (size, federal management, special permits, and the like), and, most importantly, the types of hikes available in each wilderness area. The hikes themselves have been selected as representative of the environments within each wilderness and with an eye to a variety of abilities, so as to encourage everyone to visit.

At the end of each hike description is a paragraph on road access. This information normally originates from the nearest ranger district or town to the trailhead, and includes distances, routes, road surfaces, parking facilities, and landmarks if helpful. Forest Service roads are noted by the abbreviation "FR" and a road number, such as FR 17 or FR 6500. An easy way to keep track of accumulating mileage is to set your vehicle's odometer to zero at the point of origin listed in the road access description. Mileage is usually total miles up to that point in the drive.

Be sure to keep two things in mind when hiking in Washington's wilderness areas. First, most areas have more trails to explore than are listed in this book, and I encourage you to research individual regions or wilderness areas for information on further hikes. Second, the hikes in this guide can be approached and carried out in any manner. This means doing a loop hike in reverse of what is written, hiking in just 8 miles of a 20-mile hike, or taking off on a completely different trail after hiking one found in this book. What is most important is making the time to venture out and enjoy!

Abbreviations Used in This Book

BLM	Bureau of Land Management
CR	County Road
FR	U.S. Forest Service Road
FWS	U.S. Fish and Wildlife Service
NCNPC	North Cascades National Park Complex
NF	National Forest
NP	National Park
NRA	National Recreation Area
NVM	National Volcanic Monument
NWR	National Wildlife Refuge
PCNST	Pacific Crest National Scenic Trail
RD	Ranger District (U.S. Forest Service)
RNA	Research Natural Area
US	Federal highway (preceding number)
WA	Washington; Washington State Highway (preceding number)
WIC	Wilderness Information Center (National Park Service)

Alpine meadow, Goat Rocks Wilderness

Olympic Peninsula

Soft, crumbly peaks, sharp ridgelines, and steep river valleys—shaped by both glacial retreat and the erosional knifing of rivers—radiate from the heart of the glaciated Olympics within Olympic National Park. The collision of what is now known as Mount Olympus and the Bailey and Burke Ranges, the Elwha Basin, inner and outer northeast peaks, northern ridges, and southeastern crags formed what we now call the Olympic Mountains. Major rivers like the Elwha, Gray Wolf, Dosewallips, Quinault, and Hoh spiral out from the Olympics in various directions, to the Strait of Juan de Fuca, Puget Sound, and the Pacific Ocean. High points beyond 7,969-foot Mount Olympus include Mount Angeles to the north, Mount Deception to the east, and Mount Duckabush to the south. High-mountain wildflower meadows such as those at Sol Duc Park, and beautiful cirque lakes such as those in Royal Lakes Basin, cover the ridges and high points.

To the west and sinking into the lowlands in all directions, the environments change to the classic Pacific Northwest rainforest of giant ferns; moss; and massive cedar, fir, and hemlock trees up to 15 feet in diameter and 300 feet high. West of the Olympic Mountains weather divide, this ecosystem thrives along the river bottoms such as the Hoh River Valley. An incredible display of rhododendron bushes lines the trails to the east, such as those on Jupiter Ridge in The Brothers Wilderness.

With 160 inches of annual precipitation, the Olympic Mountains are hammered by rain and snow. By contrast, the San Juan Wilderness north-northeast of Port Angeles sees on average only 26 inches of annual precipitation due to its location in the Olympics' rain shadow. This means that vegetation on many islands, islets, and rocks turns golden in the summer, and arid tree species like Rocky Mountain juniper thrive there.

Along the eastern and southeastern boundaries of the interior of Olympic National Park are five smaller wilderness areas ranging from the 2,349-acre Wonder Mountain Wilderness to the 44,258-acre Buckhorn Wilderness. Of these, only the Colonel Bob Wilderness lies outside of the Olympic Mountains' rain shadow, but even so, water is often scarce by mid-August. The terrain in these wilderness areas is mainly rugged mountains, highlighted by Mount Ellinor in the Mount Skokomish Wilderness, Mount Jupiter in The Brothers Wilderness, and the summit of Colonel Bob. Trails

Marymere Falls, Olympic National Park

in these areas parallel creeks and rivers to reach destinations like Mildred Lakes in the Mount Skokomish Wilderness, or Silver Lakes high in the Buckhorn Wilderness.

Lastly, stretching over 100 miles from Cape Flattery to past Copalis Rock (itself part of the Washington Islands Wilderness) is the Olympic coastline. Sea stacks, headlands, coves, sandy beaches, tide pools, driftwood piles, incredible bird and marine mammal life, and Sitka spruce forests define this highly unique and sparsely inhabited region. Sixty miles of this coast are accessible in the beach portion of Olympic National Park.

Moss-covered bigleaf maple, Hoh Rain Forest, Olympic National Park

The Brothers Wilderness

Duckabush River

THERE IS A PLACE where the supreme god of the ancient Romans, the gatekeeper of Christian heaven, and a monastic giant all reside together; this place is called The Brothers Wilderness. Perhaps slightly misleading but still true enough, with Mount Jupiter at 5,701 feet in the northern portion of the wilderness, St. Peter's Dome at 4,490 feet in the center, and The Brothers at 6,866 feet in the southern portion, on the border with Olympic National Park. Okay, The Brothers isn't truly a giant, but it is still the high point of a wilderness that consists of steep ridges of western hemlock, red cedar, Douglas

LOCATION: Bordering Olympic National Park south of the Dosewallips River, approximately 50 miles north of Olympia

SIZE: 17,239 acres

ELEVATION RANGE: 600 to 6,866 feet

MILES OF TRAIL: Approximately 13

TREES AND PLANTS: Douglas fir, mountain hemlock, Pacific silver fir, western hemlock, western red cedar, beargrass, blueberry, devil's club, heather, huckleberry, juniper bush, kinnikinnick, phlox, white trillium

WILDLIFE: Black bear, black-tailed deer, cougar, elk, mountain goat, golden eagle

ADMINISTRATION: Olympic NF, Hood Canal RD, 360-877-5254

BEST SEASON: Summer through fall

fir, and mountain hemlock, leading up from the deep-cut Duckabush River drainage to the north to Mount Jupiter, and to The Brothers to the south.

Two river-bottom trails and one ridgeline trail to the summit of Mount Jupiter add up to the approximately 13 miles of trail that access the 17,239-acre wilderness. The hike along Jupiter Ridge is filled with rhododendron bushes that bloom in May and June. You can follow Jupiter Ridge to the crusty rock summit of Mount Jupiter, which comes complete with views of the big Cascade volcanoes to the east and the Olympics to the west. The Brothers are a favorite destination of climbers wanting the challenge of reaching its twin peaks. The Brothers Wilderness is, I suppose, the pious one of the group of five wilderness areas protecting the southern and eastern boundaries of Olympic National Park.

DAY HIKE: MOUNT JUPITER
One-Way Distance: 7.1 miles
Elevation Range: 2,000 to 5,700 feet
Total Elevation Gain: 3,700 feet
Difficulty: Easy to strenuous
USGS Map: Mount Jupiter

This hike is a nice, easy glide for most the way, with a short rocket blast to the summit of Mount Jupiter. A moderate mile-long climb up a series of switchbacks from the trailhead will take you to a pleasant stretch along a mix of open and forested slope, just below a ridgeline, decorated with blooming rhododendron bushes from the end of May through June.

The trail slips from the south side of the ridge to the north at about mile 2.6, makes a short climb starting at mile 3 to return to the south side of the ridge, and resumes its gradual incline until mile 4. From here it climbs to the wilderness boundary at mile 4.5 and begins to wrap around the base of Mount Jupiter past a nice patch of huckleberry bushes to the north side of Mount Jupiter. At mile 5.5, make a steep push up a rocky meadow section of heather, juniper, kinnikinnick, and other wildflowers, to reach the summit of Mount Jupiter at mile 7.1.

The Brothers

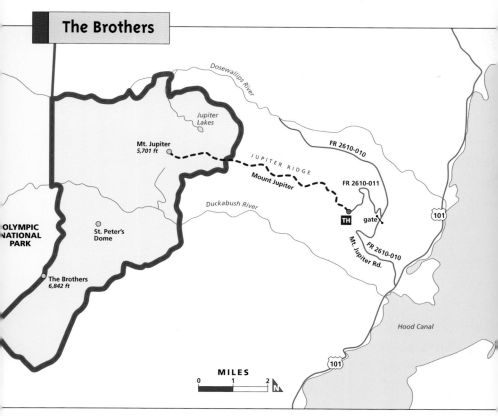

All of Washington's big Cascade volcanoes are visible: Baker, Rainier, St. Helens, and Adams, as well as the east side of the mountainous mass that makes up the Olympics, and other vantages only afforded from such a marvelous summit. Be sure to pack water.

Approximately 22 miles north of Hood Canal RD on US 101, turn left (west) onto Mount Jupiter Road (FR 2610-010). Take the left fork 0.5 mile up, following signs for the Mount Jupiter Trailhead. The road is quite rough and curvy all the way to the trailhead. Many spur roads lead from the main road, so be sure to keep following signs for Mount Jupiter. At 2.5 miles take the left fork onto FR 2610-011. A short distance beyond is a gate, which is locked from October 1 to May 1. The trailhead is another 3.5 miles.

2 Buckhorn Wilderness

View of Buckhorn Wilderness from Mount Townsend

LOCATION: 6 miles west of Quilcene and off US 101 approximately 38 miles southeast of Port Townsend

SIZE: 44,258 acres

ELEVATION RANGE: 1,000 to 7,134 feet

MILES OF TRAIL: 67

TREES AND PLANTS: Alpine fir, Douglas fir, dwarf juniper, western hemlock, beargrass, bunchberry, huckleberry, rhododendron

WILDLIFE: Black bear, black-tailed deer, bobcat, cougar, bald eagle, northern spotted owl

ADMINISTRATION: Olympic NF, Quilcene RD, 360-765-2200

BEST SEASON: Lowlands, year-round; Highlands, summer until early fall

SPLIT BY THE DUNGENESS RIVER, and contained by the Gray Wolf River to the north and Dosewallips River to the south, the Buckhorn Wilderness is the biggest of the five wilderness areas that border the eastern and southeastern sections of the interior of Olympic National Park. The smaller northern section, some 14,000 acres, is mostly a lowland environment following the path of the Gray Wolf River. The larger southern section, at some 30,000 acres, is bottom heavy with 6,900-foot-plus Iron, Buckhorn, Warrior, and Constance peaks running north to south, and lateral ridges above Boulder Creek and the Tunnel Creek Valley, which stretches to the east.

Some of the 67 miles of trail reach high points in the north and south sections of the

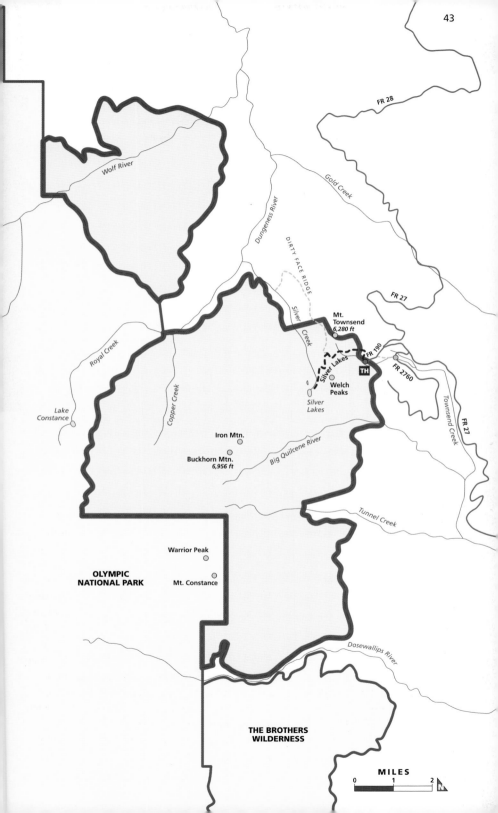

FR 28

Wolf River

Gold Creek

Dungeness River

DIRTY FACE RIDGE

FR 27

Royal Creek

Silver Creek

Mt.
Townsend
6,280 ft

FR 190

TH

FR 2760

Silver Lakes

Welch
Peaks

Copper Creek

Silver
Lakes

Townsend Creek

FR 27

Lake
Constance

Iron Mtn.

Buckhorn Mtn.
6,956 ft

Big Quilcene River

Tunnel Creek

Warrior Peak

OLYMPIC
NATIONAL PARK

Mt. Constance

Dosewallips River

THE BROTHERS
WILDERNESS

MILES

0   1   2

N

wilderness. Mount Townsend in the north, at 6,280 feet, has a broad ramping slope of a summit complete with wildflower meadows of avalanche lily, heather, phlox, and red columbine. The Tunnel Creek–Dosewallips River Divide in the south rises to 5,050 feet. Still, most trails stay in the lowlands along rivers, so expect a rich and diverse world of devil's club, ferns, huckleberry, salmonberry, and an abundance of rhododendron—the highlight of the east side of the Olympic Peninsula.

DAY OR DESTINATION HIKE: SILVER LAKES
One-Way Distance: 5.2 miles
Elevation Range: 2,900 to 5,600 feet
Total Elevation Gain: 2,700 feet
Difficulty: Moderate
Green Trails Map: Tyler Peak No. 136

The hike begins on the Upper Mount Townsend Trail through a coronation of rhododendrons up long switchbacks within a stand of taller trees. Slightly past 1 mile in, the trail reaches a meadow and huckleberry slope and begins climbing more steeply to Camp Windy at mile 2.5. Reenter the trees and reach the trail junction with Silver Lakes Trail at mile 3.

The Silver Lakes Trail veers to the left (southwest), climbing to a saddle at mile 3.2 with a fantastic view across the Silver Creek Valley and to the north of Dirty Face Ridge, before making five long switchbacks downhill as you transition from open slope to forest. Once in the trees, a short uphill climb leads to the larger of the two Silver Lakes at mile 5.2. Silver Lake lies in the bottom of a basin, with several campsites, ringed by a collection of nice peaks. The smaller lake is downhill to the north.

From the Hood Canal RD in Quilcene, travel south on US 101 for 1 mile to Penny Creek Road and turn right. Stay left at the "Y" (2.4 miles) where, in a short distance, the road will become FR 27. At 13 miles the road passes the Lower Mount Townsend Trailhead via FR 2760. Continue on FR 27 another 1.2 miles. Turn left onto a road marked "Service Road; Dead End" at 14.2 miles. The road is officially FR 190, but the road marker is nearly impossible to see. You'll reach the parking area and trailhead for Silver Lakes and Mount Townsend at 15.2 miles.

Colonel Bob Wilderness 3

Pete's Creek

ROBERT INGERSOLL WAS A LAWYER, POLITICAL ACTIVIST, ARDENT agnostic, and a colonel and commanding officer of the 11th Illinois volunteer cavalry during the Civil War. The history behind the association of his name with a mountain and later with a whole wilderness is unclear, but the story goes that an admirer of Ingersoll's had an opportunity to pay his respects by naming the mountain after him. What is definitely known is that Ingersoll, aka. Colonel Bob, was a flatlander. Like other eminent persons for whom other Washington peaks were named—Rainier, Baker, and Adams, to name a few— Ingersoll never set foot in the wildland named for him.

LOCATION: Directly northeast of Quinault Lake and US 101 some 20 miles north of Aberdeen

SIZE: 11,961 acres

ELEVATION RANGE: 300 to 4,492 feet

MILES OF TRAIL: 15

TREES AND PLANTS: Alaska yellow cedar, Douglas fir, mountain hemlock, Sitka spruce, avalanche lily, beargrass, daisy, huckleberry, salmonberry, sword fern

WILDLIFE: Black-tailed deer, cougar, mountain goat, golden eagle

ADMINISTRATION: Olympic NP, Quinault RD, 360-288-2525

BEST SEASON: Late spring through fall

The Colonel Bob Wilderness has the propped-up appearance of a steep-sided tent: From the center high point of Colonel Bob along Quinault Ridge, the slopes drop some 4,000 feet down to the Quinault River alluvial plain to the west and the West Fork Humptulips River valley to the south. Only three trails exist in the wilderness, each following the course of a creek—Ziegler, Pete's, and Fletcher—all emanating from the former lookout summit, Colonel Bob.

Like 4,492-foot Colonel Bob, other prominent peaks here, such as Gibson, Wooded, and O'Neil, do not quite reach 4,500 feet. But given the steep ascents from valley bottoms, the rough and blocky summits, and fine views of the Olympic Mountains and Pacific Ocean, each is attractive and formidable in its own right. Its location near the coast and south of the larger Olympic Mountains situate the Colonel Bob Wilderness directly in the path of 120 inches of annual precipitation. The results of all this water are displayed in fantastic examples of a temperate rainforest environment: ferns, salmonberry, vine maple, Sitka spruce, western hemlock, and western red cedar. Despite the incredible amount of rain and snow, the wilderness is quite pleasant and dry during the summer—dry enough to make potable water hard to find. But the quaint parkland of Moonshine Flats, set below the steep rise to the summit of Colonel Bob, is equipped with a running stream and rich with heather, huckleberry, and wildflowers, offering a wonderful sanctuary even late into the hiking season.

DAY HIKE: COLONEL BOB
One-Way Distance: 7.5 miles
Elevation Range: 300 to 4,492 feet
Total Elevation Gain: 4,192 feet
Difficulty: Moderate
Green Trails Maps: Quinault Lake No. 197, Grisdale No. 198

The trail moves in a southerly direction from the parking area as it climbs above the Quinault River Valley through a forest of older and taller fir and hemlock, before four switchbacks climb into the Ziegler Creek drainage. The trail moves now more toward the east and below the south slope of Wooded Peak. The trail is easy to moderate through here until it crosses Ziegler Creek—usually dry by mid-August—and climbs a steeper, more rugged section to the Mulkey Shelter at mile 4.

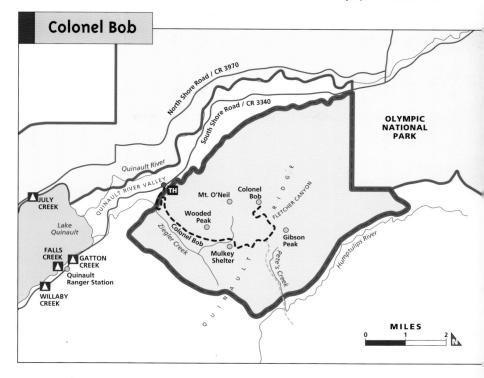

The trail continues to climb, with glimpses of Colonel Bob to the north, to reach Quinault Ridge at mile 4.7. The trail then drops through beargrass and huckleberry, by way of four switchbacks, before heading in a northeasterly direction to the Pete's Creek Trail junction at mile 5.5. From here the trail moves under the west face of Gibson Peak, climbing steeply through a thick patch of salmonberry. At mile 6.3 the trail curls to the west-northwest, past the Fletcher Canyon Trail junction, and into the marvelous miniature parkland of Moonshine Flats.

Heather, beargrass, tiger lily, and aster, among other wildflowers, along with small ponds and a creek, all contribute to the beauty of this place. Beyond the Flats at mile 6.7 the trail begins a very steep push, rising 1,100 feet in 0.8 mile to the summit. It first gains Quinault Ridge, then bends to the southwest before cutting back toward the north, west, and finally to the summit of Colonel Bob at mile 7.5. From the summit of Colonel Bob, the Olympics, Pacific Ocean, and Mount Rainier are all visible, along with many other peaks.

The parking area and trailhead for the hike to Colonel Bob are approximately 3.8 miles northeast of the Quinault RD along the South Shore Road.

4 Mount Skokomish Wilderness

View from Mount Ellinor

LOCATION: Directly north of Lake Cushman and approximately 35 miles northwest of Olympia

SIZE: 15,686 acres

ELEVATION RANGE: 2,000 to 6,434 feet

MILES OF TRAIL: 12.5

TREES AND PLANTS: Alaska cedar, Douglas fir, dwarf juniper, subalpine fir, western white pine, anemone, aster, bluebell, buttercup, kinnikinnick, thimbleberry

WILDLIFE: Black bear, black-tailed deer, mountain goat, Olympic marmot, golden eagle

ADMINISTRATION: Olympic NF, Hood Canal RD, 360-877-5254

BEST SEASON: Middle of spring through fall

TWO MUSCULAR RIDGELINES separated by the Hamma Hamma River and running southwest-northeast contain an impressive collection of 5,000- and 6,000-foot peaks that read like a who's who of major leaders of American history. Starting in the north and moving clockwise stand Mount Pershing (for Army General John J. Pershing), Jefferson Peak, Mount Washington, and Mount Lincoln. Add Mildred Lakes (for Mildred "Babe" Didrikson Zaharias, Olympic champion) to Mount Ellinor (for Eleanor Roosevelt) and Mount Rose (for Rose Kennedy) in the southern portion of the wilderness, and you've begun to mention some of the most influential women in American history.

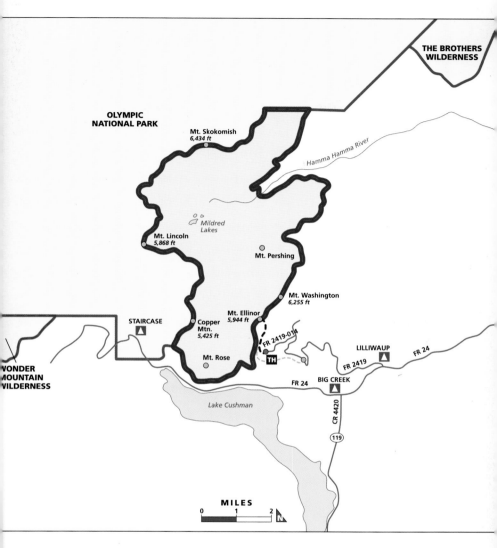

However, along the same ridgeline as Mount Lincoln and north of Mildred Lakes, the wilderness's namesake stands the tallest of all at 6,434 feet. *Skokomish* may mean "river people," but the mountains are easily the most impressive feature of the Mount Skokomish Wilderness. Peaks and ridgelines were shaped into pointed, knife-edged works of art as a result of volcanic activity prompted by oceanic and continental plate shifts followed by the movement of Pleistocene glaciers.

Impressive views across the Mount Skokomish Wilderness and into the Olympics await from high points like Mount Ellinor and Mount Washington. Equally enjoyable, en route to the summits of Ellinor, Rose, and the Sawtooth Ridge (accessed by cross-country travel only), are the meadows of anemone, aster, bluebell, buttercup, heather, and thimbleberry that paint the open slopes below rocky ridgelines.

DAY HIKE: MOUNT ELLINOR
One-Way Distance: 1.6 miles
Elevation Range: 3,500 to 5,944 feet
Total Elevation Gain: 2,444 feet
Difficulty: Strenuous
Green Trails Maps: Mt. Steel No. 167, The Brothers No. 168

Amazing for its beauty, this hike is also notable for the extremely short distance it takes to be immersed in a grand subalpine and alpine setting. However, the ascent requires some serious effort—more like climbing a ladder than hiking.

The hike begins by winding and climbing steep switchbacks along a forested rib before crossing a brief flat section, then resuming the intense climb through a rockslide. The rockslide also marks the start of a spectacular slopeside wildflower meadow. The trail through here is a combination of natural terrain and rock steps put in place to ease the ascent and reduce erosion. Once above the meadows the trail follows a ridgeline to the summit of Mount Ellinor at mile 1.6. Views include overlooks of Lake Cushman, Puget Sound, the Olympic Mountains to the northwest, Mount Skokomish to the north-northwest, and Mount Rainier to the east. Enjoy some scrambling here, including up to the summit of Mount Washington directly to the north-northeast.

From the Hoodsport RD, take Lake Cushman Road (WA 119) west and north toward Lake Cushman. Turn right (east) onto unpaved FR 24 at 9.4 miles, following signs for the Mount Ellinor Trailhead. Slightly over 1.5 miles down FR 24 turn left (north) onto FR 2419 at 10.9 miles, again following signs for Mount Ellinor Trailhead. Pass the parking area for the Lower Mount Ellinor Trailhead and continue on to FR 2419-014 at 17.6 miles to reach the Upper Mount Ellinor Trailhead. Turn left and drive 1 mile to reach the parking area and trailhead at 18.6 miles.

Olympic National Park: Beaches 5

Sea stacks at sunrise from Olympic National Park

IN GREAT WHITE PLUMES OF SPRAY, waves reach up to the raggedly torn land, struggling to hold against the ocean's forces, while sea stacks cut the misted air like tall, dark ships dangerously close to crashing on the shore. Made of harder sandstone than the coastal cliffs and headlands, these rock sea stacks look stranded beyond the run of rock, cobble, and sand beaches extending out from the headlands and coves of the Olympic Peninsula. Nearly 60 miles of this coast is preserved as part of Olympic National Park. It is indeed violence in beauty, and even beauty in violence, that give this portion of the

LOCATION: Olympic coast between Cape Flattery and South Beach, and approximately 60 miles west of Port Townsend

SIZE: 42,768 acres (25,873 acres designated wilderness)

ELEVATION RANGE: Sea level to 650 feet

MILES OF TRAIL: 57 (includes beach and forest)

TREES AND PLANTS: Pacific madrone, Sitka spruce, western red cedar, fern, kinnikinnick, moss, salal

WILDLIFE: Barnacle, mussel, purple shore crab, starfish, sea anemone, sea otter, seal, black bear, black-tailed deer, elk, raccoon, bald eagle, great blue heron, gulls, raven

ADMINISTRATION: NPS, 360-565-3130; Mora RD (seasonal), 360-374-5460

BEST SEASON: Year-round

wilderness its amazing features and attractiveness for the animal and plant life that calls this place home.

Sailing ships have an often tragic history with this stretch of coast. A Norwegian ship, the *Prince Arthur,* ran aground near Kayostla Beach in 1903, killing all crew members. A Chilean schooner barge, the *W. J. Pirrie,* wrecked on the shore 12 miles south of Sand Point in 1920. Small memorials for the *W. J. Pirrie* and the *Prince Arthur* stand near their respective wreck sites. Near Cape Alava the anchor of the American bark *Austria* is still visible today, rusting in the ocean waters since its shipwreck in 1887. Along a marvelous 2.5-mile stretch of beach called Shi-Shi, parts of hundreds of ships wash ashore every year. For sailors, the Olympic Peninsula does not partake of the beauty that hikers and beachcombers find.

The ocean strip under the management of Olympic National Park ranges from 0.3 mile to 3 miles wide, with road access stretching the entire length of the southern section but only reaching in at four points to access the more remote and wild middle and northern sections. You'll find tremendous diversity here. Offshore beyond the cobbled beaches are an assortment of sea stacks and islands, most of which are under the protection of the Washington Islands Wilderness. The line of rugged headlands is thick with weathered forests of Sitka spruce, western hemlock, and western red cedar. Along the coast the terrain alternates from serene coves, to wind-lashed beaches littered with driftwood, to the incredible expanse of Point of the Arches at the northern end of the strip. Add to all of this the amazing amount of marine and terrestrial life abounding here.

If you time it properly, you can witness and explore the various tidal zones (spray, high, middle, and low) to discover the interconnectedness of the finger limpet, California mussel, purple shore crab, sea anemone, ochre sea star, gooseneck barnacle, and sea urchin. These and other sea creatures help to sustain other species such as otters, the playful clowns of the sea; seabirds like gulls, puffins, auklets, and murres; plus dolphins, sea lions, and migratory sea life like the gray whale, filter-feeding upon the ocean's foundation of life, plankton and krill. Even land animals like deer and elk find reasons to wander the beaches, walking out to the rocks and sea stacks at low tide to feed on the grasses. Raccoons and bears look for crabs in the tide pools or for salmon that have washed up on shore (or even an unprepared and unsuspecting backpacker's food stash).

The southern section of the wilderness between the Quinault and Hoh Indian Reservations has the most convenient access via US 101. The beaches are numbered 1–6, starting in the south at South Beach and moving north to Ruby Beach, before US 101 bends to the east to parallel the Hoh River. The coast along here is mainly stretches of beach with a few headlands, sea stacks, and tide pools.

The middle section is bookended by the Hoh River and Hoh Indian Reservation in the south and by the Quillayute River and Quileute Indian Reservation to the north. Unlike the southern section, this 15 miles of coastline has road access only by Oil City to the south and by La Push to the north. The beaches at the north end, simply labeled First, Second, and Third, lie near such features as James Island, Quillayute Needles, and Teahwhit Head. These numbered beaches boast smooth sand crescents, many headlands and tide pools, and proximity to picturesque sea stacks. Campsites are on the beaches. Water sources come from the springs and creeks running out of the coastal forest toward the sea.

Sunset on the Olympic coast, Olympic National Park

From north of the Ozette Indian Reservation near Cape Alava to the Makah Indian Reservation is the northern beach wilderness. Highlights include Point of the Arches—wave-battered rock formations that resemble the wind-formed arches of the Southwest—and long stretches of sandy beach like Shi-Shi.

Many European and American ships have met their fate against the shores of the Olympic Peninsula. Ocean debris from as far away as Japan has also collected here from ships sailing hundreds and thousands of miles away. This history is brief, however, and tipped toward the tragic, compared with that of Northwest tribes who have lived in peaceful coexistence with this coast for millennia.

Discoveries of animal bones and human artifacts—tools, baskets, and weapons have established that cultures have lived along this coast for more than 12,000 years. One such tribe is the Makah, known today by its desire to revive the traditional whale hunt. Formerly the hunt played an important role in sustaining the people as well as in establishing social distinctions, since whalers were accorded great respect. The Makah also hunted other sea mammals from their cedar canoes, shoving off from whaling villages like Ozette, which provided ideal access to the migration paths of these animals. Fine woodworking and basket-making artifacts attest to a culture that had the luxury of time to nurture artistic talents.

Tribes farther south, including the Quileute, Hoh, and Quinault, also lived from the sea. They built traps for the migrating salmon and steelhead en route from the ocean upriver to spawn. These tribes also ventured inland, gathering camas to trade, hunting elk, and trapping bear. Women created incredible cooking baskets and blankets made from mountain-goat wool. By the mid- to late nineteenth century, however, Euro-American settlers on and around the Olympic Peninsula had forced the tribes onto reservations, which today are significantly smaller than their ancestral range. But if there is anything fortunate about the artificial containment of each of these tribes, it is that they are in a place that is historically their homeland, allowing them to continue their role as humble ambassadors between sea and land in this special landscape.

DAY HIKE: RIALTO BEACH TO CAPE JOHNSON
One-Way Distance: 3.5 miles
Elevation Range: Sea level to 40 feet
Total Elevation Gain: 40 feet
Difficulty: Easy to moderate
Green Trails Map: Ozette No. 130S

Give yourself some time to complete this hike. The terrain can be slow going at points, even though overall the hiking is literally a stroll down the beach. Time is needed mainly for the varying beach surfaces, the movement of the tides, and the necessity of exploration. You'll want to linger over the beached driftwood, ocean-rounded rocks, levels of life in tide pools, and dramatic coastline. Also note that the distance will be variable because of tide levels and beach surfaces. Depending on the tide level, you could be walking across sand, pebbles, cobble, rocks, boulders, driftwood, kelp (quite slick when wet), and even through a short stretch of forest, as you make your way up and back from Cape Johnson.

From Rialto Beach, pick a route through the jumble of ocean and sun-bleached driftwood (drift trees would be more accurate) and head north. At mile 1.3 you will reach a small cove and the rock formation known as Hole-in-the-Wall. The route either climbs up and around the headland if the tide is up or goes through the hole. Headland trails are marked by a round sign painted in a checkerboard pattern of red and black.

From Hole-in-the-Wall, the way crosses a more rocky section rounding a point, passing by many tide pools en route. This point, or headland, is impassible when the tide is high. Around the point lies a larger cove to explore and the Chilean Memorial at mile 3.2, honoring those lost on the *W. J. Pirrie* on November 26, 1920. The memorial stands off the beach a bit and is slightly hidden by the trees. Cape Johnson at mile 3.5 is the turnaround point merely for the sake of suggesting one. Feel free, again as levels of ocean and time permit, to continue enjoying the beach treasures, the views of the sea stacks off the coastline, and the unusual contrast of ocean and forest found all along this hike and farther up the coast.

Drive US 101 north of Forks, then turn left (west) onto La Push Road (WA 110). Drive 8 miles and turn right onto Mora Road. At 11.2 miles you will reach the Mora RD. Open seasonally, the ranger station will have information on camping as well as tide tables necessary for hiking anywhere along the Olympic NP coastline. At 13 miles you will reach Rialto Beach and parking areas.

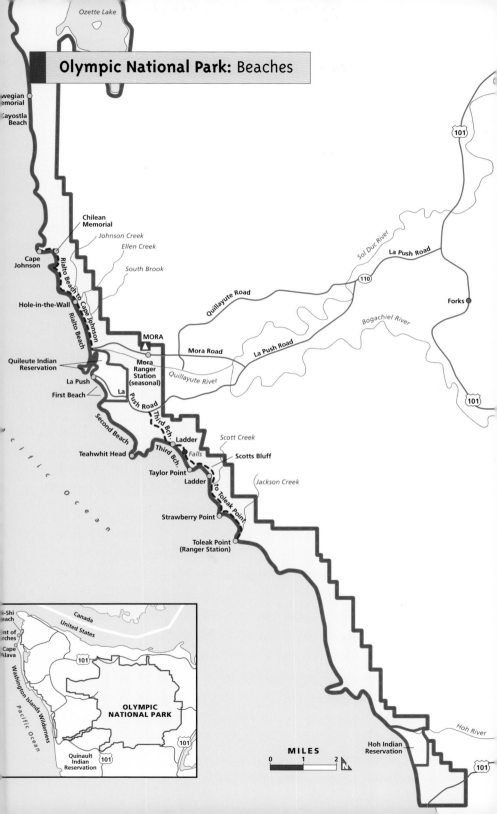

Olympic National Park: Beaches

Ozette Lake

wegian
emorial
Kayostla
Beach

101

Chilean
Memorial

Johnson Creek

Ellen Creek

Sol Duc River

La Push Road

South Brook

Cape
Johnson

Rialto Beach to Cape Johnson

Hole-in-the-Wall

Rialto Beach

Quillayute Road

110

Forks

Bogachiel River

101

MORA

Mora Road

La Push Road

Quileute Indian
Reservation

Mora
Ranger
Station
(seasonal)

Quillayute River

La Push

La

First Beach

Push Road

Second Beach

Third Bch.

Ladder

Scott Creek

Teahwhit Head

Third Bch.

Falls

Scotts Bluff

Taylor Point

Ladder

to Toleak Point

Jackson Creek

Strawberry Point

Pacific Ocean

Toleak Point
(Ranger Station)

i-Shi
each

Canada

United States

t of
rches

Cape
Alava

101

Washington Islands Wilderness

Pacific Ocean

OLYMPIC
NATIONAL
PARK

101

Quinault
Indian
Reservation

Hoh Indian
Reservation

Hoh River

101

MILES

0   1   2

N

DESTINATION HIKE: THIRD BEACH TO TOLEAK POINT

One-Way Distance: 6.3 miles

Elevation Range: Sea level to 300 feet

Total Elevation Gain: 300 feet

Difficulty: Moderate

Green Trails Map: La Push No. 163S

An easy, 1.4-mile walk through a coastal forest of ferns, Sitka spruce, and western hemlock leads down to Third Beach. The beach is a beautiful, crescent-shaped stretch of sand connected to Teahwhit Head to the north and Taylor Point to the south. Walk the beach south to the first land-route headland bypass at mile 1.8, marked by circular signs painted with a red-and-black checkerboard pattern. A steep climb up a combination of ladders and ropes brings you back into a dense coastal forest for a 1.7-mile bypass of Taylor Point.

The trail then descends, by way of a natural trail and stairs, to a short stretch of beach north of Scotts Bluff at mile 3.5. The route leaves the beach again at mile 4 to ascend via a ladder-and-rope system to another land crossing, this time around Scotts Bluff. Once back on the beach at mile 4.4, the route stays on a sand beach all the way to Toleak Point, passing tide pools, driftwood piles, and dozens of sea stacks decorating the ocean.

At mile 5.5 you will reach Strawberry Point, speckled with numerous tide pools and a long series of rock stacks jutting out into the ocean. The beach then curves around a cove for another 0.8 mile to Toleak Point at mile 6.3. Plenty of campsites lie along each of the beaches. Camping is by permit only; get one at the Mora RD, a few miles east of Rialto Beach.

Drive US 101 north of Forks and turn left (west) onto La Push Road (WA 110). Drive approximately 12 miles toward La Push to the parking area and trailhead for Third Beach.

Olympic National Park: Interior **6**

Bigleaf maple covered in moss

THE GREEK GODS OF HEAVEN lived and ruled from the heights of Mount Olympus. The mountain rose above the clouds, which acted as gates keeping both the mortals and the gods of the underworld at bay. In the calmer months of summer 1788, Captain John Meares, an Englishman flying the flag of Portugal to avoid license fees of the East India Company, sailed the Strait of Juan de Fuca, sighted the tallest of the snowy peaks on the Fourth of July, and called it Mount Olympus.

But the mountain had been identified some 14 years earlier by

LOCATION: Occupying the middle of the Olympic Peninsula and easily accessible on the east, west, and north sides from US 101

SIZE: 870,275 acres (839,193 acres designated wilderness)

ELEVATION RANGE: 80 to 7,969 feet

MILES OF TRAIL: Approximately 590

TREES AND PLANTS: Bigleaf maple, black cotton-wood, Douglas fir, Sitka spruce, western hemlock, western red cedar, avalanche lily, beargrass, devil's club, fern, heather, huckleberry, rhododendron, salmonberry

WILDLIFE: Black bear, black-tailed deer, coyote, mountain beaver, Olympic elk, river otter, chickadee, flycatcher, horned lark, junco, nuthatch, red-shafted flicker, sparrow hawk, swallow, warbler

ADMINISTRATION: NPS, 360-565-3130; Olympic NF, Quinault RD, 360-288-2525

BEST SEASON: Lowlands, year-round; highlands, summer to early fall

Spanish captain Juan Pérez of the *Santiago,* who called it *El Cerro de la Santa Rosalía.* This possibly first renaming is significant for being the earliest known instance of a European christening a geographic feature in the region. Unfortunately, this event heralded what became common practice: the imposition of hundreds of often inappropriate Euro-American names for places already recognized by the indigenous peoples.

At least "Olympus" pays homage to the grandest feature of Olympic National Park and lends its name to the entire mountain region, the Olympic Mountains. There might not be gods living on any of the three peaks of Mount Olympus (East, Middle, and West Peaks, the last the highest at 7,969 feet), but the views from any of these points, and from many others along this crazy collision of ridges and peaks, are quite divine. Mount Olympus in fact spends more time being shrouded in the clouds than rising above them, but this is because of the frequency of severe weather that pounds away on these frail mountains, none of which stands above 8,000 feet.

Most mountain ranges, including the Cascades, run in rows, but the Olympics are best described as a cluster of peaks and ridges that have collided into each other, forming twisted valleys, isolated peaks, short ranges, and hidden lakes tucked amid the chaos caused by the subduction of the oceanic and continental plates. The rock of the interior Olympics is made up primarily of siltstone, shale, and sandstone that was thrust upward from the ocean floor. Wind, water, and glacial action have all played their role in creating the dramatic effect of the Olympics. But it is also this action that has caused the demise of these weak-rocked mountains, which will continue, over millions of years, to disintegrate as if the thick forests below were devouring them. These mountains also form a kind of circle, keeping watch in each direction. From the urban vantage point of Seattle looking west across Elliott Bay, these mountains truly rise from the sea with a vertical soar equal to the Rockies' explosion from the Great Plains.

If the beacon of the mountains does not draw the curious to Olympic National Park, then the forests do, feeding the most fantastical imaginations. Sitka spruce, western red cedar, and Douglas fir trees swell here to diameters of 15 feet and rise to heights in excess of 300 feet. We are talking monstrous trees, Douglas fir especially, where the first limb looms a hundred feet above the forest floor. Locations west of the Olympic Mountains receive 160 inches of precipitation a year, feeding these giants as well as an understory of bigleaf maple, salal, giant fern, and 150 species of moss that wrap live and dead trees alike in what looks like green fur. All of these species contribute to the creation of this magnificently ghoulish and enchanting world.

The botany here varies with the life zones throughout the interior of Olympic National Park. The first, the Humid Transition Zone, lies between sea level and around 1,500 feet, dominated by spruce-hemlock nearer to the ocean, then hemlock-cedar more inland, and Douglas fir slightly higher up. The hemlock-cedar and Douglas fir forests are accompanied by rhododendron, salal, devil's club, wild rose, moss, fern, bigleaf maple, and black cottonwood, which can grow to heights of 200 feet and widths of 10 feet in diameter. Flowering plants include white trillium, starflower, twinflower, bleeding heart, fireweed, and waxen-gold buttercup.

Many more species of plants exist in this zone, dispersed between the wetter western sections and the drier eastern sections, than in higher ones. Of course the rainforests especially send the imagination loose: tall, moss-covered tree giants filtering

Lupine meadow, Olympic National Park

a heavy light spilling over the massive ferns and mushroom colonies. The stillness of the spongy ground, punctuated by the clack of water running in a creek nearby, is truly mystical.

The next-higher Canadian Zone, at 1,500 to 4,500 feet, is home to Pacific silver fir, western hemlock, white pine, Douglas fir, and western red cedar. The thick canopy of trees keep the understory sparse and open, but you can find vine maple, huckleberry, alder, devil's club, salmonberry, and glades of beargrass in the higher reaches.

The Hudsonian Zone, at 4,500 feet to timberline, hosts subalpine fir, mountain hemlock, and Alaska cedar, as well as huckleberry, blueberry, kinnikinnick, and mountain azalea. But it is the glorious wildflowers, protected and nurtured by the deep snowpack, which reign unchallenged in the upper fringes of this zone and into the Arctic-Alpine Zone.

By mid- to late summer the meadows look as if a rainbow has bedded down in the green grasses, as shooting star, bluebell, larkspur, phlox, lupine, goldenrod, columbine, daisy, glacier lily, and others make their brief but vibrant appearance. Above the "wildflower" zone, most plants are replaced by rocks, snowfields, and glaciers.

The pristine condition of Olympic National Park today is owed to both minimal direct human contact as well as to conservation. The tribes of the Olympic Peninsula did not venture too far into the interior because of superstitious beliefs. It wasn't until the winter of 1889–90, with an expedition organized by the *Seattle Press* newspaper, that anyone crossed into the heart of the Olympics and out to the sea. But even though people hadn't been crossing this area to reach the ocean, rivers had and continue to do so.

The Elwha, Gray Wolf, Dungeness, Dosewallips, Duckabush, Quinault, Queets, Hoh, and Soleduck Rivers all radiate from the central mountains to the sea like blue bicycle spokes. They are the access routes to the rainforest kingdoms for which Olympic National Park is famous, places captured in scenic photography where moss, ferns, and giant trees press against the banks of the waterways. Thankfully, efforts and money continue to come together to help remove the dams along the Elwha River, which runs south to north from Mount Barnes into the Strait of Juan de Fuca. Advocates hope to once again allow the anadromous salmon uninhibited access to their primeval spawning grounds deep in the heart of the Olympics.

From the time of the first successful cross-Olympic expedition, explorers and supporters advocated that this incredible place be preserved as a national park. However, the progression to its current status took many stops and shapes. The first was in 1897, when President Grover Cleveland set aside some 2 million acres of land as the Olympic Forest Reserve. By 1907 the name had changed to Olympic National Forest, followed by Mount Olympus National Monument in 1909. The original idea of a national park of 768,000 acres had shrunk to 620,000 acres at the beginning of its monument days. Three presidential proclamations over the next 20 years cut its size down to a sparse 300,000 acres. The greedy quest for timber in this timber-rich environment pulled at the boundaries of the monument, which unfortunately meant the loss of most of the area's oldest and largest trees in the lowlands. By the 1930s, the push for national park status began again with a proposal to include in excess of 700,000 acres.

Timber industry interests fought the expansion of Mount Olympus National Monument and seriously proposed that a national park in this area should be no more than 300 square miles, or less than 200,000 acres. But in 1936 the U.S. Forest Service established adjacent to the monument the Olympic Primitive Area, which put more land under protection from thoughtless eradication. What wasn't in place, however, was extensive enough protection of the lowlands. More than 45 years after two explorers conceived of the need to put this land under the protection of a national park, Olympic National Park finally came into existence in June 1938. Today the interior comprises 870,275 acres; some 95 percent was designated wilderness in 1988.

DESTINATION HIKE: ROYAL BASIN
One-Way Distance: 6 miles
Elevation Range: 2,680 to 5,118 feet
Total Elevation Gain: 2,438 feet
Difficulty: Moderate
Green Trails Map: Tyler Peak No. 136

The trail parallels the slate-blue Dungeness River through a stand of 100-plus-foot-tall Douglas fir and western hemlock for 1 mile to the junction with the Royal Basin Trail. From here the Royal Basin Trail begins shadowing the course of Royal Creek along its northern bank, gaining elevation gradually. At mile 2.7 the trail makes one of a couple breaks from the trees, giving views of Gray Wolf Ridge to the west before bending with the creek to the southwest and descending back into the trees closer to Royal Creek. You will pass some campsites through here.

At mile 3.5 you will cross another open section, which marks the beginning of a moderate climb for the next mile. The trail then rolls along and eventually into a beautiful meadow-marsh area with footlog crossings of numerous little creeks sliding through this lower basin. From here, climb for 0.6 mile up to Royal Lake at mile 6. Campsites around the lake and higher into Royal Basin are by permit only. The undulating basin above the lake is quite grand, decorated in a mix of trees, meadow, and rocks. Collecting around its upper rim are Mount Deception, The Needles, and other interesting rock formations.

Approximately 2.5 miles west of Sequim and 15 miles east of Port Angeles, turn south onto Taylor Cut Off Road. At 2.5 miles the road bends hard to the right and changes to the Lost Mountain Road. At 5.1 miles turn left onto Slab Camp Road and travel 1 mile to another left-hand turn onto FR 2870 at 6.1 miles, toward Gray Wolf Trailhead. The pavement ends, and the road can be narrow and rough at points. Follow the road past the Gray Wolf Trailhead and FR 2880 at 12.5 miles, staying right. Another 2.5 miles up you reach another junction; again bear to the right, now traveling on FR 2860. There are two parking areas for the start of this hike: one before and one after the trailhead at 21.6 miles.

DAY HIKE: LAKE ANGELES TO HEATHER PARK LOOP
Total Distance: 12.4 miles
Elevation Range: 1,790 to 6,046 feet
Total Elevation Gain: 4,306 feet
Difficulty: Moderate to strenuous
Green Trails Maps: Port Angeles No. 103, Mt. Angeles No. 135

This loop follows the Lake Angeles Trail out and returns on the Heather Park Trail. Until reaching the trail junction for Lake Angeles, you will stay in the trees with moderate but sustained climbing, crossing Ennis Creek at about a mile in.

From the Lake Angeles Trail junction at mile 3.4, begin a strenuous climb to Klahhane Ridge. From the junction, ascend to a gap with views across to Second Top and Mount Angeles. The path drops for a few yards before climbing again steeply over a loose dirt-and-rock surface and crossing back over to the east side of the ridge. The views begin to unfold with the efforts of the climb: Look for Lake Angeles, the Strait of Juan de Fuca, Victoria and the Vancouver Ranges on Vancouver Island, and Mount Baker to the northeast. The climb begins to lessen slightly at the start of a thick blanket of heather.

From Klahhane Ridge at mile 4.9 the Olympic Mountains come into full view and stay this way as the trail rolls along the blackish, rocky ridge, colored at points with a variety of wildflowers. Heading west, you will reach the junction with the Hurricane Ridge Trail at mile 6.1. From the junction the trail drops into a basin below Mount Angeles and over a scree slope before making a short, steep push out through a gap on the basin's west side. The trail continues along a narrow, loose-rock trail with views of the Elwha River Range to the west before turning uphill to a gap and the entrance into the upper end of Heather Park at mile 8.3.

Like the slope above Lake Angeles, heather blankets the ground through here, as the trail drops via switchbacks before straightening out to begin a long run downhill, eventually returning to the cover of trees. Once in the trees the trail will begin to make some looping switchbacks, marking its return to the parking area at mile 12.4.

From the Olympic National Park Visitor Center in Port Angeles, drive south 5.5 miles in the direction of the Heart O' the Hills entrance and Hurricane Ridge Visitor Center. Just before the official park entrance turn right, driving through an area of employee housing and onto the parking area for the hike at 5.7 miles.

MULTIDAY LOOP HIKE: SEVEN LAKES BASIN
Total Distance: 17.5 miles
Elevation Range: 1,950 to 5,200 feet
Total Elevation Gain: 3,250 feet
Difficulty: Moderate
Green Trails Maps: Mt. Tom No. 133, Mt. Olympus No. 134

Hike 0.7 mile from the parking area to just short of Sol Duc Falls to begin the loop. Bearing to the left, follow the Sol Duc River Trail in the direction of Sol Duc Park and Heart Lake. The trail moves along the Sol Duc River through the trees, crossing over creeks and elevated walkways. At mile 2.5 the trail steepens and becomes more rugged, with rocks and exposed tree roots for about a mile. Traveling over a more pleasant trail surface, you will pass a campsite before returning to more rocks and tree roots, climbing to the Appleton Pass Trail junction at mile 4. Campsites also lie near this junction. At mile 4.6 cross the Sol Duc River via footlog.

Continue up to Lower Bridge Creek at mile 5.5 and more campsites. The trail then moves through a small meadow and past a few tarns up to the start of Sol Duc Park at mile 6, with campsites available. Sol Duc Park is a beautiful basin thick with heather, wildflowers, beargrass, streams, and islands of trees. Winding up and through the park, the trail reaches Heart Lake at mile 7.3 miles and further campsites.

It is a short push from the lake to the High Divide Ridge. Enjoy an "in-your-face" view to the south of White Glacier, Blue Glacier, and Ice River Glacier, seemingly locking in the peaks of Snow Dome, Mount Mathias, Mount Olympus, and the other peaks that constitute the stout heart of the Olympics, with the Hoh River valley laid out thousands of feet below. To the north the long, treed shelf of Seven Lakes Basin sits bejeweled with lakes and ponds. Where to look first?

The trail rolls along the ridge with these views in constant companionship, eventually joining a spur trail for Bogachiel Peak at mile 9.1 and the Hoh Lake Trail junction at mile 9.3. The trail bends to the northwest, rimming above a basin across from Green Peak and popping briefly up to the ridge with final views down into the Seven Lakes Basin before continuing its high-line contour along an open slope. You will pass the spur trail down to the Seven Lakes Basin at mile 10.1. The trail wraps its way from a direction of northwesterly to westerly to northerly and finally reaches an overlook of a benched area holding a few small ponds. Then the trail descends, via switchbacks, past two of the ponds and into the trees at mile 12.

You will come to Deer Lake and campsites at mile 13.7. From here the trail winds downward, somewhat steeply, over a rock and tree-root surface, crossing over a pack bridge of Canyon Creek at mile 15.8 and reaching Sol Duc Falls at mile 16.7. The falls lie where the Sol Duc River makes a right-angle turn and drops some 20 feet into a narrow slot canyon. Over the bridge the Deer Lake Trail meets with the trail leading back to the Sol Duc Trailhead and parking area at mile 17.5.

About 30 miles west of Port Angeles off US 101 is the Sol Duc entrance to Olympic National Park and the trailhead for this hike. Go left at the sign for Sol Duc Hot Springs Resort. Drive to a large parking area at 12.5 miles. The trailhead is located at the lot's east end.

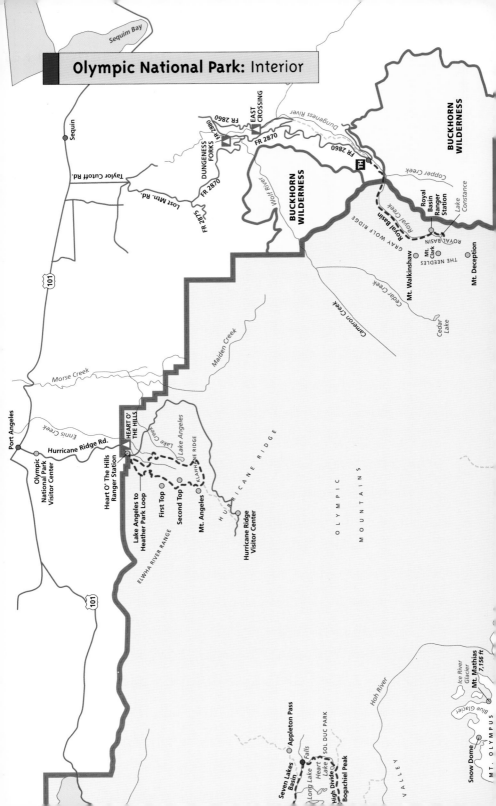

Olympic National Park: Interior

Sequim Bay

Sequim

Taylor Cutoff Rd.

Lost Mtn. Rd.

FR 2875

FR 2870

FR 2880

FR 2860

DUNGENESS FORKS

EAST CROSSING

FR 2870

Dungeness River

FR 2860

BUCKHORN WILDERNESS

BUCKHORN WILDERNESS

Wolf River

Copper Creek

Royal Creek

GRAY WOLF RIDGE

Royal Basin Ranger Station

Royal Basin

ROYAL BASIN

Lake Constance

Mt. Walkinshaw

Mt. Clark

THE NEEDLES

Mt. Deception

Cedar Creek

Cedar Lake

Cameron Creek

Maiden Creek

Morse Creek

Port Angeles

Ennis Creek

101

Olympic National Park Visitor Center

Hurricane Ridge Rd.

HEART O' THE HILLS

Heart O' The Hills Ranger Station

Lake Angeles to Heather Park Loop

Lake Creek

Lake Angeles

First Top

Second Top

Mt. Angeles

KLAHHANE RIDGE

ELWHA RIVER RANGE

HURRICANE RIDGE

Hurricane Ridge Visitor Center

OLYMPIC MOUNTAINS

101

Hoh River

Ice River Glacier

Mt. Mathias 7,156 ft

Blue Glacier

Snow Dome

MT. OLYMPUS

VALLEY

Appleton Pass

SOL DUC PARK

Seven Lakes Basin

Long Lake

Heart Lake

Falls

High Divide

Bogachiel Peak

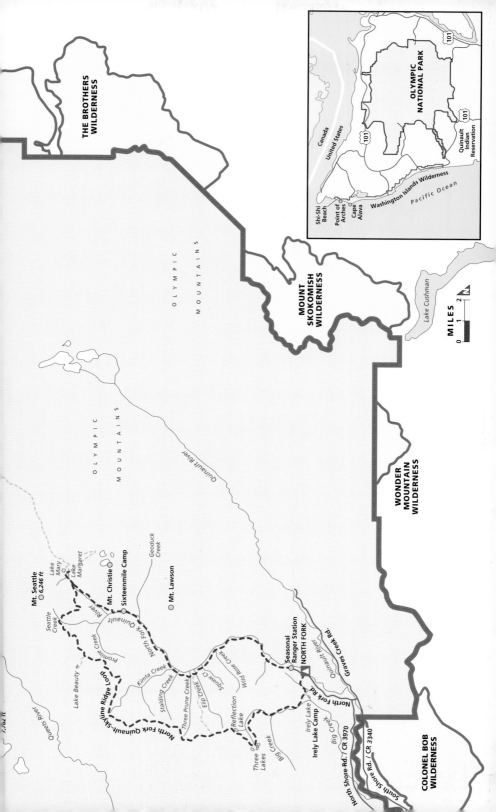

THE BROTHERS
WILDERNESS

OLYMPIC

MOUNTAINS

MOUNT
SKOKOMISH
WILDERNESS

Lake Cushman

MILES
0   1   2

WONDER
MOUNTAIN
WILDERNESS

OLYMPIC

MOUNTAINS

Quinault River

Quets River

Mt. Seattle
6,246 ft

Lake Mary
Lake Margaret

Mt. Christie

Sixteenmile Camp

Geoduck Creek

Mt. Lawson

Seattle Creek

Lake Beauty

Promise Creek

North Fork Quinault River

North Fork Quinault–Skyline Ridge Loop

Kimta Creek

Stalding Creek

Three Prune Creek

Elip Creek

Squaw Creek

Wild Rose Creek

Reflection Lake

Three Lakes

Big Creek

Seasonal
Ranger Station
NORTH FORK

Quinault River

North Fork Rd.

Irely Lake

Irely Lake Camp

Graves Creek Rd.

North Shore Rd. / CR 7 / CR 3970

South Shore Rd. / CR 3340

COLONEL BOB
WILDERNESS

Canada

United States

OLYMPIC
NATIONAL PARK

101

101

Quinault
Indian
Reservation

Shi-Shi
Beach

Point of
Arches

Cape
Alava

Washington Islands Wilderness

Pacific Ocean

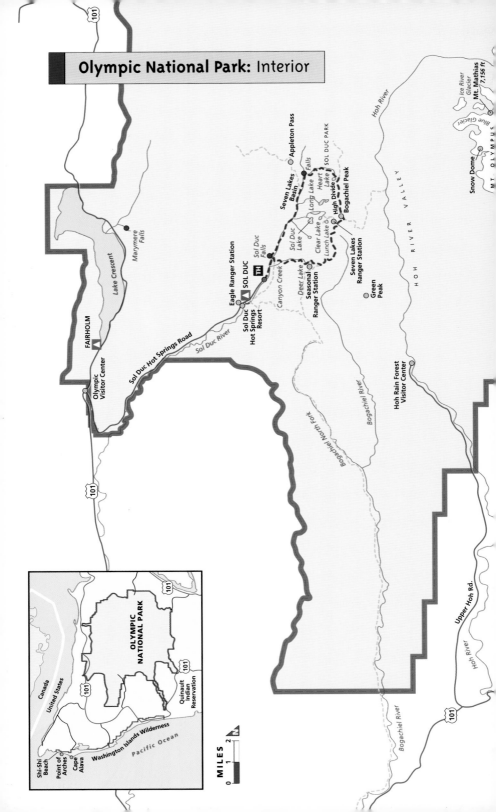

Olympic National Park: Interior

Mt. Mathias
7,756 ft

Ice River
Glacier

Blue Glacier

Snow Dome

MT OLYMPUS

Appleton Pass

Seven Lakes Basin

Falls

SOL DUC PARK

High Divide

Bogachiel Peak

Long Lake

Heart Lake

Hoh River

HOH RIVER VALLEY

Eagle Ranger Station

SOL DUC

Sol Duc Falls

Clear Lake

Sol Duc Lake

Lunch Lake

Seven Lakes Ranger Station

Canyon Creek

Marymere Falls

Lake Crescent

FAIRHOLM

Sol Duc Hot Springs Resort

Deer Lake

Seasonal Ranger Station

Green Peak

Olympic Visitor Center

Sol Duc Hot Springs Road

Sol Duc River

Bogachiel North Fork

Bogachiel River

Hoh Rain Forest Visitor Center

Upper Hoh Rd.

Hoh River

Bogachiel River

101

101

Inset map

Canada

United States

101

OLYMPIC NATIONAL PARK

101

101

Shi-Shi Beach

Point of Arches

Cape Alava

Quinault Indian Reservation

Washington Islands Wilderness

Pacific Ocean

MILES
0   1   2

N

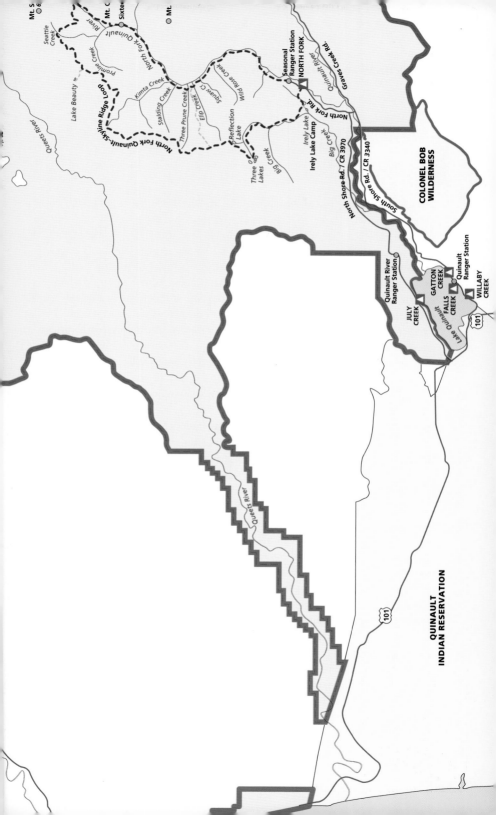

MULTIDAY LOOP HIKE: NORTH FORK QUINAULT–SKYLINE RIDGE LOOP
Total Distance: 46.1 miles (not including trips to Low Divide
and Lake Beauty)
Elevation Range: 500 to 5,100 feet
Total Elevation Gain: 6,700 feet
Difficulty: Easy to strenuous
Green Trails Map: Mt. Christie No. 166

A nice cruise along the North Fork Quinault River through an understory of ferns and between large, moss-covered trees describes the first few miles of this hike. At mile 1.8 the trail crosses two tributaries of the river—more difficult at high water—before arriving at the Wolf Bar Camp area at mile 2.5. The grassy tent sites are situated close to the river and ringed by a thick carpet of ferns.

From here the trail climbs up and slightly away from the river on a bumpier trail at mile 3.7 before leveling and smoothing out. At mile 5 the trail descends to a crossing or fording of Wild Rose Creek and to the Halfway House Shelter 0.1 mile farther. The trail then climbs over elevated walkways and a picturesque bridge crossing of Squaw Creek. Farther on, it descends to a crossing of Elip Creek at mile 6.4, distinguished by the wide, rocky floodplain. A campsite lies on the opposite bank, and just 0.1 mile up you reach the Elip Creek Trail junction.

The next section is highlighted by three high bridge crossings of creeks running down from Skyline Ridge. The sequence is Three Prune, Stalding, and Kimta Creeks. At mile 8.1 the trail passes the Trapper Shelter, then rolls along and by two sizable but unnamed creeks before reaching the confluence of Geoduck Creek and North Fork Quinault River, then crossing a third creek. This marks the approach, complete with views of Mount Lawson to the southeast, to the Twelvemile Shelter and camp area at mile 11.4. Another 0.7 miles farther, ford the river to reach Sixteenmile camp at mile 12.1.

From Sixteenmile the trail continues to climb, working over a high bridge creek crossing at mile 14.1 and up a series of switchbacks. You will enter a more open area with elevated walkways, pass through a stock gate at mile 15.1 into a beautiful narrow meadow below the southeast flank of Mount Seattle, and finally arrive at the Skyline Ridge Trail junction at mile 15.6. By passing through the second stock gate and hiking another 0.7 mile, you can reach the Low Divide camp, Lake Margaret, and slightly farther along Lake Mary.

By mile 15.6 the trail has only gained about 3,000 feet and has been mostly easy to moderate in grade. The Skyline Ridge Trail is 22.8 miles long, gains 2,300 feet in the first 7.6 miles, then gains another 1,400 feet in the next 6.5 miles by way of a grueling alternation between climbing and descending over moderate to very strenuous sections of trail. From the junction, the Skyline Ridge Trail doubles back through the meadow above the North Fork Quinault Trail, crossing two creeks and then up a series of steeper, rocky, and tree-rooted switchbacks. The trail then contours around a point and climbs out onto a beautiful open slope of heather, blueberry, and huckleberry below Mount Seattle and above Seattle Creek.

At mile 18.8 the trail descends via switchbacks to the bottom end of a lush basin and a crossing of Seattle Creek at mile 19.6. The trail then contours along the west side of the Seattle Creek drainage, climbs a set of switchbacks into a parkland area, then goes up another set of switchbacks to another parkland with views of Mount Christie to the east and Mount Lawson to the southeast. The trail continues up two more sets of switchbacks before it descends, then climbs up to a saddle and the trail junction for Lake Beauty at mile 23.2. The junction is not signed, but the lake is visible to the west-northwest of the saddle. It is 0.3 mile steeply down to campsites above the lake, spectacularly backdropped by the Olympics. Lake Beauty is the last designated camp until Three Prune, some 11 miles farther along.

Past the junction the trail stays briefly on the North Fork Quinault River side of the ridge before descending a short distance to the Queets River side. The trail returns to the North Fork side, alternating between steep ascents and descents. At approximately 1.8 miles from the Lake Beauty junction you enter a barren, rocky basin where the trail can be very difficult to follow or find. Bear in mind two things: first, look for cairns; second, if the cairns are hard to find, make it through this section by angling high, always ascending around the basin, but not so high that your route either enters denser stands of trees or becomes very difficult to traverse.

A peak will be visible to the southeast, along with a ridgeline that curls around to it. The Skyline Ridge Trail will end up on that ridge, at a point where a dead stand from an old burn meets a live stand at mile 26.2. The trail drops over this ridge and heads in a westerly direction, eventually climbing up to the headwaters of Kimta Creek at mile 28. Be aware that, later in the hiking season, water is scarce to nonexistent along the some 6 miles from Kimta Creek to Three Prune.

The trail dips and rises along a ridge, heading in the direction of a prominent peak to the south. You will pass through a meadow at mile 30.4 before moving behind the peak and onto the Queets side. The trail finally relents and cruises along, alternating from the Queets to the North Fork side of the ridge. At mile 33.4 you'll round a point and enter a basin, where at mile 34 you reach the Three Prune camp.

From Three Prune the trail climbs 1.5 miles to the Elip Creek Trail junction at mile 35.5. It continues to climb for another 0.4 mile before descending to a shallow shelf basin, crossing through more meadow areas by Reflection Lake at mile 36.7 and into the trees down to Three Lakes at mile 38, where you'll find campsites. It is, for the most part, all downhill from here—2,700 feet—starting gradually before moving to a set of steeper switchbacks to a bridge crossing at mile 40.8 and on to the Irely Lake Trail junction at mile 44.3. From the junction the trail climbs slightly, crosses over Irely Creek, and reaches the Irely Lake Trailhead at mile 45.4. Note that permits are needed for camping.

Turn off US 101 onto South Shore Road toward Quinault Lake. At 2.2 miles you will reach the Quinault RD. Continue northeast toward the North Fork Trailhead. The road changes to gravel at 10.9 miles. At 16 miles cross the North Fork Quinault River and continue now more to the north for the Irely Lake and North Fork Trailheads. At 19.3 miles are the Irely Lake Trailhead and parking area. You can leave a vehicle here, which is the endpoint for the loop hike, or drive another 0.7 mile and park at the North Fork Trailhead, the start of the hike.

7 San Juan Wilderness

Colorful starfish on Matia Island

LOCATION: In Puget Sound between Victoria, British Columbia, and Bellingham

SIZE: 353 acres

ELEVATION RANGE: Sea level to 174 feet

MILES OF TRAIL: No hiking access except for a short trail on Matia Island

TREES AND PLANTS: Douglas fir, lodgepole pine, Pacific madrone, Rocky Mountain juniper, bluegrass, wheatgrass

WILDLIFE: Dall's porpoise, harbor seal, minke whale, orca whale, pilot whale, black brant, black oystercatcher, Brandt's cormorant, rhinoceros auklet, tufted puffin

ADMINISTRATION: FWS, Washington Maritime NWR Complex, 360-457-8451

BEST SEASON: Year-round

THOSE WHO LOVE BUILDING PUZZLES might have a great urge to try to put together the 700 islands of big, small, long, smooth, and jagged-edged shapes that constitute the San Juan Archipelago and see what sort of image might appear. The geologic picture, though, shows that these islands weren't a single landmass but were instead the results of tectonic plate movements, volcanic activity, and glacial shaping. In fact these islands should really be seen as mountains, with only their summits—rounded, bare, grassy, or forested—rising above the waterline where the Straits of Juan de Fuca and Georgia come together in Puget Sound. These island-mountaintops are in the Olympic Mountains' rain shadow, which limits annual precipitation to 25 inches and creates a relatively arid environment suitable for the growth of Pacific madrone and Rocky Mountain juniper.

"Islands" also fails to describe all the geographic features of this puzzle. The San Juans are a collection of islands, islets, reefs, and rocks that host numerous bird species including auklet, cormorant, gull, oystercatcher, and puffin, as well as hundreds of species of migratory birds. Harbor seals sun on rocks and reefs. Porpoises, along with pilot, minke, and orca "killer" whales, swim in the waters.

Of the 700 (let's call them) geographic pieces of the San Juans, only 200 have names. The large islands—Lopez, Orcas, San Juan, and Shaw—constitute the vast majority of the landmass of the archipelago and have communities on them like the popular tourist destination Friday Harbor. The San Juan Islands National Wildlife Refuge comprises 84 of the smaller pieces; 81 of these 84, or 353 acres, are also under wilderness designation as the San Juan Wilderness. The 81 pieces of the San Juan Wilderness, with names like Bare Island, Bird Rock, Flower Island, Gull Reef, Puffin Island, Shark Reef, and White Rocks, are only to be viewed from afar: Land access is not allowed. In fact, the only parcel within the wilderness open to human intrusion is a 5-acre piece of Matia Island, which is part of a state park. Here you'll find camping, coves for anchorage and moorage, and a short hiking trail along the shoreline.

8 Washington Islands Wilderness

LOCATION: Off the west coast of the Olympic Peninsula, extending from Cape Flattery to Copalis Rock

SIZE: 485 acres

ELEVATION RANGE: Sea level to 223 feet

MILES OF TRAIL: No trails; this wilderness is not open to the public.

TREES AND PLANTS: Sitka spruce, salal, salmonberry

WILDLIFE: Fur seal, gray whale, harbor seal, humpback whale, Pacific right whale, piked whale, sea lion, sea otter, auklet, bald eagle, cormorant, gull, murre, oystercatcher, peregrine falcon, petrel, tufted puffin

ADMINISTRATION: FWS, Washington Maritime NWR Complex, 360-457-8451

BEST SEASON: Year-round

FOR NEARLY 100 MILES from Cape Flattery to Copalis Rock run the 870 islands, reefs, and rocks of the Washington Islands Wilderness. The wilderness actually comprises three national wildlife refuges: 125-acre Flattery Rocks, 300-acre Quillayute Needles, and 60-acre Copalis Rock. All were first designated as migratory bird sanctuaries in 1907, then became wildlife refuges in 1940, then were named wilderness in 1970. These islands include such sea stack features as Point of the Arches, Flattery Rocks, Giants Graveyard, and Destruction Island that can be seen from the beaches of Olympic National Park. Tunnel Island, Copalis Rock, and dozen or so other rock formations north of Ocean Shores and south of South Beach are also part of the wilderness.

These islands, reefs, and rocks are the result of tectonic plate collisions more than 50 million years ago. Running in size from less than an acre up to 36 acres, most of the islands are unable to host any sort of tree and plant species because of the thin layer of soil. The islands and rocks that can provide a nutrient-rich environment host Sitka spruce, salal, and salmonberry. But lifeless these places are not, as they host thousands of birds like auklet, bald eagle, cormorant, gull, oystercatcher, peregrine falcon, and tufted puffin, along with thousands of migratory birds.

In the waters that define these 485 acres of Washington Islands are a number of whale species like gray, humpback, piked, and Pacific right. Also present, either in the waves or sunning on the rocks, are fur seal, harbor seal, and sea lion. This stretch of coast also contains a healthy underwater forest of kelp, which is an ideal habitat for the sea otter, reintroduced 30 years ago after being hunted to near extinction. To protect this vibrant life zone of land birds, sea birds, and sea mammals, the Washington Island Wilderness has a "You can look, but please don't touch" policy—no public entry.

A coastal sunset with sea stacks

9 Wonder Mountain

LOCATION: Bordering the south-eastern corner of Olympic National Park and approximately 50 miles northwest of Olympia

SIZE: 2,349 acres

ELEVATION RANGE: 1,741 to 4,848 feet

MILES OF TRAIL: No maintained trail system

TREES AND PLANTS: Douglas fir, Pacific silver fir, western hemlock, huckleberry, slide alder, thimble-berry, vine maple

WILDLIFE: Black-tailed deer, mountain goat, Olympic marmot

ADMINISTRATION: Olympic NF, Hood Canal RD, 360-877-5254

BEST SEASON: Summer through fall

An area of wilderness is…an area of unde-veloped Federal land retaining its primeval character and influence…of sufficient size as to make practicable its preservation….

AS DELINEATED IN THE WILDERNESS ACT of 1964, this criterion explains the existence of the undersized, pie slice–shaped Wonder Mountain Wilderness. The bill actually sets forth 5,000 acres as a preferable minimum size, but 2,349-acre Wonder Mountain became a wilderness area in 1984 by dint of the "of sufficient size" clause.

Like large sections in the Stephen T. Mather and Glacier Peak Wilderness Areas, and like Juniper Dunes, it has no trail system. The combination of rugged and thickly forested slopes can make the cross-country-only travel difficult but also rewarding in its solitude. Wonder Mountain sits in the Olympic rain shadow, keeping its annual precipitation around 60 inches—half of what the Colonel Bob Wilderness, located just a few miles to the west, receives. A half dozen or so lakes are clustered around the rugged center ridgeline and high point, 4,848-foot Wonder Mountain. Routes into the wilderness begin either from the southwest or southeast and require pressing up the steep, tree-covered slopes to reach open ridgelines and the lakes region.

The Wilderness Act of 1964 also qualifies a wilderness as an area that "generally appears to have been affected primarily by the forces of nature, with the imprint of man's work substantially unnoticeable." I think the unmolested Wonder Mountain Wilderness meets this criterion as well.

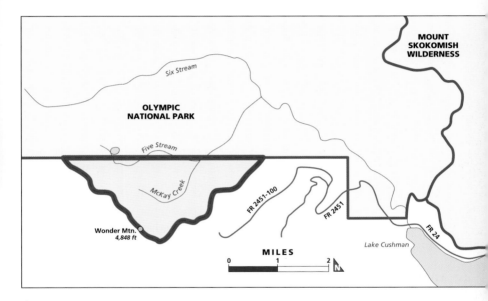

North Cascades

The Cascade Range, on one level, is but a part of the American Cordillera running 12,000 miles from Alaska to the tip of South America. Looking closer in, the Cascade Range runs from southern British Columbia into northern California like a charm bracelet of massive volcanoes—Mount Baker, Mount Rainier, Mount Adams, Mount Hood, Mount Jefferson, Mount Shasta, Mount Lassen—separated by lowland geography. Looking even closer, though, it is Washington's North Cascades that display by far the most impressive collection of subalpine and alpine scenery in the entire range.

Water, both fluid and frozen (rivers and glaciers, respectively), has taken what the subduction of the oceanic plate beneath the continental plate provided and turned the landscape into an area of intimidating mountains and steep-sided valleys like the Picket Range, Jack Mountain, Colonial Peak, and the area around Boston and Eldorado Peaks. Although much of the North Cascades National Park Complex is without trails because of the formidable terrain, hikes to Cascade Pass and Desolation Peak can offer some accessible and closer perspectives.

On the western edge of the North Cascades region are the quaint Anderson Lakes, floating in rolling meadows high above Baker Lake in the Noisy-Diobsud Wilderness. In the Mount Baker Wilderness, the pink and white heather meadows pool on Hannegan Pass, having run down the wildflower slopes below Hannegan Peak. The Pasayten Wilderness grabs a slice of the North Cascade mountain environment but then creates its own world with dozens of ridgelines full of tall peaks. Buckskin Point, Monument Peak, Remmel Mountain, Cathedral Peak, and Windy Peak run eastward into the amazing Pasayten Highlands, lush with grasses, wildflowers, and overviews of peaks and valleys in every direction. Hikes to Corral Lake and Horseshoe Basin will treat visitors to all these splendors.

More so than any other in Washington, the North Cascades region requires long, multiday hikes to truly appreciate its vastness—and to access some extremely remote destinations.

The Pleiades, Mount Baker Wilderness

10 Mount Baker Wilderness

View of Mount Baker from Park Butte

LOCATION: Approximately 25 miles east of Bellingham on the Canadian border

SIZE: 117,528 acres

ELEVATION RANGE: 1,800 to 10,781 feet

MILES OF TRAIL: Approximately 75

TREES AND PLANTS: Alaska yellow cedar, Douglas fir, mountain hemlock, bistort, blueberry, cinquefoil, heather, huckleberry, glacier lily, lupine, paintbrush

WILDLIFE: Black bear, black-tailed deer, fisher, hoary marmot, black-capped chickadee, crow, ferruginous hawk, ptarmigan, raven, Steller's jay

ADMINISTRATION: Mount Baker–Snoqualmie NF, Mount Baker RD, 360-856-5700. Glacier Public Service Center (Friday–Monday), 360-599-2714

BEST SEASON: Midsummer to early fall

LOOKING EASTWARD from Bellingham Bay, Mount Baker floats like a white island above a dark sea of forest. In the time of great sea conquests by the European sailing powers, to be "first" meant possession. We are presented, for obvious reasons, a Eurocentric view of the history of the United States, including the so-called discovery of the West by explorers on ship, horseback, and foot. Like other horizon-dominating Cascade volcanoes, Mount Baker has a story of "discovery."

Spanish legend has it that Greek captain Apostolos Valerianos, known more popularly as Juan de Fuca, sighted the volcano in 1592. If he did indeed lay eyes on what the Lummi tribe called Koma Kulshan, it is not written anywhere that this "new" mountain would be called

El Monte del Rey Felipe II after the king of Spain. For the next 200 years, no map, ship log, or other chronicle of voyages made any mention of the peak. In 1790 Spain was again credited with identifying the mountain, labeling it on a map as *La Gran Montaña del Carmelo* in honor of the Catholic Carmelite order.

However, it was an English name that stuck in 1792. A lieutenant named Joseph Baker sighted the volcano from the deck of Captain George Vancouver's ship near New Dungeness, which was east of Port Angeles and some 70 miles southwest of Mount Baker. According to the captain's log, the summit was "a very conspicuous object, bearing by compass N 43 E, apparently at a very remote distance." With the grace and honor important to men of that time, Captain Vancouver bestowed the name Mount Baker upon the peak, giving what time proved to be permanent credit to his third lieutenant.

The Spanish explorers, the British explorers, the French who "owned" this area as a part of the Louisiana Territory, and even the climbers, trappers, miners, and loggers who came to occupy camps and towns in the late nineteenth century around the present-day Mount Baker Wilderness, only *saw* this mountain. They did appreciate this incredible wonder; they did not understand the respect it deserves as a volcano—active as recently as 1975. By contrast, the Lummi, Nooksack, and other local tribes had awe for the bounty as well as the wrath of the volcano. Legend tells of an angry god who unleashed his fury by striking the mountain with a lighting bolt, wounding the great white peak, and causing it to shed blood of molten rock. Rivers were choked with ash, killing fish and leaving the waters barren. The Lummi tribe's name for the mountain-volcano, *Koma Kulshan,* means "Damaged Mountain" or "Wounded Mountain."

Cloaked in 10,000 acres of glaciers, Mount Baker is the massive centerpiece of the Mount Baker Wilderness, which comprises 117,528 acres but also adjoins a 45,000-acre roadless area and an 8,600-acre national recreation area. Many trails in the wilderness lead to climbing routes on the various glaciers covering Mount Baker. Three maintained trails also climb up the spectacularly fierce Mount Shuksan—in my opinion, the most perfect example of a jagged alpine peak in the American West. It is hard not to pause in the presence of these giants and be humbled by their hulking mass, as you would in the presence of Glacier Peak, Rainier, St. Helens, or Adams.

So it is surprising to those who have in fact climbed Mount Baker (and even those who never will) that the summit, called Grant Peak, is a 35-acre, nearly level ice mound, unlike the sharper-topped Sherman Peak standing more than 600 feet lower on a rim above the summit crater. Both Mount Baker and Mount Shuksan (actually in the Stephen T. Mather Wilderness) attract hundreds of climbers throughout the year. But other marvels lie in these V- and U-shaped valleys, up on ridgelines, along the creek drainages, by the cirque-filled lakes, and within the splendid alpine meadows.

An ideal outing for someone wanting it all is the Heather Meadows–Galena Chain Lakes loop. Heather Meadows is one of nature's finest landscape undertakings, thick with heather, cinquefoil, glacier lily, paintbrush, and many other wildflowers. Trails wind their way through this garden of nature collected around the Bagley Lakes, up and over a rocky gap, and into the beautiful and somewhat hidden Galena Chain Lakes area—Arbuthnet, Hayes, Iceberg, and Mazama Lakes—set in a marvelous basin. The journey continues to circumnavigate Table Mountain while both Mount Shuksan and Mount Baker loom in the near distance. It must be close to perfection.

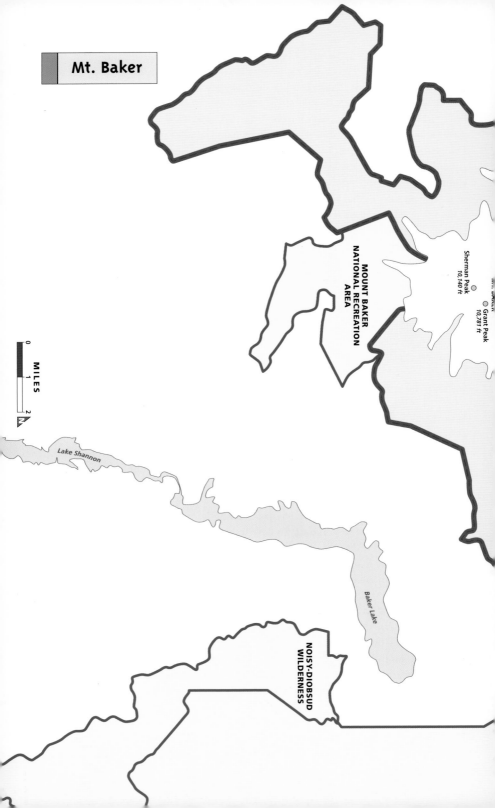

Mt. Baker

MILES
0
1
2

MOUNT
BAKER
NATIONAL
RECREATION
AREA

Sherman Peak
10,140 ft

Grant Peak
10,781 ft

Lake Shannon

Baker Lake

NOISY-DIOBSUD
WILDERNESS

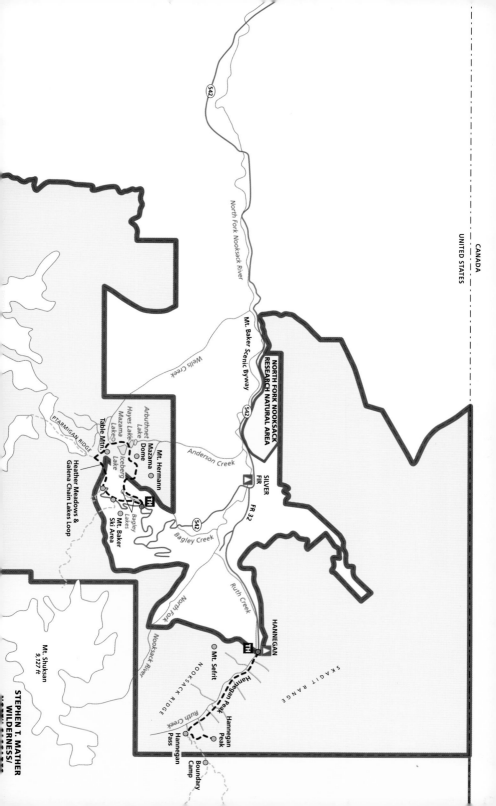

CANADA

UNITED STATES

North Fork Nooksack River

Mt. Baker Scenic Byway

542

542

Wells Creek

NORTH FORK NOOKSACK
RESEARCH NATURAL AREA

Anderson Creek

SILVER
FIR

FR 32

PTARMIGAN RIDGE

Table Mtn.

Arbuthnet
Lake

Hayes Lakes

Mazama
Dome

Mazama
Lakes

Iceberg
Lake

Mt. Hermann

Heather Meadows &
Galena Chain Lakes Loop

Bagley
Lakes

Mt. Baker
Ski Area

Bagley Creek

North Fork

Ruth Creek

HANNEGAN

Nooksack River

Mt. Sefrit

Hannegan Peak

NOOKSACK RIDGE

Ruth Creek

Hannegan
Pass

Hannegan
Peak

Boundary
Camp

SKAGIT RANGE

Mt. Shuksan
9,127 ft

STEPHEN T. MATHER
WILDERNESS/
NORTH CASCADES

> **DAY HIKE: HANNEGAN PEAK**
> One-Way Distance: 5.4 miles
> Elevation Range: 3,100 to 6,185 feet
> Total Elevation Gain: 3,085 feet
> Difficulty: Moderate
> Green Trails Map: Mt. Shuksan No. 14

The trail follows gently along the bottom of Ruth Creek with views of the Nooksack Ridge to the south. At mile 1.8 you reach two quick switchbacks before the trail continues with its gentle climb above the creek. At mile 3 the grade steepens to become more moderate. You'll come to the spur trail leading down to Hannegan Camp at mile 3.9. After passing the spur trail, the main trail becomes slightly steeper, passing through a mix of treed and open sections before reaching the lovely heather meadows of Hannegan Pass at mile 4.4.

From the pass, the trail leading to Hannegan Peak cuts to the left, passing through wonderful meadows. Eventually the trail makes its way completely out of the trees and at mile 5.4 up to Hannegan Peak, which is more like a high point on a broad ridge. The views from this southernmost high point of the Skagit Range include the Picket Range to the east, the north face of Mount Shuksan to the south, and the Cascade volcano Mount Baker to the southwest.

From the Glacier RD, go east 13.1 miles on WA 542. Turn left onto FR 32 toward Hannegan Pass and Nooksack Cirque Trail. You'll reach the Hannegan Pass Trailhead at 18.5 miles.

> **DAY HIKE: HEATHER MEADOWS AND GALENA CHAIN LAKES LOOP**
> Total Distance: 7.3 miles
> Elevation Range: 4,200 to 5,300 feet
> Total Elevation Gain: 1,500 feet
> Difficulty: Moderate
> Green Trails Map: Mt. Shuksan No. 14

From the parking area, begin on Trail #682 down to the western shoreline of the first and bigger of the Bagley Lakes. The trail is rocky, edging beneath the sheer slopes of Mount Herman with spectacular views of Mount Shuksan to the east. At 0.6 mile you come to a stone bridge leading to the east; pass this bridge and continue on to the second Bagley Lake, set below Table Mountain. Once past the second lake the trail climbs steeply via switchbacks up a rock slope to a gap at mile 3 between Mazama Dome and Table Mountain. Take in the views down to Iceberg and Hayes Lakes, the first two of the Galena Chain Lakes. The trail winds down and cuts between Iceberg and Hayes, continuing on to Mazama Lake at mile 4.6. There are camps around all of these lakes as well as at Arbuthnet Lake north of Hayes.

From Mazama Lake, the trail begins to climb around the southwest flank of Table Mountain to Ptarmigan Ridge at mile 5.5. Ptarmigan Ridge is one of the approach trails for climbers attempting Mount Baker, which stands larger than life to the southwest. The loop hike trail hugs close to the southeast flank of Table Mountain, wrapping around and down to a large parking lot at mile 5.7. From the parking lot follow the Heather Meadows Trail. The trail drops through a magnificent alpine world of heather and wildflowers above the east shoreline of the first Bagley Lake, then returns to the trailhead at mile 7.3.

From the Glacier RD on WA 542, travel east 21.5 miles to the Wild Goose–Bagley Lakes Loop Trailhead. The trailhead and parking area are on the right, a short distance past the ski resort.

Mount Shuksan, east of Mount Baker in the adjoining Stephen T. Mather Wilderness

Noisy-Diobsud Wilderness

LOCATION: Between Baker Lake and the western edge of the North Cascades National Park Complex, approximately 35 miles northeast of Sedro-Woolley

SIZE: 14,133 acres

ELEVATION RANGE: 1,600 to 6,234 feet

MILES OF TRAIL: 12

TREES AND PLANTS: Douglas fir, mountain hemlock, western red cedar, western hemlock, devil's club, elderberry, Oregon grape, salal, vine maple

WILDLIFE: Black bear, black-tailed deer, mountain goat, northern spotted owl, peregrine falcon

ADMINISTRATION: Mount Baker–Snoqualmie NF, Mount Baker RD, 360-856-5700

BEST SEASON: Summer to early fall

TO REACH THE NORTHERN PORTION of the Noisy-Diobsud Wilderness and the largest percentage of the scant 12 miles of maintained trails, you must first cross over the Baker Lake Dam. High above this 1960s-esque military-like compound of concrete and chain-link, the wilderness sits in a compact and narrow strip of steep and rugged terrain. The road ascends above the dam, Baker Lake, towns, and highways. It's a mixed view, one of balance (wilderness) and imbalance (clear-cuts), taken in from the high points like Anderson Butte.

Below Anderson Butte, wrapped in forest and pocket meadows, are the Watson and Anderson Lakes. Mount Watson lies to the southeast, Baker and Shuksan appear to the northwest and west, and the peaceful crowding of formidable peaks of North Cascades National Park (NCNP) rise to the east and northeast. More than 4,600 feet of elevation separate the low points along the creek bottoms of Noisy and Diobsud Creeks and the pivot point of the Noisy-Diobsud Wilderness, 6,234-foot Mount Watson.

The wilderness's yin and yang spill forth, Noisy Creek running north and Diobsud Creek flowing south. The handful of creeks here are easily as impressive defensively—with their legions of ferns, moss, salal, devil's club, elderberry, and salmonberry—as the rocky ridgelines and peaks that cut through the tree line of old-growth fir, cedar, and hemlock. Up the Anderson, Thunder, and Jackman Creek drainages near the west and southwest boundary of the Noisy-Diobsud Wilderness, clear-cuts stand out as reminders of economic progress. The balance, in the form of preservation, unfolds to the east in the NCNP. Noisy-Diobsud is an extension of the protected park and a symbolic barrier to the advancement of the swell of civilization.

Watson Lakes

The odd name of this wilderness makes it distinctive in relation to other Washington wilderness areas, even if the intent behind its formation was to add to an already existing preserve (NCNP). However, the Noisy-Diobsud Wilderness is significant for both the beauty it possesses and the mix of land uses that lie around it. You don't want to miss the quaintness of Anderson Lakes and nearby meadows at the foot of Mount Watson, or the meditative effects of standing on the ridgeline of Anderson Butte contemplating the land touched by man with both affection and aggression.

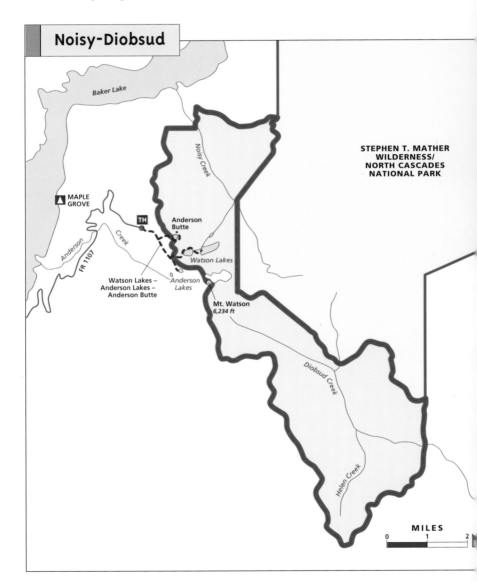

DAY HIKE: WATSON LAKES–ANDERSON LAKES–ANDERSON BUTTE
One-Way Distance: 3.7 miles
Elevation Range: 4,300 to 5,420 feet
Total Elevation Gain: 1,220 feet
Difficulty: Moderate to strenuous
Green Trails Map: Lake Shannon No. 46

The trail works nicely through the trees, winding and switchbacking up a moderate grade as it crosses over elevated walkways and 3-foot bridges before entering an open area. You will reach the spur trail up to Anderson Butte at 0.7 mile. The trail to Watson Lakes climbs through the open area before ducking back into the trees and descending into another open section and the trail junction for Watson and Anderson Lakes at mile 1.3. Heading straight will take you to Watson Lakes; bear to the right for Anderson Lakes.

The trail to Watson Lakes climbs steeply for 0.2 mile up to a notch before descending down switchbacks to the upper lake at mile 2. The trail wraps around the west and north shore of the upper lake, cuts across a marshy meadow area and the upper lake's outlet, climbs up a short hill, then heads down to lower Watson Lake at mile 2.5. Enjoy great views of Anderson Butte, very close to the north, and the glaciated Mount Watson farther to the south.

The trail to the Anderson Lakes passes through the open area into a rock and boulder section before beginning a steep descent through the trees. At 0.4 mile from the junction the trail enters a beautiful, marshy meadow that rolls along in all directions and contains the Anderson Lakes. Explore multiple lakes and ponds from here, the majority situated to the east in a rocky basin above a band of surmountable cliffs.

The trail up to Anderson Butte climbs steeply to reach a notch and the ridge at 0.6 mile. Follow just below or on the ridge to the north-northwest for another 0.2 mile to the location of a former lookout at 0.8 mile, with more grand views of Mount Baker and Shuksan.

NOTE: The distances to the Anderson Lakes and Anderson Butte are from the corresponding trail junctions, not from the trailhead. Also, feel free to explore this area in any manner you wish, hiking to any number of these destinations. The Noisy-Diobsud makes a fantastic place to skulk around in for a day, in whatever direction you choose.

About 5 miles east of Hamilton off WA 20, turn north onto Baker Lake Road (FR 11). At 14 miles turn right (east) onto Baker Lake Dam Road (FR 1106) toward Kulshan Campground. The road changes to gravel; you'll reach the campground at 15.2 miles. Continue straight, following signs for Anderson and Watson Lakes and crossing Upper Baker Dam. Follow the sign for the Watson Lakes Trail and FR 1107 at 17.1 miles. The road climbs high above Baker Lake. At 26.2 miles, turn left onto FR 022. At 27.4 miles you reach the trailhead and parking.

12 Pasayten Wilderness

Lupine meadows

LOCATION: Between the Canadian border and WA 20, east of Ross Lake and west of the Okanogan Valley, approximately 25 miles north of Winthrop

SIZE: 530,031 acres

ELEVATION RANGE: 2,550 to 9,066 feet

MILES OF TRAIL: over 600

TREES AND PLANTS: Alaska cedar, Douglas fir, Engelmann spruce, grand fir, larch, lodgepole pine, ponderosa pine, western hemlock, cinquefoil, huckleberry, lupine, phlox, sedge

WILDLIFE: Bighorn sheep, black bear, cougar, gray wolf, grizzly bear, lynx, mule deer, white-tailed deer, wolverine, blue grouse, Clark's nutcracker, mountain chickadee, northern flicker, red-breasted nuthatch, red-tailed hawk, Steller's jay

ADMINISTRATION: Okanogan NF: Methow Valley RD, 509-996-4003; Tonasket RD, 509-486-2186

BEST SEASON: Midsummer to late fall

THIS IS A LAND OF CASCADE PEAKS, rolling highlands, flower-filled meadows, and wetlands. *Okanogan* means "rendezvous," and for 8,500 years people have done so in what we now call the Pasayten Wilderness. Nomadic natives frequented what is now the Lost River Gorge, and Okanogan tribes on both sides of the current U.S.–Canadian border gathered for potlatches of fish and wild game in the Pasayten. In 1879, President Rutherford B. Hayes designated the Pasayten area as the Moses Reservation, set aside for the Columbia tribe led by Chief Moses. The containment policy was of course brought on by the insistence of white settlers, who wanted undisputed and safe claim to the surrounding lands. Chief Moses, however, refused the artificially contrived homeland, since his people's ancestral home was to the southeast—much closer to the Columbia River. Pressures from miners and stockmen soon led to subsequent designation of mining and grazing areas within the northern portion of the vacant reservation. By 1885, the reservation was abolished and the land returned to public domain.

On February 22, 1897, President Grover Cleveland signed a proclamation facilitating the formation of 13 forest reserves covering 21 million acres in the western states. The Okanogan, Wenatchee, and Mount Baker–Snoqualmie National Forests, established in the early 1900s, were once part of this forest reserve system. Even with preserve and national forest status in place, though, the Pasayten 100 years ago had a more diverse collection of people "rendezvousing" within its boundaries than it does today.

Trappers, hunters, stockmen, miners, climbers, horseback riders, and hikers all shared this diverse and immense area. Sheep grazed quite heavily from 1912 until as recently as 2000. Tungsten mining had a 15-year history during the time of World War I in the area around Scheelite Pass. Long a mainstay of inhabitants, trapping became illegal here in the 1960s. The Civilian Conservation Corps built numerous fire lookouts here in the 1930s public-works era and constructed hundreds of miles of trails to reach these manned mountain locations on places like Bunker Hill, Remmel Mountain, and Windy Peak. Designated in the second wave of congressional wilderness acts in 1968, and expanded in 1984, the Pasayten Wilderness is today largely under the jurisdiction of the Okanogan National Forest, though its far western edge lies in the Mount Baker–Snoqualmie National Forest. Over time some groups have faded away, while others (especially backpackers and equestrians) have remained and continue to explore the Pasayten.

More than 600 miles of trail work through the 530,031 acres. The Boundary Trail runs 73.1 miles over the beautiful high parkland of Horseshoe Pass and into the sanctuary of the Cathedral Peak region before rolling on many more miles to the west at the boundary with the North Cascades National Park Complex. The final leg—or the beginning stretch, depending on your direction—of the Pacific Crest Trail cuts through the Pasayten in a north-south direction, cresting eight passes and totaling 32.5 miles. The Hidden Lakes–Larch Pass Loop (see p. 96) has everything: glorious ridgelines, creek crossings, lakes, dozens of spectacular peaks above 7,500 feet, and even the cathartic experience of breaking from the trees into the high, open, bouldered grasslands that are the signature of the northeastern portion of the Pasayten. The Pasayten is home to rare plants like inky gentian and tiny gentian, not to mention the largest concentration of lynx in the lower 48 states. It is also roaming territory for grizzly bear and gray wolf.

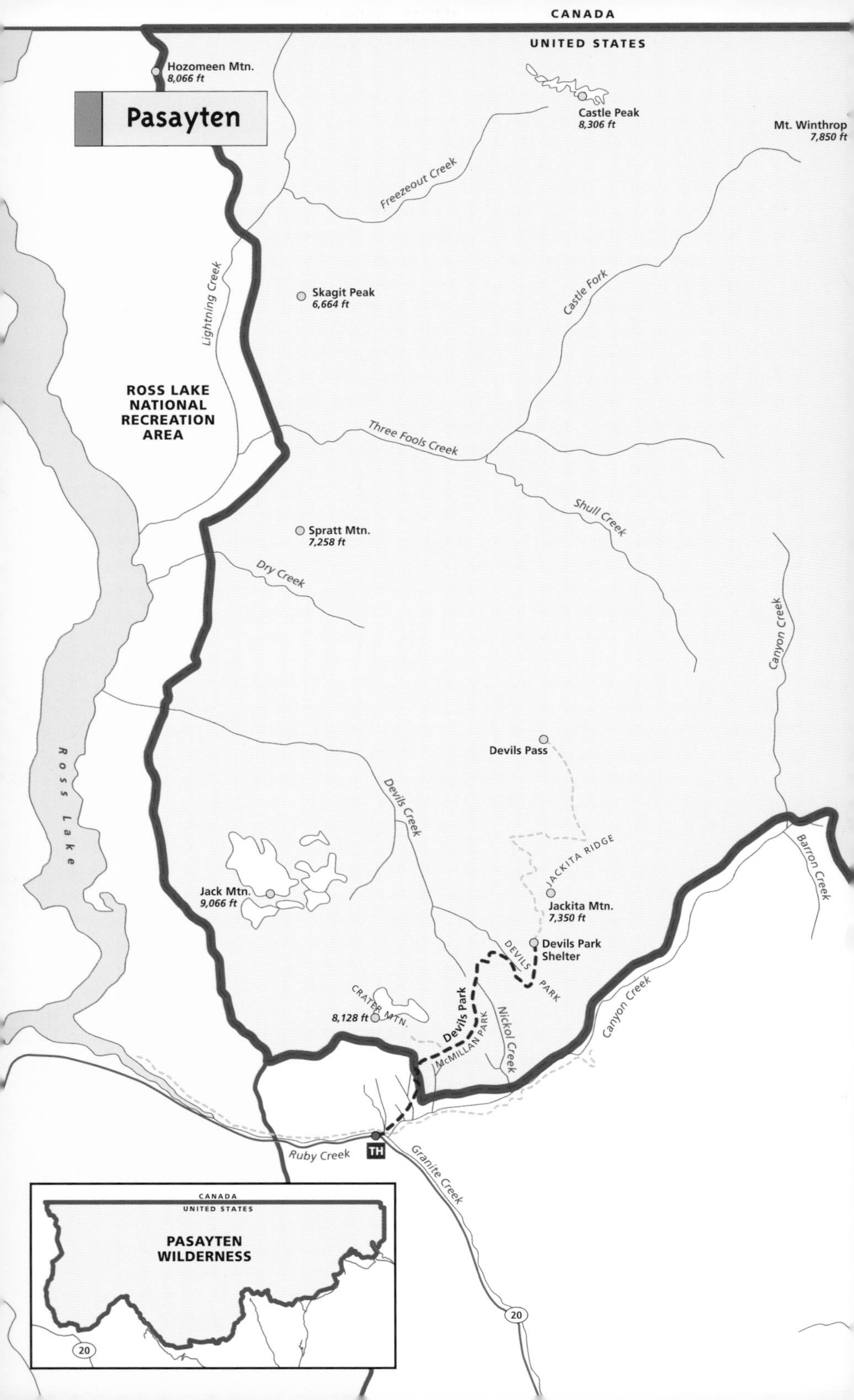

Pasayten

CANADA
UNITED STATES

Hozomeen Mtn.
8,066 ft

Castle Peak
8,306 ft

Mt. Winthrop
7,850 ft

Freezeout Creek

Castle Fork

Lightning Creek

Skagit Peak
6,664 ft

**ROSS LAKE
NATIONAL
RECREATION
AREA**

Three Fools Creek

Shull Creek

Spratt Mtn.
7,258 ft

Dry Creek

Canyon Creek

Devils Pass

Devils Creek

JACKITA RIDGE

Jack Mtn.
9,066 ft

Jackita Mtn.
7,350 ft

Barron Creek

Devils Park
Shelter

Canyon Creek

CRATER MTN.

DEVILS PARK

8,128 ft

Devils Park

Nickol Creek

McMILLAN PARK

Ruby Creek

TH

Granite Creek

20

CANADA
UNITED STATES

**PASAYTEN
WILDERNESS**

20

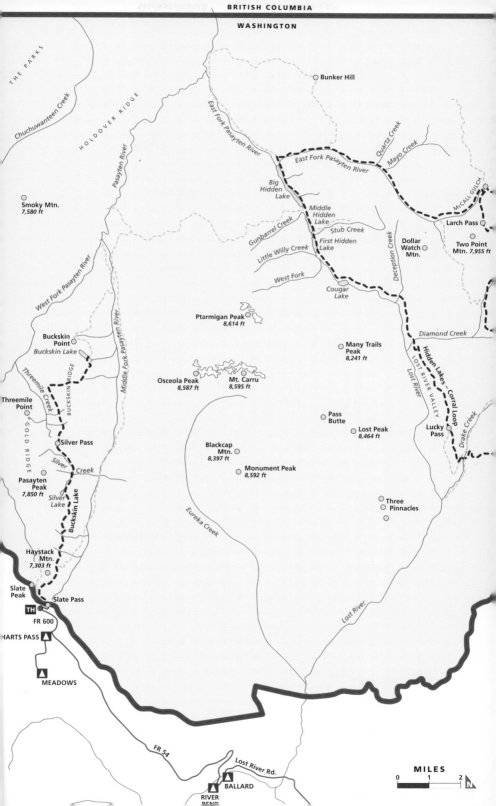

THE PARKS

Chuchuwanteen Creek

HOLDOVER RIDGE

Pasayten River

East Fork Pasayten River

Bunker Hill

Quartz Creek

Mayo Creek

East Fork Pasayten River

McCALL GULCH

Smoky Mtn.
7,580 ft

Big
Hidden
Lake

Middle
Hidden
Lake

Larch Pass

Gunbarrel Creek

Stub Creek

Dollar
Watch
Mtn.

Two Point
Mtn. 7,955 ft

First Hidden
Lake

Little Willy Creek

West Fork

Deception Creek

West Fork Pasayten River

Cougar
Lake

Ptarmigan Peak
8,614 ft

Many Trails
Peak
8,241 ft

Diamond Creek

Middle Fork Pasayten River

Buckskin
Point
Buckskin Lake

BUCKSKIN RIDGE

Osceola Peak
8,587 ft

Mt. Carru
8,595 ft

Hidden Lakes – Corral Loop

LOST RIVER VALLEY

Threemile Creek

Threemile
Point

GOLD RIDGE

Pass
Butte

Lost Peak
8,464 ft

Lost River

Lucky
Pass

Drake Creek

Silver Pass

Silver Creek

Blackcap
Mtn.
8,397 ft

Pasayten
Peak
7,850 ft

Silver
Lake

Buckskin Lake

Monument Peak
8,592 ft

Three
Pinnacles

Eureka Creek

Haystack
Mtn.
7,303 ft

Slate
Peak

Slate Pass

TH

FR 600

HARTS PASS

Lost River

MEADOWS

FR 54

Lost River Rd.

BALLARD

RIVER
BEND

MILES

0   1   2

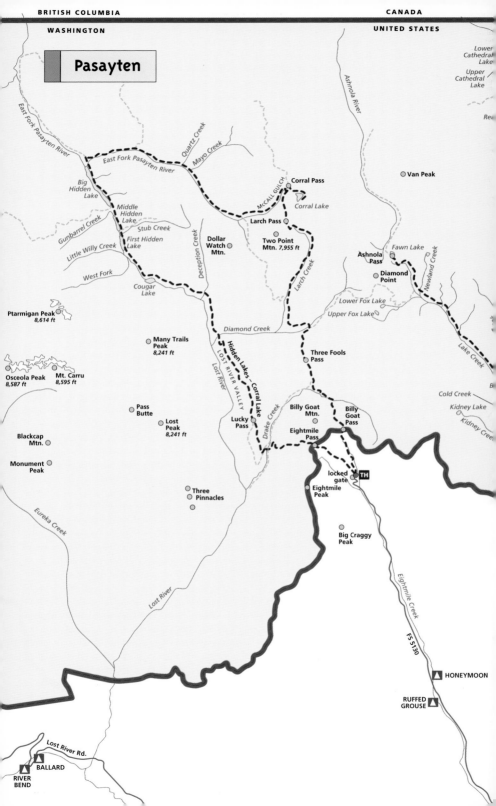

Pasayten

Lower Cathedral Lake
Upper Cathedral Lake

East Fork Pasayten River

Quartz Creek

Mayo Creek

East Fork Pasayten River

Van Peak

Big Hidden Lake

Middle Hidden Lake

Gunbarrel Creek

Stub Creek

First Hidden Lake

Little Willy Creek

West Fork

Cougar Lake

Deception Creek

Dollar Watch Mtn.

McCALL GULCH

Corral Pass

Corral Lake

Larch Pass

Two Point Mtn. 7,955 ft

Larch Creek

Ashnola Pass

Fawn Lake

Newland Creek

Diamond Point

Ptarmigan Peak 8,614 ft

Diamond Creek

Lower Fox Lake

Upper Fox Lake

Lake Creek

Many Trails Peak 8,241 ft

Hidden Lakes — Corral Lake

Three Fools Pass

Osceola Peak 8,587 ft

Mt. Carru 8,595 ft

Lost River Valley

Cold Creek

Kidney Lake

Pass Butte

Lost Peak 8,241 ft

Lucky Pass

Drake Creek

Billy Goat Mtn.

Billy Goat Pass

Kidney Creek

Blackcap Mtn.

Eightmile Pass

Monument Peak

locked gate   TH

Eureka Creek

Three Pinnacles

Eightmile Peak

Big Craggy Peak

Lost River

Eightmile Creek

FS 5130

HONEYMOON

RUFFED GROUSE

Lost River Rd.

BALLARD

RIVER BEND

BRITISH COLUMBIA

WASHINGTON

Cathedral
Peak 8,601 ft

Cathedral
Pass

Amphitheater
Mtn.

Wolframite
Mtn.

Scheelite
Pass

Crawford

BAUERMAN RIDGE

Teapot
Dome

Haig
Mtn.

Loudon
Lake

Rock
Mtn.

Horseshoe Pass

HORSESHOE BASIN

Cathedral Creek

Apex
Pass

Apex
Mtn.

Tungsten
Lake

Cinch Creek

Tungsten Creek

Horseshoe Creek

Big Horn Creek

Saddle
Peak

Topaz
Mtn.

Windy
Peak
8,331 ft

Clutch Cr.

Chewel Creek

Windy Peak – Boundary Loop

Middle Fork Toats

Coulee Creek

Four
Point
Lake

Four Point Creek

Chewuch River

Basin Creek

Windy Creek

TH

FR 500

FR 39

Toats Coulee Creek

FR 300

Queen Creek

Windy Creek

Ashnola Pass

South Fork Toats Coulee Creek

TH

Chewuch River

FR 250

FR 5160

Lake Creek

FR 100

FR 51

CAMP
FOUR

FR 100

CHEWUCH

Chewuch River

MILES

0   1   2

CANADA

UNITED STATES

PASAYTEN
WILDERNESS

20

DAY OR DESTINATION HIKE: DEVILS PARK
One-Way Distance: 5.3 miles
Elevation Range: 1,900 to 5,600 feet
Total Elevation Gain: 3,700 feet
Difficulty: Moderate
Green Trails Maps: Jack Mountain No. 17, Mt. Logan No. 49

This hike follows Jackita Ridge Trail #738, which heads from the parking area into the trees to a footbridge crossing of Granite Creek. A short distance beyond the crossing the trail forks; to the right is the Canyon Creek Trail, to the left is Jackita Ridge. Bear left to a footlog crossing of Canyon Creek and begin a long climb up and away from the creek. At approximately mile 3 you'll reach a junction with an unmaintained trail, #746, which leads to two abandoned lookout sites on Crater Mountain (summer home of poet Gary Snyder in 1952). Continue on Trail #738 toward Devils Park through a marvelous stretch of meadows and marshland called McMillan Park, all situated beneath the southern face of Crater Mountain.

After the glide through the park, the trail makes a short drop down to Nickol Creek at mile 4.1 before working uphill through patches of huckleberry bushes to Devils Park. An open forest and meadow environment, Devils Park has plenty of tempting grassy slopes to hike and views to take in, all accessible from the Devils Park Shelter at mile 5.3. You'll find a few sleeping bunks in the shelter and plenty of areas around it in which to set up camp.

From Winthrop travel west on WA 20 for 52.2 miles, then turn right into the parking area for Canyon Creek.

DESTINATION HIKE: ASHNOLA PASS
One-Way Distance: 12.3 miles
Elevation Range: 3,200 to 6,200 feet
Total Elevation Gain: 3,000 feet
Difficulty: Moderate
Green Trails Maps: Billy Goat Mountain No. 19, Coleman Peak No. 20

The hike to Ashnola Pass follows Lake Creek Trail #500 through a broad section of the drainage containing a mix of trees and rockslides, which in some spots will have wild raspberry growing out from between the rocks. Set between two ridgelines and various drainages running into Lake Creek, the trail slowly gains about 800 feet in elevation over the 5 miles to the southeastern end of Black Lake. You can camp on either end of the lake; access the northwestern end by continuing along the skinny blackish green lake on its northeastern shoreline.

Beyond the lake the trail continues, gradually passing through a rocky section before leaving the floor of the drainage at mile 6.3, winding its way upslope. At mile 9 the trail goes through a section of heavy blowdown before continuing its elevation gain, crossing over four footbridges and reaching the junction with the

Diamond Point Trail at mile 10.3. As you continue on Lake Creek Trail #500, two more sections of increasingly steep uphill follow before you reach Ashnola Pass and the pleasant surprise of Fawn Lake at mile 12.3. The setting—Diamond Point nearby to the southwest, Van Peak farther to the north—as well as the available water source in Fawn Lake, make this an ideal location to overnight.

From Winthrop, take WA 20 west to West Chewuch Road in 0.2 mile. Turn right and drive to the stop sign, then at 7 miles continue straight on FR 51. At 14 miles you'll see a sign for FR 100; do *not* take this road but continue on FR 51. The road number will change to FR 5160 at 18.3 miles. Turn left onto FR 100 at 21.6 miles toward the Lake Creek Trailhead, reached at 24.1 miles.

DESTINATION HIKE: BUCKSKIN LAKE
One-Way Distance: 9.8 miles
Elevation Range: 6,800 to 7,300 feet
Total Elevation Gain: 1,600 feet
Difficulty: Strenuous
Green Trails Maps: Pasayten Peak No. 18, Washington Pass No. 50

The breathtaking views begin even before one step is taken: the expanse of the Pasayten to the north and ridgeline after ridgeline of North Cascade peaks to the west and south. Make a short push uphill on Trail #498 to Slate Pass, and a whole new world emerges. You're in the classic, grassy highland slopes of the Pasayten. View the trail running below Gold Ridge, along with a myriad of looming peaks like Monument, Blackcap, and Ptarmigan across the Middle Fork Pasayten River valley to the east.

From the pass, the trail drops into a basin before beginning its gentle, descending course below Gold Ridge. Along early sections of the trail you can spy the Slate Peak Lookout. At mile 2.1 the trail passes through a rockslide and makes a short climb uphill before leveling out. The next short climb comes at mile 2.8, with a somewhat steep push up to the ridgeline before dropping down the other side into the trees to the trail junction for Silver Lake at mile 3.2. The left fork goes to Silver Lake, where you'll find campsites. The right fork continues its descent to a creek crossing at mile 3.8. You'll then climb at a moderate incline to Silver Pass at mile 4.8, with a nice overlook of the Threemile Creek drainage.

Work down a series of switchbacks to a level path that alternates from grassy sections to forest before bending to the right at mile 5.7 and climbing steeply up tight switchbacks for 0.5 mile. You will continue to climb briefly up more relaxed switchbacks before contouring mid-slope beneath Buckskin Ridge on a narrow, rocky, and loose surface. The higher vantage, a path suitable for a mountain goat, and views of the big, craggy peaks to the west make this a thrilling section of the hike.

At mile 6.9 the trail drops into a talus basin occupied by stands of larch. After passing through the basin and winding through the trees at mile 7.2, the trail begins climbing up to Buckskin Ridge at mile 8.2. From the ridge the trail works its way steeply down another basin, this time on the east side of the ridge, passing by some small ponds and cutting cross-slope. You'll again see various peaks across the Middle Fork Pasayten River valley, then arrive on the shores of the southeast end of Buckskin Lake at mile 9.8. The lake sits in a long, narrow talus basin overlooked by Buckskin Point to the north-northwest. Campsites are available.

From the Methow Valley RD in Winthrop, travel west 13.2 miles on WA 20 to the Mazama turnoff. Turn right and drive 0.4 mile to a "T" intersection. Turn left to continue on Lost River Road toward Harts Pass. At 20.3 miles, shortly before the road surface turns to gravel, Lost River Road becomes FR 54. Approximately 5 miles up on FR 54, proceed with caution along a 0.5-mile stretch of quite narrow and exposed but still drivable road. At 32.7 miles you'll reach Harts Pass; bear to the right, following the signs for Slate Peak. From here you will be on FR 600. It is 1.8 miles up to the trailhead, at 34.5 miles. There is no parking area; you must park along the road.

MULTIDAY LOOP HIKE: HIDDEN LAKES–CORRAL LAKE
One-Way Distance: 31.3 miles
Elevation Range: 4,800 to 7,500 feet
Total Elevation Gain: 7,200 feet
Difficulty: Moderate
Green Trails Maps: Pasayten Peak No. 18, Billy Goat Mountain No. 19

From the north side of the parking area, follow the trail behind the locked gate to begin the hike. Stay to the right where another trail cuts downhill. After gaining some elevation and rounding a bend, Trail #477 begins at about mile 0.2; you'll see the sign for Cougar Lake and Hidden Lakes. The trail stays high on an open slope along the east side of the steep-sided Eightmile Creek drainage, opposite the impressive northeastern faces of Big Craggy and Eightmile Peaks. After mile 1.2 the trail will reach a high point, Eightmile Pass, before dropping 1,000 feet in elevation through the trees to an established camp area and footbridge crossing of Drake Creek at mile 3. Continue on Trail #477 after the junction with Trail #502b, climbing above the drainage before heading north through an old burn just prior to Lucky Pass at mile 4.5.

Over the pass (more like a broad saddle), the trail again cuts across a slope, slowly losing elevation over the next 4.8 miles, high above the amazing Lost River Valley. Look for massive mountains like Three Pinnacles, Lost Peak, Pass Butte, and Many Trails Peak to the southwest and west. Water can be scarce along this stretch during late summer and early fall. You'll find a camp approximately 1.2 miles past Lucky Pass called Hoot Owl as well as other dispersed campsites farther down the trail.

The trail crosses Diamond Creek at mile 7.7, then continues dropping down to the confluence of Deception Creek and Lost River at mile 9.3. Through here the trail stays low alongside Lost River en route to Cougar Lake and the three Hidden Lakes. The river gets its name because it will eventually disappear underground past Cougar Lake. At mile 10.5 you will reach emerald-colored Cougar Lake; campsites lie on the east end. The trail continues around the north shoreline, through open and treed sections, and past a lake at mile 11.4 before reaching First Hidden Lake at mile 11.7.

A camping area lies on the north end, along with a sheltered eating area and a guard station built in 1954. There is a noticeable contrast between the high, open slopes above the Lost River Valley and the valley bottom, which has thicker stands of trees and rounder, shorter mountains. No established campsites exist around Middle Hidden Lake, but you can find a few sites at the south end of Big Hidden Lake.

Leaving the Hidden Lakes, the trail makes two creek crossings and passes by a lean-to shelter before reaching the junction with Trail #451 at mile 14. Take Trail #451 east, following signs for Bunker Hill. The trail stays mainly in the trees except for a few open wooded areas around the junction with Trail #456 at mile 15.1. Continue on #451 toward Corral Lake, gaining elevation all along.

The trail crosses Quartz and Mayo Creeks and a short stretch of elevated wooden walkways at mile 18 before coming into view of Dollar Watch Mountain and the junction with Trail #548 to Corral Lake at mile 18.2. Trail #548 cuts uphill via a series of switchbacks above McCall Gulch before bursting out from the cover of trees into a high-mountain world of rolling, grassy slopes at the junction with Trail #502 at mile 19.7. A small creek runs through this basin, which has some great places to pitch camp, especially in the fall when the turning of the larch trees makes a fiery yellow glow in Larch Pass to the south.

To continue on toward Corral Lake, take Trail #502 north up the basin to Corral Pass at mile 20.3. From the pass, head to the right (east-southeast) below the ridgeline to a spectacular overlook of Corral Lake and the endless flow of peaks to the north and east at mile 20.8. The trail drops another 0.5 mile down to the lake, ringed by larch trees. Plenty of campsites are available.

From Corral Lake, backtrack to the trail junction with Trail #548, continuing on Trail #502 to Larch Pass at mile 23.3, northeast of Two Point Mountain. Through the pass make sure to take the left fork of the trail, switchbacking downhill into the trees below Two Point before swinging to the opposite side of the Larch Creek drainage. The trail keeps dropping in elevation, going from wooded to open valley environments, all the way to a campsite at mile 25.2.

After two footbridge crossings of Larch Creek, the trail reenters the trees and begins a moderate ascent past Trail #451 at mile 25.7 and up to Three Fools Pass at mile 27.1. Campsites lie both shortly before and on the pass; note that a water source at the pass may be scarce later in the season. The trail drops again, this time down to a crossing of Drake Creek at mile 27.8, then climbs through a mix of moderate and steeper sections around the northeastern side of Billy Goat Mountain and up to Billy Goat Pass at mile 29.6. The pass literally takes just a few strides to get over. The trail then begins a 1.5-mile rapid run down a series of switchbacks, with 1,000 feet in elevation loss, returning to the trailhead at mile 31.3.

From downtown Winthrop, take WA 20 west to West Chewuch Road in 0.2 mile. Turn right, drive to the stop sign, then continue straight on FR 51 at 7 miles. Turn left at 9.5 miles onto FR 5130 toward Billy Goat Corral. The road surface turns from pavement to gravel at 14.7 miles. The road ends at the trailhead, at 26.1 miles.

MULTIDAY LOOP HIKE: WINDY PEAK–BOUNDARY LOOP
One-Way Distance: 45.6 miles
Elevation Range: 4,200 to 8,000 feet
Total Elevation Gain: 6,200 feet
Difficulty: Moderate
Green Trails Maps: Coleman Peak No. 20, Horseshoe Basin No. 21

The trail is wide at the start, more like a skinny road than a trail as it drops some elevation through a mixed conifer forest. Windy Peak is visible to the left (northwest) about halfway to the Clutch Creek Trail #343 junction at mile 0.5. Follow the Clutch Creek Trail as it descends through a stand of aspen with a lush grass and wildflower understory. At approximately mile 1.2 is another trail junction; follow the sign to the left for Windy Peak, and cross over Middle Fork Toats Coulee Creek a short distance further. The trail climbs from here, initially in the trees before breaking out onto an open grassy slope at mile 2.2 with views of the valleys, ridges, and rounded, tree-covered peaks to the south. The trail alternates nicely between forested, open, and mixed environments on its way to the trail junction with the Long Swamp Trail #342 at mile 3.8. Head north (right) on Trail #342 for the push up to Windy Peak.

Worlds change again as the trail leaves the open slope and enters a well-cairned rockscape environment with stunted trees, stiff bunchgrasses, and other plants. The trail levels out onto a plateau below Windy Peak, which can be an amazing campsite abounding with panoramic views—but be sure to pack water if the snowpack has melted. At mile 5.5 a spur trail leads to the top of Windy Peak. After you head straight at the sign for Horseshoe Basin, the trail drops down to a saddle between Windy Peak and Topaz Mountain, crosses to the northeast side of the ridge, and drops back into the trees to the junction at mile 6.6 with Basin Creek Trail #360, which leads to the Chewuch River.

The Basin Creek Trail alternates between losing and gaining elevation before making a steady descent through the trees, with the last mile dropping quickly down a series of switchbacks to Chewuch River Trail #510 at mile 13.3. A campsite lies 0.1 mile south of this junction, alongside Basin Creek. Continue on Trail #510 north as it parallels the river, staying low through another pleasant corridor of trees. At mile 14.8 is another campsite and footlog crossing where Trail #510 passes Trail #534 toward Tungsten Mine in another 0.1 mile. Follow the trail toward Remmel Lake. The trail continues to follow the Chewuch River and then Remmel Creek but starts to gain more elevation as it passes more campsites at mile 15.6, the junction for Four Point Lake at mile 17.6, and finally the Remmel Lake junction at mile 20.9.

There's no sign at the Remmel Lake junction, but if you continue straight through the old stock gate, you'll reach Remmel Lake, and campsites, in about 0.7 mile. Heading right, the trail climbs above the lake and into a marvelous long meadow, or pasture corridor, lush with grasses and wildflowers in the shadow of

Canyon Creek in the Pasayten Wilderness

Amphitheater Mountain to the east-northeast. The trail into the Amphitheater dead-ends, but it still makes a great lunch spot for a day hike in the Cathedral area.

From this pasture and before the trail curls around Amphitheater Mountain, you'll come to the junction at mile 22.6 with Boundary Trail #533, which also takes you in 0.9 mile to the junction with Lower Cathedral Lake. Heading right, another 1.5 miles takes you to Upper Cathedral Lake at mile 24.1. Upper Cathedral Lake is nestled against the blocky wall of the northwest ridge of Amphitheater Mountain; the pointy-topped Cathedral Peak looms a short distance to the northeast. Campsites abound at both lakes, making for ideal base camps from which to explore the area.

Climb 0.6 mile from Upper Cathedral Lake to Cathedral Pass, after which the trail begins its marvelous, high-line run into Horseshoe Basin. From the pass the trail makes a long swing around the Cathedral Creek drainage, then ascends to Apex Pass at mile 27.3 before making a much shorter swing around the Tungsten Creek drainage to the abandoned Tungsten Mine at mile 28.9. An old cabin and other remnants of the mining operation still linger, even though nature is doing its best erase them. Camping is available here, as is a water source.

The trail continues its high route, staying mainly on the edge of the treeline with fantastic views of Windy Peak, with Cathedral and Amphitheater behind. The trail passes over Scheelite Pass at mile 32.1 (some campsites are here), below Bauerman Ridge, under Teapot Dome, around Rock Mountain and Loudon Lake, and into the high-mountain grasslands of Horseshoe Basin at mile 40. Be advised that water is scarce in this section later in the hiking season.

Horseshoe Basin is an amazing setting of rolling, grassy slopes, with bonus high-mountain views across the Pasayten. Plenty of campsites lie in the basin; choose one that is established. At mile 40.3 is the Goodenough Peak Trail #340 junction. Continue on Trail #533, wrapping around a point, past Albert Trail and Trail #342 to Windy Peak, before reentering the trees and descending along the Clutch Creek drainage on a broad, easygoing trail. At mile 45.1 Trail #533 meets Trail #341; the last 0.5 mile returns to the Irongate Trailhead at mile 45.6.

From Tonasket, cross over the Okanogan River. Turn right onto Highway 7 (Loomis-Oroville Road) and drive about 16 miles west to Loomis. Drive through and north (right) out of town another 2.2 miles, then turn left at the road sign for Chopaka Lake (at 0.8 mile in, the road is marked FR 39). At 26.2 miles, bear to the left at the sign for the Irongate Trailhead. At 32 miles, turn right onto FR 500. The road is dirt and rough. It is 6 miles from here to the trailhead, at 38 miles.

Stephen T. Mather Wilderness/ North Cascades National Park Complex   13

Mix-up Peak near Cascade Pass

> From a national standpoint, the area is unquestionably of national park caliber, is more valuable used as such than for any other use now ascertainable. . . . Such a Cascade park will outrank in its scenic, recreational, and wildlife values, any existing national park and any other possibility for such a park within the United States.
> —*National Park Service, "Northern Cascades Area Report," 1937*

THE STEPHEN T. MATHER WILDERNESS, some 93 percent of the North Cascades National Park Complex (NCNPC), is perhaps the closest of any of the larger nonisland wilderness areas in Washington to being truly left to its

LOCATION: Between the Canadian border and Lake Chelan, and approximately 35 miles east-northeast of Sedro-Woolley

SIZE: 634,614 acres (wilderness); 684,600 acres (NCNPC)

ELEVATION RANGE: 400 to 9,210 feet

MILES OF TRAIL: 390

TREES AND PLANTS: Bigleaf maple, black cottonwood, Douglas fir, mountain hemlock, Sitka alder, whitebark pine, cinquefoil, glacier lily, heather, huckleberry, kinnikinnick, red columbine, tiger lily

WILDLIFE: Beaver, black bear, elk, lynx, marmot, moose, mountain goat, pika, raccoon, river otter, white-tailed deer, wolverine, black-capped chickadee, blue grouse, ferruginous hawk, northern spotted owl, pileated woodpecker, ptarmigan, ruffed grouse, Steller's jay

ADMINISTRATION: NPS 360-856-5700; Chelan RD, 509-682-2576; North Cascades Visitor Center, 206-386-4495

BEST SEASON: Midsummer to late fall

own devices, with only limited human alteration. The most obvious reason for this status is the terrain itself. The centers of the larger northern portion of the park and the smaller southern portion contain incredibly mountainous terrain. The logjam of sharp ridgelines, steep valleys, and raging rivers make it a challenge for even the hardiest adventurer.

The 684,600-acre park complex is broken down into three major parts: North Cascades National Park (NCNP) has 505,000 acres; Ross Lake National Recreation Area (NRA) has 117,600 acres; and Lake Chelan NRA has 62,000 acres. Each region has within its boundaries designated wilderness: Ross Lake has about 63 percent, Lake Chelan about 90 percent, and only 386 acres of the huge NCNP are *not* wilderness. These several portions collectively form the 634,614-acre Stephen T. Mather Wilderness, enacted in 1988.

Holding true to the park complex's confusion of designations, unfortunately, is the oft-forgotten fact that the Stephen T. Mather Wilderness was named for the first director of the national park system. Appointed in 1916, Mather (1867–1930) had already devoted a large portion of his life to the protection, support, and stewardship of wildlands. His legacy is still very much present in our national parks system. Some 15 years on, many users still call the area North Cascades National Park, perhaps for simplicity's sake.

The numbers and designations of the NCNPC may be complex, but what is not is the deep, simple splendor radiating from this vast region of fierce-looking mountains, steep-sided, glacially shaped valleys, high meadows, waterfalls, cirque lakes, rivers, and tens of thousands of acres left virtually inaccessible to humans. In the north the signature feature of the Picket Range—Whatcom Peak, Mount Challenger, Crooked Thumb, and Mount Fury—effectively keeps nearly 200,000 acres trailless and accessible only to those with mountaineering experience. In the same manner, Eldorado Peak, Boston Peak, and Mount Logan help to keep 130,000 acres without trail access in the southern portion of the park, in and around Cascade Pass.

To see and experience these remote places, or really any of the more easily accessible terrain of the NCNPC, you need to hike—or take a floatplane. The North Cascades Scenic Highway (WA 20) and Lake Chelan are the only two major access routes to the trailheads of a vast number of long, multiday hikes. There are no bus tours, concessions stands, or guided tours to Whatcom Peak or up to Rainbow Lake. (By comparison, Mount Rainier National Park at one-third the size has only 80 fewer miles of trail than the park complex.) As with the other national parks, hunting is prohibited. However, note that hunting is permitted within the national recreation areas, subject to state laws.

Ironically, part of the allure of the park complex is an unintended consequence of intervention in and alteration of the area. Humans, indigenous and pilgrim, have left their mark on the region. The most noticeable contemporary legacy, if now taken for granted by most, is the presence of the four largest lakes: Ross, Diablo, Gorge, and Chelan. As early as 1917 the city of Seattle had begun to investigate the development of hydroelectric power along the Skagit River. By 1927 federal permission was granted to begin the construction of the first of three dams, called Diablo. By 1937 construction had begun on the next, Ruby Dam, later renamed Ross Dam after John D. Ross, the visionary behind the dam projects and superintendent of Seattle City Light Company. By 1961 all three dams had been built: Diablo, Ross, and Gorge High, eradicating more than 40 miles of valley bottomland. Ross Dam was also enlarged over three phases from its original height of 305 feet to 540 feet. Enough time has passed since 1961 that these lakes are now part of the accepted landscape.

Today, Ross Lake is the most popular area within the complex for multiuse recreation, both for the easy highway access and for the shorter trails into the region's signature radiance of formidable peaks and incredible vistas. Ross Lake NRA also offers motorboat launches on Diablo Lake and on the southern end of Ross Lake (boats up to 14 feet can also be portaged from Diablo Lake to Ross Lake). Site of such amenities as lodge accommodations, boat rentals, and portage and water-taxi services, some 43,600 acres lie outside of wilderness designation in Ross Lake NRA. Lake Chelan NRA, on the other hand, is predominantly wilderness, with only 6,000 acres unclassified because of private landholdings in and around Stehekin, on the north end of Lake Chelan.

If 51-mile Lake Chelan owes its shape primarily to glacial movement, it too has not avoided the mining of its hydroelectric capacity. But its human history is longer than that. Mineral mining activity in the Stehekin Valley dates back to the 1880s. As with other mining claims and operations, small waves of support businesses followed in the wake of the miners, along with homesteaders wanting to make a life in the lower valley. Mining operations in the Stehekin Valley began their slide into extinction by the early twentieth century, though a few squeezed out production in Horseshoe Basin until 1959. You can still visit the Black Warrior Mine, which is on the National Register of Historic Places; take the Horseshoe Basin Trail off the old Mine-to-Market Road or get there from Cascade Pass.

Boats that ferried goods and supplies to support mining and the needs of homesteaders also brought a contingency of tourists. Passage from Chelan to Stehekin and back was a two-day journey via wood-fueled steamers and required travelers to stay overnight. Among other lakeside inns, travelers could stay in Stehekin at a small two-story hostel called the Argonaut, built by a settler named George Hall. In 1892 Hall sold the Argonaut to Merritt E. Field, a Coloradan who proceeded to greatly improve and expand it. Rechristened the Hotel Field, it retained a modest exterior but was elegant and well-appointed within. The 60-room hotel became easily the most famous lodging on the lake. In 1927, however, the outlet at the southern end of Lake Chelan was dammed. To avoid inundation, the Hotel Field at the head of the lake had to be dismantled and moved to higher ground; today it is the NPS Golden West Visitor Center and Museum at Stehekin (renovations to be completed by summer 2004).

Conservationists have recognized the Stehekin Valley, as well as the other regions of the North Cascade National Park Complex, for their beauty and wealth not in timber and ore but in the preservation of the natural cycles without direct human influence. As early as 1906 the Mazamas mountaineering club advocated for a national park in this area. With their efforts and those of many others over six decades, the national park and the two recreation areas were legally solidified in October 1968. Because of NPS acquisitions since then, private property holdings in the Stehekin Valley are only a third of what existed in 1968. Construction of the North Cascades Highway began in 1958 between Newhalem and Thunder Creek, the section from Methow to Washington Pass was undertaken in 1962, and the highway was finally completed in 1972. No other wilderness area in Washington has a highway, or any road for that matter, cutting right through its center. But on the other hand, no other wilderness area in Washington has so many awe-inspiring, trailless acres.

NORTH CASCADES NATIONAL PARK
DAY OR DESTINATION HIKE: THORNTON LAKES
   One-Way Distance: 5.4 miles
      Elevation Range: 1,700 to 5,700 feet
   Total Elevation Gain: 4,000 feet
         Difficulty: Strenuous
   Green Trails Map: Marblemount No. 47

Enjoy the first 2 miles of trail along an old logging road, casually contouring a hillside and crossing three or four small creeks. The first section will also be quite brushed in, but that won't seem so bad after you begin the climb.

Worlds collide as the trail leaves the road bed and begins a 2.7-mile, brutal ascent up a twisting trail. Rocks, stumps, logs, and exposed tree roots in the trail add to the challenge of reaching the crest. The trail to the first Thornton Lake heads to the left with the main trail leading straight, bringing you to the scramble up to the top of Trappers Peak (approximately 0.7 mile), with marvelous views of the Picket Range to the north and Teebone Ridge to the south. The trail down to the lake is very steep, narrow, rocky, and slippery. Be careful descending.

At the trail's end at mile 5.4, three campsites are set along the banks of Thornton Lake, still sometimes frozen into August. Permits are needed to camp. You can take a route along the west shoreline from the first lake to middle and upper Thornton Lakes. The setting is quite tantalizing and well worth a day or two to explore from—or just to stay put to enjoy the solitude.

From Marblemount travel 11.5 miles east on WA 20. Turn left at the sign for Thornton Lakes. The road to the trailhead is rough and steep in sections. The trailhead lies at 16.5 miles from Marblemount. Alternatively, from the Newhalem Visitor Center travel 3.3 miles west on WA 20 to reach the turn for Thornton Lakes.

NORTH CASCADES NATIONAL PARK
DAY HIKE: CASCADE PASS TO BLACK WARRIOR MINE
One-Way Distance: 8.4 miles
Elevation Range: 3,600 to 5,400 feet
Total Elevation Gain: 3,000 feet
Difficulty: Moderate
Green Trails Map: Cascade Pass No. 80

Begin the ascent up to Cascade Pass from the parking area. Nearly three-quarters of this section could be rated an Easy to Moderate. Climb the hillside via 30 switchbacks before taking a more direct and slightly steeper route up to Cascade Pass at mile 3.7. The pass lies within a parkland environment, beautifully pressed by Cascade Peak and The Triplets. You'll also be treated to astounding views down the Stehekin River Valley. The route up to the pass is quite popular, so be prepared for company and make sure to be sensitive to the plant life, as always.

From the pass the route drops through a rockslide area, past the trail for Pelton Basin Camp at mile 4.2, and through a gap into the upper end of the Stehekin River Valley. The trail drops more steeply through brush and brilliant wildflowers like tiger lily and red columbine before coming to a ford of Doubtful Creek, which displays a wonderful waterfall as the creek rushes from Doubtful Lake and glaciers higher above. Later in the season it's possible to pick a route over exposed rocks in the creek.

Out of the brush, work along the north wall of the river valley to a switchback and junction with the Basin Creek Trail at mile 6.8. A short, stocky sign indicates Horseshoe Basin; this path leads up to the Black Warrior Mine. Note that the lower portion of the basin is brushed in, and during the melt period the trail can also double as a creek. The trail moves into the open toward the upper end of the basin, with views of multiple waterfalls clinging to rock walls crowned by Ripsaw Ridge. You will reach the mine, to the left, at mile 8.4.

A byproduct of the Gold Rush of the 1880s, the Black Warrior Mine eventually occupied a 4-mile-long tunnel connected to Thunder Creek to the north. The mine and a rail line operated sporadically from the 1920s to the 1940s before avalanches became too much. The mine was reactivated for a brief time after World War II, when certain minerals like copper and zinc were at a premium. However, since 1959 it has been quiet, leaving the sounds of falling water, rocks, and snow to dominate. You can explore the mine, but be prepared for a damp and cool environment, and make sure to have a reliable light source.

From Marblemount cross over the Skagit River and follow the Cascade River Road to its end at Johannesburg Camp. The road is paved for the first 7 miles, then intermittently toward the road's end at 23.6 miles.

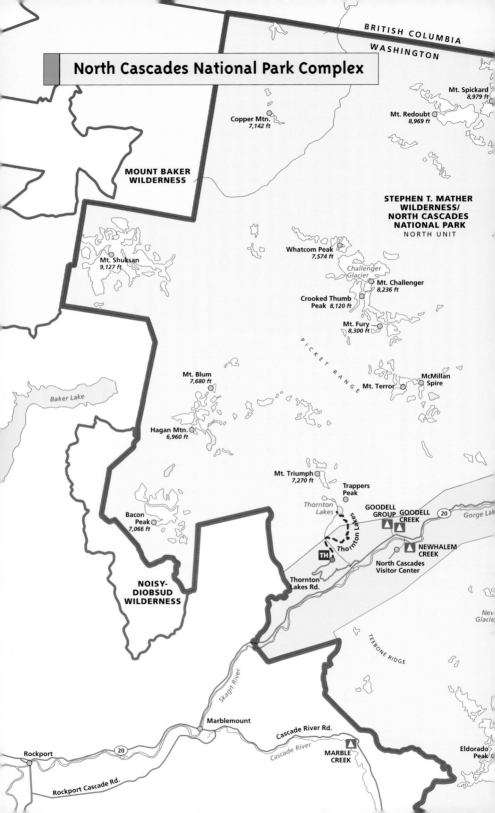

North Cascades National Park Complex

BRITISH COLUMBIA
WASHINGTON

Mt. Spickard
8,979 ft

Copper Mtn.
7,142 ft

Mt. Redoubt
8,969 ft

MOUNT BAKER
WILDERNESS

STEPHEN T. MATHER
WILDERNESS/
NORTH CASCADES
NATIONAL PARK
NORTH UNIT

Whatcom Peak
7,574 ft

Mt. Shuksan
9,127 ft

Challenger
Glacier

Mt. Challenger
8,236 ft

Crooked Thumb
Peak 8,120 ft

Mt. Fury
8,300 ft

McMillan
Spire

Mt. Blum
7,680 ft

PICKET RANGE

Mt. Terror

Baker Lake

Hagan Mtn.
6,960 ft

Mt. Triumph
7,270 ft

Trappers
Peak

Thornton
Lakes

GOODELL
GROUP

GOODELL
CREEK

Bacon
Peak
7,066 ft

Thornton Lakes

20

Gorge Lake

TH

NEWHALEM
CREEK

North Cascades
Visitor Center

NOISY-
DIOBSUD
WILDERNESS

Thornton
Lakes Rd.

New
Glacie

TEEBONE RIDGE

Skagit River

Marblemount

Cascade River Rd.

Rockport

20

Cascade River

MARBLE
CREEK

Eldorado
Peak

Rockport Cascade Rd.

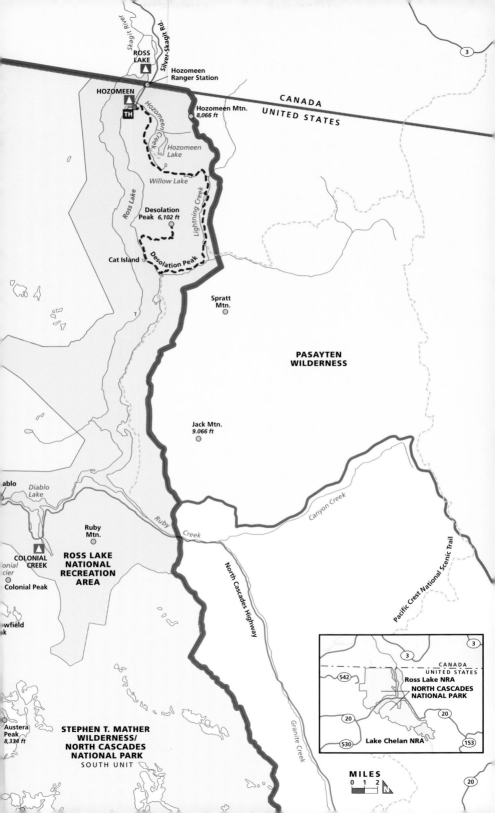

Skagit River

Silver-Skagit Rd.

ROSS
LAKE

Hozomeen
Ranger Station

HOZOMEEN

TH

Hozomeen Creek

Hozomeen Mtn.
8,066 ft

CANADA
UNITED STATES

Hozomeen
Lake

Willow Lake

Ross Lake

Desolation
Peak *6,102 ft*

Lightning Creek

Cat Island

Desolation Peak

Spratt
Mtn.

PASAYTEN
WILDERNESS

Jack Mtn.
9,066 ft

Canyon Creek

ablo

Diablo
Lake

Ruby
Mtn.

Ruby Creek

COLONIAL
CREEK

onial
cier

Colonial Peak

ROSS LAKE
NATIONAL
RECREATION
AREA

North Cascades Highway

Pacific Crest National Scenic Trail

wfield
k

Austera
Peak
8,334 ft

STEPHEN T. MATHER
WILDERNESS/
NORTH CASCADES
NATIONAL PARK
SOUTH UNIT

Granite Creek

3

CANADA
UNITED STATES

542

Ross Lake NRA
NORTH CASCADES
NATIONAL PARK

20

20

530

Lake Chelan NRA

153

MILES

0   1   2

20

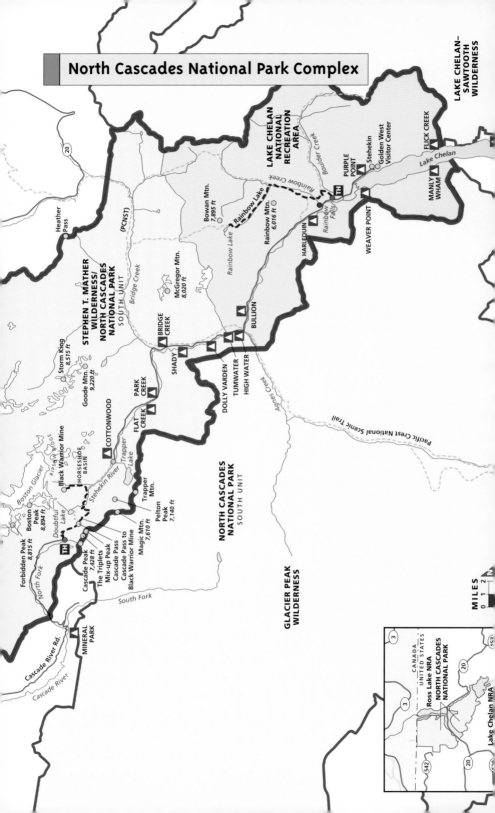

North Cascades National Park Complex

LAKE CHELAN–SAWTOOTH WILDERNESS

LAKE CHELAN NATIONAL RECREATION AREA

Golden West Visitor Center

Stehekin

PURPLE POINT

Lake Chelan

FLICK CREEK

MANLY WHAM

WEAVER POINT

HARLEQUIN

Rainbow Falls

Boulder Creek

Rainbow Creek

Bowan Mtn. 7,895 ft

Rainbow Lake

Rainbow Mtn. 6,016 ft

(PCNST)

Heather Pass

20

STEPHEN T. MATHER WILDERNESS/ NORTH CASCADES NATIONAL PARK SOUTH UNIT

Bridge Creek

McGregor Mtn. 8,020 ft

BRIDGE CREEK

SHADY

DOLLY VARDEN

TUMWATER

HIGH WATER

BULLION

Agnes Creek

Pacific Crest National Scenic Trail

Storm King 8,515 ft

Goode Mtn. 9,220 ft

PARK CREEK

COTTONWOOD

FLAT CREEK

Trapper Lake

HORSESHOE BASIN

Black Warrior Mine

Stehekin River

Trapper Mtn.

Pelton Peak 7,140 ft

Magic Mtn. 7,610 ft

Boston Glacier

Forbidden Peak 8,815 ft

Boston Peak 8,894 ft

Doubtful Lake

North Fork

Cascade Peak 7,428 ft

The Triplets

Mix-up Peak

Cascade Pass

Cascade Pass to Black Warrior Mine

South Fork

NORTH CASCADES NATIONAL PARK SOUTH UNIT

GLACIER PEAK WILDERNESS

MINERAL PARK

Cascade River Rd.

Cascade River

MILES
0 1 2

CANADA
UNITED STATES

Ross Lake NRA

NORTH CASCADES NATIONAL PARK

Lake Chelan NRA

3

20

153

542

3

ROSS LAKE NATIONAL RECREATION AREA
MULTIDAY DESTINATION HIKE: DESOLATION PEAK
One-Way Distance: 19.3 miles
Elevation Range: 1,659 to 6,102 feet
Total Elevation Gain: 6,137 feet
Difficulty: Moderate (Lightning Camp); Strenuous (Desolation Peak)
Green Trails Maps: Ross Lake No. 16, Jack Mountain No. 17

The hike starts on the Hozomeen Lake Trail, climbing up a set of switchbacks before changing to a more rolling climb in a fairly dense forest of fir and cedar, with ferns, moss, and lichen in the understory. You will reach the Hozomeen Lake spur trail to the left at approximately mile 3. Bear right toward Willow Lake over similar terrain, crossing one creek and making two short pushes uphill before reaching the west end of Willow Lake and Willow Lake Camp at mile 4.8.

Continue on the Willow Lake Trail along the north shoreline of the lake, passing through an awesome stand of older-growth cedar, fir, and hemlock, following the outlet of Willow Lake to its confluence with Lightning Creek. Past the large trees the trail winds steeply down to a small bridge, crossing to the west side of Lightning Creek, where it then climbs, drops, levels out, and drops again via a short set of switchbacks to Nightmare Camp at mile 8.5 and a pack-bridge crossing of Lightning Creek. Now on the Lightning Creek Trail, ascend a short distance above the creek before moving along quite pleasantly through the trees. At mile 10.1 the trail passes Deer Lick Camp. You will reach the Three Fools Trail junction 0.2 mile farther, then make the last crossing, via pack bridge, of Lightning Creek at mile 10.4.

The trail climbs above the northwest side of the Lightning Creek drainage, eventually affording views of Spratt Mountain to the southeast and at mile 12.4 the first views of Ross Lake. At mile 13 the trail begins its steep descent via switchbacks to the junction with the Desolation Peak and East Bank Trails at mile 13.6. A short distance farther you will come to the Lightning Creek Camp, along the shoreline north of the suspension bridge over Lightning Creek. Enjoy great views into the glacier-filled crater of Jack Mountain and of peaks like Ruby Mountain and Colonial Peak beyond the south end of Ross Lake in the Stephen T. Mather Wilderness.

From the campground, backtrack up to the trail junction with the Desolation Peak Trail as it heads north above the east shoreline of Ross Lake, passing by the Cat Island Camp and on to a turn east at mile 15.3. The trail from here is all steep climbing, initially through the trees before coming out onto a huckleberry-filled slope at mile 17.3 and staying in the open past Desolation Camp at mile 17.8. Note that the only water source is lingering snowpack, which in most years is gone by July. Continue through a subalpine setting of heather and wildflowers, and on to the rocky, barren summit of Desolation Peak at mile 19.3, its lookout made famous by Jack Kerouac in his novel *Desolation Angels*.

From the lookout point, the prominent peak to the north is Hozomeen Mountain; to the east are the highlands of the Pasayten; to the south you'll have a higher vantage into the spectacular mouth of Jack Mountain; and toward the west you can spy the Picket Range and Mount Baker. The lookout, closed to public access, is still in use when needed, so please respect it whether it's occupied or not. Camping in the designated camp areas is by self-registration at the Hozomeen Ranger Station.

This hike may require proof of U.S. citizenship, because its driving access is by way of Canada. From Hope, British Columbia, approximately 100 miles east of Vancouver, turn off Highway 1 onto Flood-Hope Road heading west. At mile 1.7, turn left (south) onto the Silver-Skagit Road, which is marked by a flashing yellow light. The road changes from asphalt to gravel at 4.1 miles. It will be 38.2 miles to the International Boundary and the Hozomeen Ranger Station, which may or may not be attended. At 39.5 miles, turn left (east) to reach the Hozomeen Lake Trailhead. The parking area and trailhead are 0.1 mile up. You can also access this hike by way of private or hired boat from Ross Lake Resort, but note that these options can be costly. Contact Ross Lake Resort at 206-386-4437 or www.rosslakeresort.com.

Pink mountain heather, Stephen T. Mather Wilderness

LAKE CHELAN NATIONAL RECREATION AREA
DESTINATION HIKE: RAINBOW LAKE

One-Way Distance: 8.7 miles
Elevation Range: 1,200 to 5,630 feet
Total Elevation Gain: 4,430 feet
Difficulty: Moderate
Green Trails Map: Stehekin No. 82

NOTE: Plan your boat schedule ahead, before starting on this hike.

Off the Stehekin Road, start on the lower trail of the Rainbow Loop, climbing gradually through an open forest for approximately 0.5 mile. The trail continues to climb, now more steeply, for 0.7 mile before the grade eases. The trail then drops to a campsite and bridge crossing of Boulder Creek at mile 1.6. Past the creek crossing, climb for another 0.4 mile to the Rainbow Creek junction at mile 2. From the junction hike along the west side of the Rainbow Creek drainage to Rainbow Ford Camp at 4 miles.

Cross the creek over a rickety rope bridge or ford it to reach the other side and continue uphill to the Rainbow Lake Trail junction and Bench Creek Camp at mile 4.7. The trail descends to another crossing of Rainbow Creek before it begins a steady 1.3-mile climb. At mile 7 the trail passes the Rainbow Meadows Camp, intermittently crossing through sections of meadows, then climbs through the trees and up a set of switchbacks that move through a rockslide. The trail then straightens to take a more direct path to Rainbow Lake. The trail passes through a lovely meadow before reaching the trail for Rainbow Lake Camp at mile 8.7; Rainbow Lake lies a short distance beyond. The cirque lake is beautifully situated, surrounded by ridges and peaks, the largest being Bowan Mountain to the northeast. Camping anywhere along this hike is by permit only. Permits can be obtained at the visitor center in Stehekin.

Leave the car behind on this one. The only access to this hike comes by way of boat or floatplane—if you don't feel like hiking 20 or 30 miles to reach the trailhead. The easiest and most economical access is to book passage on a boat from the Lake Chelan Boat Company in the town of Chelan. Take the boat to Stehekin, and then either hike 2.5 miles to the trailhead or take the bus from the Stehekin Landing (for a fee). Different schedules and costs apply depending on season, itinerary, and class of boat. Contact the Lake Chelan Boat Company at 509-682-2224 or www.ladyofthelake.com.

Central Cascades

For many Washington residents, the Central Cascades region *is* the Cascades. They crowd in to see features like the prominent Stuart Range and a magnificent collection of mid- and high-mountain lakes of the Alpine Lakes Wilderness. They admire the steep-sided, cirque- and glacier-decorated 8,000- and 9,000-foot peaks extending from border to border around the center point of Glacier Peak in the Glacier Peak Wilderness. This is a region, a result in part of the forceful yet delicate hand of glacial activity, where you have to hike up from the valleys and drainages to find the sun. Roam among wildflower meadows at Cloudy Pass in Glacier Peak Wilderness; discover numerous water bodies, such as Twin Lakes in the Henry M. Jackson Wilderness; and marvel at the extent of this central Cascade geography from peaks like Surprise Mountain in the Alpine Lakes Wilderness or Three Fingers in the Boulder River Wilderness.

The Central Cascades rightfully earn their popularity for their beauty. Another advantage is that the state's two busiest west-east highways (I-90 and US 2) carry hikers and backpackers to their trailheads. Whether day hikers skipping into the Douglas fir forests along Snoqualmie Pass or more ambitious trekkers connecting with the Pacific Crest Trail to head northward into the Henry M. Jackson or Glacier Peak Wilderness Areas from Stevens Pass, recreationists have benefited from the convenient access roads.

Nineteenth-century explorers knew and present-day visitors find out how difficult cross-country travel is in this region. The Central Cascades are covered with thick forests of Douglas fir, western hemlock, and western red cedar. Understory plants like devil's club, salal, salmonberry, and fern line river valleys and creek drainages. By sticking to the trails you will find meadows on ridgelines like Goat Flats in the Boulder River Wilderness. You will also discover more than a thousand lakes, some easily accessed like Blanca Lake in the Henry M. Jackson Wilderness, others tucked away in places few people reach, like Venus Lake in the Alpine Lakes Wilderness.

Granite peaks like Mount Stuart, volcanoes like Glacier Peak, and sharp, shale peaks like Three Fingers, part of the backbone of the Boulder River Wilderness, are all gathered here. Accompanying the myriad lakes and ponds, hundreds of creeks and rivers, and countless number of peaks, there are more than 1,000 miles of trail in just these four Central Cascades wilderness areas, an area of approximately 1.1 million acres. What are you waiting for?

Lake Brynhild, Alpine Lakes Wilderness

14 Alpine Lakes Wilderness

Robin Lake

LOCATION: Between Stevens Pass on US 2 and Snoqualmie Pass on I-90, approximately 10 miles west of Leavenworth

SIZE: 362,670 acres

ELEVATION RANGE: 1,000 to 9,415 feet

MILES OF TRAIL: 450

TREES AND PLANTS: Alpine larch, Douglas fir, Engelmann spruce, mountain hemlock, western red cedar, whitebark pine, avalanche lily, balsamroot, bluebell, huckleberry, snow lily, twinflower

WILDLIFE: Beaver, black bear, black-tailed deer, bobcat, cougar, mountain goat, chestnut-backed chickadee, Clark's nutcracker, hermit thrush, raven, ruffed grouse, Steller's jay

ADMINISTRATION: Mount Baker–Snoqualmie NF: North Bend RD, 425-888-1421; Skykomish RD, 360-677-2414. Wenatchee NF: Cle Elum RD, 509-674-4411; Leavenworth RD, 509-548-6977; Lake Wenatchee RD, 509-763-3103.

BEST SEASON: Summer through fall

THE AMOEBIC SHAPE OF Alpine Lakes Wilderness is not the result of natural boundaries or barriers but the culmination of nearly eight years of human effort to preserve as much of the acreage as conservationally, privately, industrially, and politically allowable. David Knibb, former president of the Alpine Lakes Protection Society (ALPS), wrote about this arduous process in his book, *Backyard Wilderness: The Alpine Lakes Story.* Formed in October 1968, ALPS had a simple mission: to preserve an area of the Cascades chock full of some 700 lakes and decorated with perhaps the most spectacular valleys, meadows, creek drainages, and mountains in all of Washington. Knibb recounts the story of this small but dedicated group, who worked as lovingly as fearful parents would do for their child to establish what was already then, and still is today, one of Washington's premier wildlands.

For ALPS, it took poring over maps, reading through government documents, and consulting with both other conservation groups and "everyday" hikers to determine exactly what should be considered and what was at stake. Ownership of the lands ran the gamut from the U.S. Forest Service to logging operations to mining claims to private and commercial real estate. Compromise would prove to be unavoidable, but ALPS leaders felt especially empowered to negotiate. A unified coalition of conservation groups came together in 1974, six years after ALPS had come into existence. By that time, the organization was more about political posturing and positioning than romantic notions of a hiking paradise. The point was to garner political power centered around a cohesive and unified plan.

ALPS debated the best approach to the protection of the land. Should they push for a national park, as was accomplished by the North Cascades Conservation Council (NCCC) in 1968 with the formation of the North Cascades National Park Complex? Would they have more success creating a proposal that kept the core 243,000-acre wilderness but surrounded it with lands under the guidelines and management of a national recreation area? With the support of the NCCC, Sierra Club, and The Mountaineers, ALPS finally agreed to push for a 575,000-acre National Recreation Area (NRA).

Along this slow journey other proposals were drafted, with requisite maps, by the logging industry and the Forest Service. If you place all these maps in line, starting with the original designation by ALPS followed by the Forest Service, industry, and the final congressional designation of the Alpine Lakes Wilderness, it resembles not just an amoeba but a giant ice sheet, both in its natural attributes and in its imposed perimeters. The political posturing and bluffing, not to mention the usual procedural pace, made time seem positively glacial.

Beyond the membership of ALPS, very few of the key decision makers had even set foot in any portion of the Alpine Lakes Wilderness. Paper is what they had: maps and proposals to decide the area's fate. Nature was debated, pulled and pushed at, propagandized, and eventually given an airing in cities like Seattle and Washington, D.C. Backroom, formal, and informal meetings; public, committee, and subcommittee hearings; continuous lobbying from every interested position; along with setbacks, failures, and successes over a nearly eight-year period finally landed House bill H.R. 7792 in the U.S. House of Representatives in 1976.

A principal politician in bringing the Alpine Lakes legislation to fruition, Rep. Lloyd Meeds (D), said:

This bill is supported by the entire Washington State House delegation, the timber companies, recreation-vehicle users, rock hounders, horsemen, and a whole bunch of other people. It is supported by all conservation groups in our State and in the Nation. It is supported very strongly by the Governor of our State, Dan Evans. In short . . . it is supported by almost everyone.

The bill was voted on with unanimous consent, then moved on to the Senate, where Sen. Henry M. "Scoop" Jackson (D) helped to shoot the bill through at lightning speed to land at its final stop, the desk of President Gerald R. Ford. On July 12, 1976, Ford signed the bill into law establishing a 362,670-acre Alpine Lakes Wilderness.

This action was of course a triumph of great consequence for ALPS, conservationists, and recreationists alike. But what the bill did not do is to protect natural beauty from being defaced. Yes, logging is prohibited in wilderness areas. Yes, group sizes are limited to no more than 12 people. Yes, places like the Enchantments are only accessible via a designated permit, issued for the high season on a lottery basis from applications received months before the trails (given the usual snowpack) will even allow a weekend hiker access.

But protection of the wilderness comes not from bills or management by the Forest Service: It is a product of us—backpackers, canoeists, climbers, anglers, hikers, equestrians, hunters, and kayakers—and of our interactions with the surroundings. Wilderness longevity is a result of how we choose to preserve the trails, campsites, delicate meadows, and sensitive waterways. The comment has been made about a number of wilderness areas that people are "loving the wilderness to death," and Alpine Lakes is no exception.

The 47 trailheads at Alpine Lakes are accessible from nearly every direction from several major, paved roadways. Proximity to Seattle—the state's largest city, with some 600,000 people—combined with the fact that over half of the entire state of Washington's population lives within a one-hour drive of some portion of the wilderness, make it extremely popular. Alpine splendor and lakes galore abound in Alpine Lakes Wilderness, which receives, according to Forest Service estimates, some 150,000 visitors a year—only a fraction of the 2 million who visit Mount Rainier, but enough to make a noticeable impact.

Alpine Lakes is a splendid and diverse wilderness with multiple life zones split by the Cascades. The lower sections of the western side are treed with Douglas fir, western hemlock, western red cedar, and red alder; covering the forest floor here are salmonberry, devil's club, and Oregon grape. At these elevations you can find black-tailed deer, beaver, and elk. Pushing up the slopes into the front range of the subalpine meadows, the terrain hosts such edibles as blackberry, elderberry, and currant. Rainforest trees are replaced by Pacific silver fir, mountain hemlock, and noble fir. In the subalpine zone the meadows come alive with avalanche lily, bluebell, phlox, and paintbrush, while forested areas are made up of subalpine fir and larch. Craggy, open slopes are home to the mountain goat.

The west side runs the gamut with Douglas fir, ponderosa pine, western hemlock, lodgepole pine, and balsamroot in the understory. Higher elevations pass through hemlock, white fir, and grand fir. The forest floor here is mixed with sedge, huckleberry, elderberry, and vine maple. Across the crest at the highest elevations are the common eastern slope mix of spruce; whitebark pine; and subalpine, white, and silver firs.

A chance to work up the steep, bouldered gully to Aasgard Pass and stand on the western edge of the Enchantments to take in the world of glacially smoothed, white granite rock, with pools of ice-blue water seemingly scattered about and lit by torches of golden autumn larch, can be cathartic. Preparing for a hike in Tucquala

Meadows immersed in a rainbow of greens, with the unmistakable Cathedral Rock looming like an Easter Island statue over the western ridge of the spectacular high loop around Hyas Lakes, will also force a reflective pause. Lounging in the sun on the water-smoothed rocks of the Denny Creek waterslide before continuing up to Keekwulee Falls can make a weekend afternoon memorable. It is our responsibility to preserve the wilderness by allowing it to preserve itself.

DAY OR DESTINATION HIKE: DENNY CREEK TO MELAKWA LAKE
One-Way Distance: 4.1 miles
Elevation Range: 2,240 to 4,510 feet
Total Elevation Gain: 2,360 feet
Difficulty: Moderate
Green Trails Map: Snoqualmie Pass No. 207

Denny Creek Trail #1014 to Melakwa Lake is quite pleasant, with an easygoing path through old-growth trees. Never mind the concrete interstate overhead at the start: As you move along the creek and up farther into the woods, you soon separate from the manmade world into that of the nature-made, full of complex splendors. The sound of the creek overpowers the sound of highway vehicles fairly early on. At mile 1.1 a second footbridge crosses over Denny Creek. Here large, smooth rocks are exposed, creating a picturesque setting known as the Denny Creek waterslide —a pleasant place to pause. Cross the bridge and continue upstream, still contained in the trees, before breaking out into a more open area with heavy brush lining the trail. As you stand amid a grayish rockslide at mile 1.6, the magnificent Keekwulee Falls are in view pouring over a cliff into an amphitheater-like setting.

From here the trail makes a series of tight but gently inclined switchbacks for 0.4 mile, gaining a vantage point over the creek, which has sunk into the narrow, rock-walled canyon visible just off the trail. Returning for a short while into the trees, the trail again comes in alongside the creek and a footlog crossing at mile 2.2, between Low Mountain to the southwest and Denny Mountain to the northeast. From here the trail heads through a mix of wooded and open, rocky terrain as it climbs switchbacks to Hemlock Pass at mile 3.5. It is a short downhill stretch from here, once again under the cover of trees, to Melakwa Lake at mile 4.1.

The secluded feel of the lake comes from the basin it sits in and the company of trees and rock outcroppings surrounding it. Limited camping is available. You'll have plenty to explore in the area. Take an excursion to Upper Melakwa Lake by going around the west side of Melakwa Lake. Consider also a longer journey to Tuscohatchie Lake, an extra 6 miles round-trip downslope to the west of Melakwa Lake.

From the North Bend RD take I-90 east for 14.1 miles to Exit 47 and follow the signs for Denny Creek Campground. At 14.6 miles turn left on FR 58. Drive past Denny Creek Campground at 16.7 miles, then turn left onto FR 5830 at 17 miles toward Denny Creek and Melakwa Lake. The parking area and trailhead are at 17.2 miles.

Alpine Lakes

Skykomish

South Fork Skykomish River

FR 68

West Fork Foss River

Ba
Pe

Silver
Peak

Lake
Malachite

Copper
Lake

Delta
Lake

Jewel
Lake

och
atrine

e
belle

Lake
Dorothy

Bear Lake

Little
Heart
Lake

Big Heart
Lake

Lock
La

Snoqualmie
Lake

Dear Lake

Angeline Lake

Chetwoot
Lake

Nordrum
Lake

Crawford
Lake

Hester
Lake

Pratt River

Middle Fork Snoqualmie River

Hatchet
Lake

Derrick
Lake

Wildcat
Lakes

Lake
Caroline

PCNST

Spe
La

Kaleetan
Lake

Snow
Lake

Lundin Peak
6,057 ft

Red Mtn.
5,890 ft

Alaska
Lake

Melakwa
Lake

Commonwealth
Basin

Lake
Kulla
Kulla

Hemlock Pass

Denny Creek to
Melakwa Lake

DENNY MTN.

Denny Creek

Pratt
Lake

Tuscohatchie
Lake

TH

Snoqualmie
Pass

Granite
Mtn.

TH

DENNY
CREEK

90

South Fork Snoqualmie River

FR 58

Keechelus
Lake

MILES

0   1   2

N

> **DAY HIKE: COMMONWEALTH BASIN**
> One-Way Distance: 4.6 miles
> Elevation Range: 3,000 to 5,350 feet
> Total Elevation Gain: 2,350 feet
> Difficulty: Moderate
> Green Trails Map: Snoqualmie Pass No. 207

The beginning of this hike runs along the Pacific Crest Trail, which is moderately inclined as it works through a predominantly Douglas fir forest. A break from the trees comes at mile 1.9 alongside a collection of rockslides before the junction with Commonwealth Basin Trail #1033 at mile 2.5. Take in nice views of the mountainscape, especially Lundin Peak and Red Mountain, as the trail follows the bottom of the basin. After crossing over a spring runoff creek bed at mile 2.9, the trail ascends a steep rib before reaching a small benched area at mile 4.1. The trail continues to the right, gaining elevation over Red Pond and heading toward a ridgeline connecting Red Mountain to Lundin Peak. The visibly maintained trail follows the ridgeline to the left before ending at mile 4.6 at Red Pass. Achieving an elevation gain of 2,350 feet awards hikers with some spectacular views in all directions but especially to the northeast, as the ridge drops dramatically away into Goat Creek Basin.

From the North Bend RD take I-90 east for 19.1 miles to Exit 52. Take a left turn at the intersection, going under the overpass. The parking lot for the PCT and the start of this hike will be the first right turn.

> **OVERNIGHT HIKE: CATHEDRAL ROCK LOOP**
> Total Distance: 14.7 miles (add another 2 miles for the
> Peggy's Pond excursion)
> Elevation Range: 3,400 to 5,600 feet
> Total Elevation Gain: 2,700 feet
> Difficulty: Moderate
> Green Trails Map: Stevens Pass No. 176

Creating one of the most dramatic beginnings of any wilderness hike in Washington, Cathedral Rock looms over the forest to the northwest. From the Tucquala Meadows parking area, cross the Cle Elum River on Cathedral Trail #1345 over a tilting and weathered pack bridge and begin climbing up a series of moderate switchbacks before reaching the junction with the Trail Creek Trail at mile 1.8. Continue past the junction toward Squaw Lake (overnight camping by reservation) and Cathedral Rock. The trail makes its way through a mix of trees and open sections with views of Granite Mountain to the northeast, the Wenatchee Mountains to the east, and, rising slightly higher and farther to the east of the Wenatchees, a mountain called The Cradle. Shortly before reaching the junction with the Pacific Crest Trail, the trail passes by a series of small lakes, each with sites to pitch a tent. You can appreciate the full grandness of Cathedral Rock at mile 4.5 and can also take a side trip before continuing the loop.

Follow the PCT west a short distance to reach a breathtaking overlook of Deep Lake and the Spinola Creek Valley running away from it. Head downhill to the first switchback, where an unmaintained but easily hiked trail leads around the southern base of Cathedral Rock for approximately 0.7 mile to Peggy's Pond. From here, enjoy an alternate view of the valley below and of glaciated Mount Daniel to the west-northwest.

The Cathedral Rock Loop continues through on the PCT to the north, skirting underneath Cathedral Rock before losing some elevation down a series of switchbacks with overlooks of Hyas Lake in the Cle Elum River Valley. The trail continues along the upper west side of the valley, crossing over two creeks (the first of which has campsites) and passing by views again of Mount Daniel. At mile 7 a spectacular slot canyon squeezes together another creek to be crossed.

Past here the trail begins to gain elevation as it makes its way to Deception Pass and the upper head of the valley at mile 9.7. From the pass, take Trail #1376 in a southerly direction toward Little and Hyas Lakes. The trail glides downhill from here under trees filtering light, with views of Lynch Glacier on Mount Daniel to the west. After passing Little Hyas Lake at about mile 12.7, you will be halfway along the east shore of Hyas Lake and next to campsites. The trail continues beside the lake, descending and flattening out as it moves through the trees and by a small meadow before reaching the Tucquala Meadows Trailhead at mile 14.7.

Drive north from the Cle Elum RD on WA 903. The pavement ends at 18.6 miles. Continue on FR 4330 toward Tucquala Lake. The parking lot for the trailhead is to the left, near the road's end at 31.1 miles.

DESTINATION HIKE: NECKLACE VALLEY
One-Way Distance: 8.2 miles
Elevation Range: 1,600 to 4,800 feet
Total Elevation Gain: 3,200 feet
Difficulty: Moderate
Green Trails Maps: Skykomish No. 175, Stevens Pass No. 176

The trail begins in a fairytale-like setting of cedar, fern, moss, and shadows along the East Fork Foss River. The trail continues over modestly rolling terrain, crossing creeks and elevated wooden walkways put in place to reduce the erosion caused by the year-round marshy ground. At mile 2.7 the trail dips down to meet the East Fork Foss River and enters a more open setting containing thick brush and alder as well as views of Bald Eagle Peak to the west. A footlog provides access to the west side of the East Fork Foss River at mile 4.5, while a second log crossing shortly thereafter leads to a rockslide scramble and the continuation of the trail up to Necklace Valley.

After climbing a natural rock staircase in a corridor of small trees with views to the northwest of Silver Eagle Peak, the trail reenters a more wooded area and works its way up what feels like a brushed-in creek bed, climbing over slick rocks and tree roots, eventually arriving at Jade Lake, the first of the Necklace

Valley Lakes, at mile 7.5. You'll find campsites at the south end of the lake. The trail continues on to Emerald Lake at mile 7.8 and Opal Lake at mile 8.2. The best campsites are at Emerald.

Absorb the splendors of this landscape: Within a 3-mile radius of these Necklace Valley lakes are ten other lakes to explore or camp by. The difficulty of access to each lake varies, so refer to available maps and talk to a ranger to get the lay of the land. The Necklace Valley is an enchanting place in which you could easily invest several days.

From the Skykomish RD drive US 2 east for 0.5 mile to Foss River Road (FR 68). Turn right and follow the paved then gravel road 4.2 miles to the trailhead for Necklace Valley Trail #1062.

OVERNIGHT HIKE: SURPRISE LAKE–SURPRISE MOUNTAIN
One-Way Distance: 9.9 miles
Elevation Range: 2,200 to 6,330 feet
Total Elevation Gain: 5,030 feet
Difficulty: Moderate
Green Trails Map: Stevens Pass No. 176

This hike starts very pleasantly, making its way over elevated walkways and through an airy forest with a footlog crossing of Surprise Creek at 1.2 miles. Past the crossing the trail continues through the trees over more walkway and into a lengthy brushed-in section at mile 2. From here, climb up a series of switchbacks to Surprise Lake at mile 4, which is at the beginning of the subalpine zone. Plenty of campsites lie around the north end of the lake.

Trail #1060 continues alongside the lake before gaining elevation on a benched area and reaching the junction with the Pacific Crest Trail. Continue on the PCT southward to the larger Glacier Lake at mile 5.2. Notice that both lakes lie between Spark Plug and Thunder Mountains. Trail access to Glacier Lake is just past the large boulder field, along with campsites. More campsites are also available a short distance beyond the south end of Glacier Lake.

Continuing on, the trail enters a brilliant basin of white rock set beneath Surprise Mountain, with thoughtfully placed switchbacks up the west side of the basin. The higher you get, the more you can see to the north: great overlooks of both Surprise and Glacier Lakes, and an awesome view of the pyramid-shaped Glacier Peak. The closer you get to Pieper Pass at mile 7.4, the more trees and huckleberry surround you. During the descent to Deception Lakes at mile 8.6, take in some magnificent views across the valley: Lake Clarice, seemingly clinging to the mountainside; the craggy, glaciated peaks of Mounts Hinman and Daniel in the southwest; and Cathedral Rock to the south. Deception Lakes make for an ideal camp setting, good for fishing and exploring around.

Here, Trail #1063 will lead you up and above the first lake, initially in the direction of the horse camp, before the trail forks at 0.3 mile from the lake. The right spur heads to the horse camp, and the left continues the somewhat steep climb to Surprise Gap at mile 9.4. (You can also see this gap from the amphitheater as you head toward Pieper Pass from Glacier Lake.) From here continue to the west, wrapping around the southeast side of Surprise Mountain for another 0.5 mile before topping out on its peak at mile 9.9. The panoramic views are plentiful from here, with grander takes on many of the natural features seen earlier, as well as new ones, including Mount Stuart and Colchuck and Dragontail Peaks to the southeast. After descending back to Surprise Gap, take an easy-to-follow trail that drops into the bottom of the white rock basin, then connects back up with the PCT, which will return you to Glacier and Surprise Lakes and the trailhead.

From the Skykomish RD drive 9.7 miles east on US 2, approximately 0.7 mile past milepost 58, and turn right onto an unmarked road. Take the road to the left, crossing over a bridge and railroad tracks. Once across the tracks, follow the spur to the right approximately 0.3 mile to the small parking lot and wilderness sign-in at 10.1 miles. The trailhead is another 0.1 mile up the road.

> ## DESTINATION OR MULTIDAY LOOP HIKE: WAPTUS LAKE
> Total Distance: 21.7 miles
> Elevation Range: 2,900 to 5,600 feet
> Total Elevation Gain: 3,700 feet
> Difficulty: Moderate
> Green Trails Maps: Stevens Pass No. 176, Kachess Lake No. 208

From the parking area in Tucquala Meadows you will have a great view to the northwest of Cathedral Rock, which you will pass beneath en route to Waptus Lake. Begin the hike by crossing the Cle Elum River on Cathedral Trail #1345 via a rickety pack bridge and climbing a series of moderate switchbacks to the Trail Creek Trail junction at mile 1.8. Stay on the Cathedral Trail, passing by Squaw Lake and through a mix of trees and open sections with fine mountain views. You will then go past a collection of small lakes before reaching the junction with the Pacific Crest Trail and a wonderful view of Cathedral Rock. Continue the hike, now on the PCT, in a westerly then southerly direction, edging around the southern base of the rock before plunging down to Deep Lake some 1,300 feet below.

The scenery is quite impressive as you descend a series of switchbacks: the lake below, mountain peaks lined out to the west, and, in the distant south, views of Mount Adams and Goat Rocks. At the bottom, the trail emerges from the trees into a meadow at the outlet of Deep Lake at mile 7.7. Camping is available here. The trail to Waptus Lake continues to the south along the west side of Spinola Creek, dropping in elevation the entire time.

After leaving Deep Lake you'll make two creek crossings. After the second crossing the trail will fork at 0.2 mile; make sure to take the path to the right. The trail goes through a mix of wooded and open areas from here down to the junction with Spinola Creek Trail #1310A at mile 11.2. Another 0.9 mile on #1310A, then 0.4 mile on #1310, will bring you to the outlet of Waptus Lake at mile 12.4, where you can access campsites.

From the junction with Trail #1310A you could also continue to the west on the PCT and then descend on a small access trail (#1337) to the midpoint of Waptus Lake at mile 2.4. Here you'll again meet Trail #1310, which goes northwest along and above the northern shore toward the head of the lake. If you climb in the other direction (north and northwest) on Trail #1337, in 3.4 miles you will reach Spade Lake, another excellent location for a camp or destination for a short day hike from Waptus Lake.

The setting is truly dramatic, with Waptus Lake extending to the northwest, the forest spilling down the mountainsides around the entire shoreline, and nature's sculptures of Bears Breast Mountain and Summit Chief Mountain standing boldly in the distance beyond the head of the lake. If you can find a reason to leave, then take Trail #1310 to the southeast and cross over Waptus Lake's outlet and the beginning of the Waptus River. From the lake it is approximately 2 miles to the junction with Trail Creek Trail #1322. Cross the river, which may require fording, and begin climbing alongside Trail Creek, gaining 1,400 vertical feet in the next 2.5 miles to mile 16.9.

At first you'll have intermittent views of Bears Breast and Summit Chief Mountains and Waptus Lake before a ridgeline to the west blocks the views. After the elevation gain the trail levels out onto a benched area, making its way past a few small meadows before crossing over Trail Creek and climbing gradually up to the junction with Cathedral Trail #1345 at mile 19.9. Don't be deceived by the apparent closeness of the Wenatchee Mountains to the east as an indicator of the proximity of the junction; count on about 1.5 miles from the point they come into view. Return to the Tucquala Meadows Trailhead via Cathedral Trail #1345 at mile 21.7.

Drive north from the Cle Elum RD on WA 903. The pavement ends at 18.6 miles. Continue on FR 4330 toward Tucquala Lake. The parking lot for the trailhead is to the left, near the road's end at 31.1 miles.

Glaciated Mount Daniel, Alpine Lakes Wilderness

> ## MULTIDAY HIKE: THE ENCHANTMENTS
> One-Way Distance: 17.4 miles
> Elevation Range: 1,300 to 7,800 feet
> Total Elevation Gain: 4,600 feet
> Difficulty: Moderate to strenuous
> Green Trails Map: The Enchantments No. 209S

NOTE: The Enchantments are only accessible for camping via a designated permit, issued for the high season on a lottery basis from applications received in advance. Applications are accepted beginning in February of each year. Contact the Leavenworth RD, 509-548-6977, for details on how and when to apply.

The way to the Enchantments begins humbly but with measured steps reveals natural splendors in doses from manageable to completely overwhelming. The hike begins on Trail #1599, which leads to both Lake Stuart and Colchuck Lake. You'll have a gradual grade through the trees and alongside huckleberry bushes before reaching a sturdy footlog crossing of Mountaineer Creek at mile 1.2. Climb for a distance to a short drop at the junction with Colchuck Lake Trail #1599A at mile 2.1. From here you also have the first glimpses of some of the craggy peaks of the Stuart Range to the south and southwest. You'll cross another creek a short distance in from the junction as the trail skirts along the bottom end of a boulder field before beginning a steep climb up to Colchuck Lake at mile 3.7. Camping is available; it is worthwhile to stay and watch the jewel-like blue of the lake play against the reddish rock and craggy, glaciated peaks of Colchuck and Dragontail, standing in their massiveness beyond the head of the lake.

The trail to Aasgard Pass follows the west shoreline then rounds the south end of the lake, picking its way through a cairned boulder field to the base of the chute. The route is steep, rocky, and difficult to follow, even with cairns in place. It is important to stay to the left of the falls farther up the chute. You will have to scramble to make it over the last steep section, ending up in a small shelf basin below the last short push to Aasgard Pass at mile 5.7. The pass is the gateway into the string of lakes, which is deservedly referred to as the Enchantments.

Where to look first? The fiery yellow blaze, in September and October, of the stunted larch trees, stuck like torches between glittering white rock; the front-row views of Dragontail Peak and the tempting north face of Little Annapurna; and of course the lakes, the premier attractions here, placed about like forgotten blue-green planets. Prepare to be mesmerized as the trail winds its way over the glacially smoothed, white rock landscape. Pass between lakes of various shapes and sizes aptly given such names as Tranquil, Isolation, Inspiration, and Perfection; and skirt islands of thick, green mountain grass. Depending on the time of year and snowpack, the route is easy to follow via cairns and trail signs. You'll find numerous campsites, many with pit toilets.

It is a downhill glide until the short climb from Lake Viviane to the gap at mile 9.1 above the Snow Lakes. The trail picks its way down through a rockslide before reaching Upper Snow Lake. From here you can skirt either the southeast or northwest side of the lake—both end up between the upper and lower lake at mile 10.9. Continue on Snow Lake Trail #1553 in the direction of Nada Lake. At this point you have lost 2,400 vertical feet and will lose another 4,100 vertical feet by the time you reach the Snow Creek Trailhead. Stay along the northwest shoreline of Nada Lake, crossing a creek and then, well above the brushy bottom of the Snow Creek drainage, heading down past the Snow Creek Wall and over a bridge spanning Icicle Creek to the trailhead at mile 17.4.

Although you have a couple of options for approaching this area, I am describing the path from Lake Stuart Trailhead to Snow Lake Trailhead. Because of the distance between the two, it's advisable to have a vehicle at each trailhead. To reach the Snow Creek Trailhead from the Leavenworth RD take US 2 west for 1 mile and turn left onto Icicle Creek Road. Travel another 4.3 miles to the parking area at 5.3 miles, on the left-hand side of the road just above Icicle Creek. For the Lake Stuart Trailhead, continue another 4.2 miles on Icicle Creek Road to FR 7601. Turn left and drive 3.8 miles to the trailhead at 13.3 miles.

Larch trees in autumn at Leprechaun Lake, Alpine Lakes Wilderness

15 Boulder River Wilderness

Cascades on the Boulder River

AS WITH MANY OF THE WILDERNESS AREAS IN WASHINGTON, geologic history has shaped the human history associated with Boulder River Wilderness. This story is a triumphant one, mainly because of formidable terrain. Tectonic plate movements more than 50 million years ago gave this area its initial shape, followed by a common Pacific Northwest occurrence of volcanic activity more than 10 million years ago. However, it was the receding of high mountain glaciers during a period from 2 million to as recently as 12,000 years ago that sculpted the present-day features we attribute to the Boulder River Wilderness. A wall of mountains—Whitehorse, Bullon, Three Fingers, Big Bear, and Liberty—run through the center of the wilderness with dense, mossy forests of western hemlock, Douglas fir, and western red cedar running below the slopes of these sharply broken shale peaks.

LOCATION: South of Darrington

SIZE: 48,674 acres

ELEVATION RANGE: 1,000 to 6,850 feet

MILES OF TRAIL: Approximately 22

TREES AND PLANTS: Alaska cedar, Douglas fir, mountain hemlock, Pacific silver fir, subalpine fir, western hemlock, western red cedar, blueberry, devil's club, dwarf lupine, fern, huckleberry, paintbrush, salmonberry, vine maple

WILDLIFE: Black bear, black-tailed deer, elk, flying squirrel, mountain goat, Barrow's goldeneye, great horned owl, pileated woodpecker, Steller's jay

ADMINISTRATION: Mount Baker–Snoqualmie NF, Darrington RD, 360-436-1155; Verlot Public Service Center, 360-691-7791 (weekends)

BEST SEASON: Year-round along river bottoms; midsummer to early fall in the highlands

Given the heavy mining activity around Monte Cristo in the present-day Henry M. Jackson Wilderness to the southeast, gold fever in the 1880s ran too high to keep prospectors from venturing into the Boulder River area. Its fierce beauty proved to be its saving grace, though, as miners learned that their efforts far outweighed their rewards. Most of the rugged prospector trails fell into disuse and returned to a natural state. Logging operations in the lowlands grew (so to speak) here in the 1920s and 30s. Yet well before Congress officially designated this 48,674-acre area a wilderness in 1984, loggers had also lost interest in it. Even in a relatively accessible area like Boulder River, the terrain was such that loggers were simply unable to maintain profitable operations.

Hikers and conservationists now benefit from what remains as essential wildlife habitat: the fantastic stands of cedar, hemlock, and fir, some more than 200 years old, with diameters reaching 6 feet and heights topping 100 feet. Before the end of mineral exploration and logging, the trail along Boulder River went past its current 4-mile length all the way to Tupso Pass (this section is no longer maintained). Today, Trail #641 begins near the pass and continues on to the high ridge meadow of Goat Flat (with tremendous views of Mount Baker), on to Tin Can Gap and somewhat precarious glacier travel, and finally to the even more exposed ascent up a series of ladders to the Three Fingers Lookout. The Civilian Conservation Corps in 1932–33 took on the task of blasting some 10 to 15 feet off the top of the South Peak of Three Fingers to build this lookout.

Only a handful of maintained trails access the wilderness. The Boulder River Trail to the northwest and the Marten Creek Trail to the southeast both stay low in the valleys and only forge into brushy environments a short distance. The middle core—the most rugged area of the wilderness—remains rough and trailless, with the exception of the Goat Flat Trail to the top of Three Fingers. The size of the wilderness, its location near the more popular Henry M. Jackson and Glacier Peak areas, and the dearth of trails all keep the number of hikers to a minimum in Boulder River. As a result, more common animals like black bear, elk, and black-tailed deer live in healthy populations alongside more rare species like the flying squirrel, northern spotted owl, and marbled murrelet, all of which continue to survive in the old-growth forests remaining in the Boulder River Wilderness.

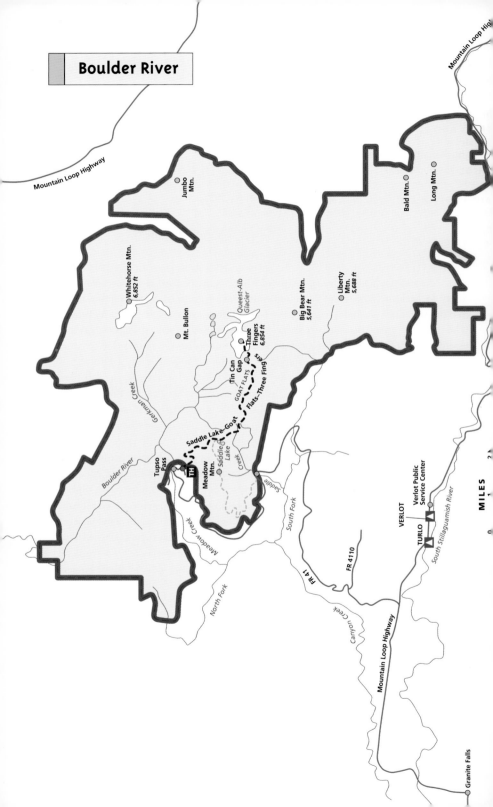

Boulder River

Jumbo Mtn.

Bald Mtn.

Long Mtn.

Whitehorse Mtn.
6,852 ft

Mt. Bullon

Quest-Alb Glacier

Big Bear Mtn.
5,641 ft

Liberty Mtn.
5,688 ft

Three Fingers
6,854 ft

Tin Can Gap

GOAT FLATS

Saddle Lake-Goat

Flats–Three Fing

Gerkman Creek

Boulder River

Tupso Pass

Meadow Mtn.

Saddle Lake

Creek

Saddle

South Fork

Meadow Creek

North Fork

FR 41

FR 4110

Canyon Creek

Verlot Public
Service Center

VERLOT

TURLO

South Stillaguamish River

Mountain Loop Highway

Mountain Loop Highway

Mountain Loop Highway

Mountain Loop Hig

Granite Falls

MILES

0   1   2

DAY OR DESTINATION HIKE: SADDLE LAKE–GOAT FLATS–THREE FINGERS LOOKOUT

One-Way Distance: 6.7 miles
Elevation Range: 3,050 to 6,854 feet
Total Elevation Gain: 3,804 feet
Difficulty: Moderate
Green Trails Maps: Granite Falls No. 109, Silverton No. 110

The trail begins in a heavily wooded area over a rocky and tree-rooted trail, climbing moderately. The thick tree canopy makes for cool hiking even in the heat of July and August. Flora attractions include salmonberry and sizable cedar trees. At mile 1.5 the trail curves downhill into a small, marshy drainage before continuing to climb. About 0.1 mile from Saddle Lake, a break in the trees gives you the first glimpse of Three Fingers in the distance. Saddle Lake is a small, shallow pool offering primitive campsites at mile 2.5. The trail becomes easier to travel by mile 3.4 but still gains elevation, entering a marshy meadow, vivid with green foliage and dashes of yellow, white, pink, violet, and purple wildflowers in season. At this point the tree type also changes, from cedar and Douglas fir to mountain hemlock and subalpine fir.

At Goat Flats (mile 5) the meadow area broadens to its widest point, along the benchlike ridge the trail has been following. You will find numerous campsites, a wilderness toilet, and water sources in the forms of pools and lingering snow patches. Enjoy spectacular views of mountains including Three Fingers, White Horse, Mount Baker, and other peaks to the north.

Follow the trail out of Goat Flats to reach Tin Can Gap and Three Fingers Lookout. The trail continues through a rockslide before switchbacking upward to the gap. Depending on the time of year and snowpack, you may be crossing over snow. Tin Can Gap at mile 6 is a small, rocky gap that provides access for those wanting to venture farther on to the lookout. The gap is also a great turnaround point, with a view of the lookout as well as of the Queest-Alb Glacier that fills the couloir below the gap.

At mile 6.7, by crossing glacier and rock to a set of ladders below, you reach the Three Fingers Lookout, perched on the summit of South Peak. The lookout is no longer used for fire spotting, but it is maintained and accessible. Overnight stays are allowed on a first-come, first-served basis. Take an ice ax and crampons for the glacier travel.

From the Verlot Public Service Center, travel 3.9 miles west on the Mountain Loop Highway. Turn right (north) at the top of the hill onto FR 41 (the road sign appears in about 200 feet). At 5.7 miles follow the left fork; the road changes from paved to gravel. From this point to the trailhead it is a combination of dirt and gravel. You will reach Trail #641 to Saddle Lake–Goat Flats at 21.9 miles, with parking before and after the trailhead.

16 Glacier Peak Wilderness

Meadows on Green Mountain

LOCATION: Bordering the North Cascades National Park Complex and Lake Chelan, north of US 2 and about 25 miles north of Leavenworth

SIZE: 572,338 acres

ELEVATION RANGE: 1,150 to 10,541 feet

MILES OF TRAIL: 450

TREES AND PLANTS: Cottonwood, Douglas fir, lodgepole pine, mountain hemlock, subalpine fir, western hemlock, western red cedar, anemone, aster, daisy, heather, huckleberry, lupine, monkeyflower, paintbrush, sedge

WILDLIFE: Black bear, black-tailed deer, elk, gray wolf, grizzly bear, hoary marmot, lynx, marten, mountain goat, wolverine, Clark's nutcracker, goshawk, gray jay, grouse, red-shafted flicker, northern spotted owl, peregrine falcon

ADMINISTRATION: Mount Baker–Snoqualmie National Forest: Mount Baker RD, 360-856-5700; Darrington RD, 360-436-1155. Wenatchee National Forest: Chelan RD, 509-682-2576; Entiat RD, 509-784-1511; Leavenworth RD, 509-548-6977; Lake Wenatchee RD, 509-763-3103.

BEST SEASON: Midsummer to mid-autumn

We have rejected the pleas of miners who would shatter the wilderness calm with the roar of helicopters because such use would make their work easier and more efficient. We have used primitive equipment and travel methods in administering Wilderness when modern motorized equipment would have been more convenient. I have urged the Kennecott Copper Corporation to forgo development of large copper deposits in favor of priceless, yet intangible, national treasures of the Glacier Peak Wilderness in Washington. . . . We held then, and we hold now, that economics *alone* is not sufficient basis for determining whether wilderness shall survive or die.

—*Orville L. Freeman, U.S. Secretary of Agriculture, 1968*

IT IS TRUE THAT THE GLACIER PEAK WILDERNESS WAS ONE of a number of geographic areas to be so designated as part of the Wilderness Act of 1964, which designated an area of some 464,300 acres. Freeman was responding to the Kennecott Copper Corporation's proposal to mine Plummer Mountain along Miners Ridge—a legal right they would hold until 1984. Since Kennecott had proposed development of a pit mine, opposition forces quickly assembled, claiming that such an open pit would be visible from the moon. This of course was not true, but public pressure proved real and kept the mine from being developed. In 1984, the same year that 19 new wilderness areas were added in Washington, Glacier Peak grew in size while maintaining its original designation within the cycles of nature, not humanity.

If mining was a part of the Glacier Peak Wilderness for nearly 80 years, it was railroad companies seeking an east-west crossing that promoted the first attempts at redesigning the natural landscape. Railroad builders hoped to cash in on the increasing trade in eastern Washington wheat bound for Asia via Seattle-based shipping operations. But there is nearly always someone who has gone before in stories of the West, and it is no different when looking at the history of railroads in the Cascades.

It was the fall of 1859 when a prospector-engineer named Ed Cady found, after hard brushed-in travels up the North Fork of the Skykomish River, a pass south of the present-day boundaries of Glacier Peak Wilderness. The impetus for exploring Cady Pass, as it is known today within the Henry M. Jackson Wilderness, came from west-side port communities and particularly from a speculator named E. C. Ferguson, who sought a means to connect the eastern Washington gold-rush fever to the west. In the end, funding from the interested parties dried up, halting the road's construction some five miles from the pass. But the idea remained that a railroad could cross this formidable divider of the state.

The Northern Pacific Railroad conducted explorations in 1867, and then again in 1870, up the Suiattle River and Sulphur Creek near Dome Mountain to the north, and along the Sauk River south to a point near Indian Head Peak. A Massachusetts engineer named D. C. Linsley led the journeys. From the top of Indian Head he could see no other passable route over what is today called Linsley Pass on the north side of the peak. Snoqualmie Pass was already known, as was Stampede Pass, both situated farther to the south near the present-day Alpine Lakes Wilderness. With higher cost estimates for the construction of a rail line over Linsley Pass, along with reports of the greater intensity of snowfall through here, the Northern Pacific chose to run its line over Stampede Pass, which they completed in 1887.

The Great Northern Railroad (GNR) had yet to find a suitable route, so they employed John Frank Stevens, perhaps the world's foremost civil engineer (who later oversaw of the construction of the Panama Canal). Stevens had found Marias Pass at the south end of Glacier National Park in Montana for the GNR. After exploring options over Cascade Pass north of the current wilderness, and along the Entiat River, whose headwaters originate in the wilderness, Stevens discovered what is known today as Stevens Pass. Even though Stevens Pass does not adjoin the boundaries of the Glacier Peak Wilderness, present-day US 2 crosses the pass, mostly parallels the rail line, and remains a major access road to trailheads into the south end of the wilderness.

The quests for rail and road passage over the Cascades eventually led to the construction of I-90 over Snoqualmie Pass far to the south and the incredibly scenic North Cascades Highway (WA 20) to the north, which provides some access to the wilderness. Forest Service roads, along with water access via Lake Chelan, provide the remaining access to trails on the east side of Glacier Peak, and spur roads off both WA 530 and the Mountain Loop Highway between Darrington and Silverton provide access to trails on the west side. Very few trails traverse the northern portion of Glacier Peak bordering North Cascades National Park because of extremely rugged mountain terrain. Even with mountains named Formidable, Sinister, Disappointment, and Fortress, and despite the railroads' failures to find adequate passage through this challenging land, miners still managed to pull minerals from various locations in Glacier Peak.

Gold prospectors in the 1880s and '90s initially made claims in areas around the Chiwawa River valley and the Phelps Creek drainage. Along with gold they found copper, silver, lead, zinc, and molybdenum. The Royal Development Company processed low-grade copper extracted from mines at Red Mountain and along Phelps Ridge until it was no longer profitable. The company's large mill in Trinity ceased operations in the early 1940s, and the company dissolved in 1948. The Howe Sound Company, the largest copper mill in the state, operated in the town of Holden, up Railroad Creek from the Lake Chelan shoreline town of Lucerne. This 2,000-ton mill extracted minerals, including 600,000 ounces of gold, from 1939 to 1957. As had happened to Royal Development in Trinity, operations at the Holden mill were no longer profitable after the big drop in copper prices in 1957. Many of the buildings of Holden still stand today; the town now operates as a year-round, ecumenical Lutheran retreat.

Human history in the Cascades, long driven by the commerce of trappers, miners, loggers, and railroads, began of course with the Indians. The central Washington –based Wenatchee, Chelan, and Entiat tribes foraged for edible plants and hunted deer and mountain goat. They also engaged in trade with other tribes, such as the Skagit, Sauk, Skykomish, and Stillaguamish tribes from the coast, creating trails such as those over Cloudy, Indian, and White Passes. Trappers and traders used these Indian trails. Some of the trails can also be attributed to the shepherds who drove their flocks from the lowlands up to lush alpine meadows in summer. But despite these impacts, the 572,338-acre Glacier Peak Wilderness contains only about 450 miles of trail, proving human limits to adventure as well as profit.

Working up the Surprise Mountain Trail toward Pieper Pass in the Alpine Lakes Wilderness, you can see an incredible view of Glacier Peak, the mountain, to the north. A giant, horizon-dominating, glaciated mass, Glacier Peak has an equally impressive trailing ridgeline of peaks like Disappointment, Tenpeak, and Clark, that scale down slightly in height from west to east. Glacier Peak seems to possess the ability to stop you in your tracks with thoughts of humanity in relation to nature—not least because Glacier Peak is classified as an active volcano. It is very similar to the way Rainier, Adams, Hood, or Shasta can fill the sky and hijack a mind with wonder. But unlike those others, the deserved prominence isn't gained by a prospect from the lowlands tens of miles away but only reveals itself from higher vantage points that ring the center of the wilderness.

Glacier Peak is also the most remote of the state's Cascade volcanoes sought after by climbers. Rainier, Adams, Baker, Hood, and Shasta have nothing of an approach: Drive your car to a parking lot and begin your climb. By contrast, no road comes within eight miles of what many Indian tribes called the "White Mountain." (The Skagit tribe calls it *Da-Kobed,* meaning "parent" or "mother.") Most hikes start from closer to 10 miles away and cross rugged, formidable terrain.

Glacier Peak is of course glaciated and was shaped by the continental ice-sheet movements that began some 1 million years ago and ended about 12,000 years ago. This glaciation was responsible for the detailing of valleys, peaks, cirques, and bowls, now occupied by more than 200 lakes, along with dozens of lower-elevation peaks clad in alpine skirts and hanging glaciers. Indeed, Glacier Peak is the most active glaciated region in the lower 48 states. If glaciation's handiwork can take the credit for its appearance, the area's foundation is attributable to both an earlier movement of the earth's crust and to a later series of volcanic eruptions.

Starting some 700,000 years ago, the cone of Glacier Peak formed atop the western edge of the Cloudy Pass batholith. Lava flows, building the mountain's side, worked toward both the Suiattle River valley and the White Chuck River drainage. Further eruptions have been credited with such creations as the extruded dactite formation on a rib to the south of Glacier Peak, known today as Disappointment Peak. A series of closely spaced blasts some 12,000 years ago, with an intensity rivaling the 1980 blast of Mount St. Helens, distributed ash and pumice to eastern areas of the wilderness upwards of 12 feet thick and caused gigantic mudslides.

The terrain of the Glacier Peak Wilderness ranges from 1,150 feet at the Devore Creek Trailhead off Stehekin River Road, up to 10,541 feet at the summit of Glacier Peak. Peaks above 9,000 feet include Disappointment, Fernow, Seven Fingered Jack, Maude, and Bonanza. Dozens more range between 7,500 and 8,500 feet. Thick forest, sharp-edged ridgelines, steep valley walls, and ice-cold creeks just add to the glory and awesome presence you will discover inside this wilderness. At home in the forest areas and around the creeks and lakes are black-tailed and mule deer; a scattering of elk, black bear, and lynx; along with squirrel, chipmunk, marten, and fisher. In the rocks and cliffs expect to see large animals like mountain goat in addition to pika, marmot, and ptarmigan. Hunting birds in the wilderness include goshawk, red-tailed hawk, and great horned owl, with rarer sightings of spotted owl and peregrine falcon.

Actions by trappers and hunters from the mid-1800s onward greatly reduced the numbers of gray wolf, grizzly bear, and wolverine until such hunting became illegal in the mid-1960s. These three creatures are rarely glimpsed within the wilderness. Much has been preserved by the designation of wilderness areas like Glacier Peak, but so much has been altered or taken away in other areas outside the wilderness—but still within the natural habitat of roaming creatures like the gray wolf and grizzly bear—that it is ever more difficult for them to survive.

DAY HIKE: GREEN MOUNTAIN LOOKOUT
One-Way Distance: 3.5 miles
Elevation Range: 3,500 to 6,500 feet
Total Elevation Gain: 3,000 feet
Difficulty: Moderate
Green Trails Map: Cascade Pass No. 80

The hike begins pleasantly by working through a tightly canopied old-growth forest over spongy ground with very little understory. At mile 1.1 the trail breaks from the forest onto hillside meadows, which typically explode with wildflowers in July. The trail contours the hillside from south to east via long switchbacks through meadows and a huckleberry patch, eventually reaching a more treed environment of spruce and hemlock.

After climbing up to an open section in the woods, the trail descends at mile 2.2 into a marvelous rolling meadow containing a pair of small tarns. Campsites are available. The trail to the lookout passes through this area to the base of a thick grassy slope at mile 2.6, which marks the start of the steep climb up to the ridge to the Green Mountain Lookout. You'll reach the ridge at mile 3.3 and the lookout at mile 3.5. Built in 1933, the lookout commands views of Mount Baker and Canada beyond to the north, Glacier Peak and an incredible array of mountain peaks to the east and south, and Puget Sound to the west.

From the Darrington RD drive 7.2 miles north on WA 530 to Suiattle River Road (FR 26) and turn right. The pavement changes to gravel and dirt at 17.2 miles. At 26.3 miles turn left onto FR 2680 toward the Green Mountain Trailhead. The road is bumpy. The trailhead at 35.1 miles is uphill to the left, approximately 0.1 mile before the road's end. There is no parking area, so pull as far to the side of the road as possible.

DAY OR DESTINATION HIKE: SPIDER MEADOW AND SPIDER GAP
One-Way Distance: 7 miles
Elevation Range: 3,500 to 7,100 feet
Total Elevation Gain: 3,600 feet
Difficulty: Easy (through the meadows); Strenuous (to Spider Gap)
Green Trails Map: Holden No. 113

Here's the dreaded news—this is a popular hike. Try to avoid high season on weekends and holidays. Weekdays during high season and the off-season—early to late fall—are ideal times to visit. So prepare for a wonderful treat.

The trail is wide in the beginning before it narrows down, following an up-and-down route above Phelps Creek in and out of the trees, with occasional views of Phelps Ridge to the west. After 4 miles of easy hiking, the trail enters Spider Meadow, which lies between the rock walls of Phelps Ridge and a ridgeline connecting Seven Fingered Jack and Dumbell Mountain. Wildflowers abound in the grassy meadow along the glacially chilled Phelps Creek. You will find campsites at the entrance and a few more after the meadow at mile 4.5, not far from the trail junction at mile 5.3 to Spider Gap and Phelps Creek Basin.

The trail to Spider Gap climbs very steeply—1,800 vertical feet in 1.7 miles —up a rocky trail, momentarily leveling out at mile 6.1, where a point juts out for a great view over Spider Meadow down below. This is also a splendid campsite— arrive early to secure it. From here, head north up the rib edging the east side of Spider Glacier or into the couloir up the glacier itself.

Given good conditions, I recommend glacier travel. You can take an ice ax, but ski poles or a hiking stick should provide enough stability on your climb. At mile 6.8, cross through a small cirque affording a great view of Dumbell Mountain, or skirt along the upper right-hand side to reach Spider Gap at mile 7. Below your feet will be a chain of small lakes and the terminus of Lyman Glacier; in the distance is Lyman Lake and a collection of dramatic peaks rising above it, notably 9,511-foot Bonanza Peak. In all, a splendid display of fine high-alpine features.

From the gap, descend the glacier if you wish and climb over rocks to a trail along the east side of the chain of lakes. In another 2.5 miles you will reach Lyman Lake.

Travel west on US 2 from the Leavenworth RD 15.6 miles to WA 207, then turn right (north) toward Lake Wenatchee. At 21 miles turn right onto Chiwawa Road, and at 22.2 miles turn left onto Meadow Creek Road (FR 62). Follow the paved road about 6 miles, where it changes to sometimes bumpy gravel. At 39.3 miles take the right fork to the Phelps Creek Trailhead at 41.7 miles. Parking is limited.

DAY HIKE: MOUNT DAVID
One-Way Distance: 7.7 miles
Elevation Range: 2,300 to 7,420 feet
Total Elevation Gain: 5,120 feet
Difficulty: Strenuous
Green Trails Map: Wenatchee Lake No. 145

Be sure to start this day hike early. Expect miles of sustained climbing, and note that there are no established campsites up high. From the parking area cross over the bridge, 25 to 30 feet above White River, and take your first left at the sign for Mount David, cutting back parallel to the river. This section is easy traveling, staying above the river in a predominantly cedar forest. At 0.7 mile take the right fork in the trail, again following a sign for Mount David. Approximately 0.2 mile farther along, the trail forks once more; bear right onto Mount David Trail #1521.

From this second fork, the climbing is at first minimal but soon picks up in its incline, alternating between moderate to strenuous, but staying sustained the entire way up the slope and high above the White River valley and Lake Wenatchee to the south. At mile 4.6 the trail reaches the ridge and begins a fantastic progression, swinging from the ridge's northeast to southwest sides, affording grand views in both directions. The trail eventually climbs above the treeline and through the

continued on p. 142

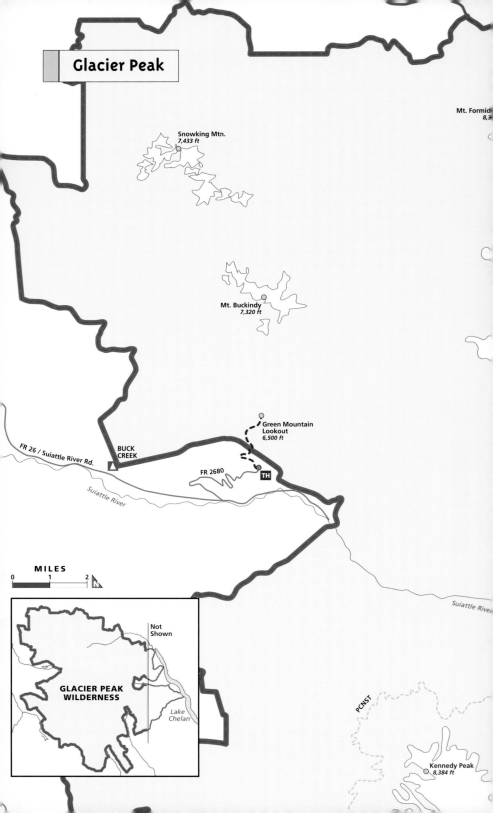

Glacier Peak

Mt. Formid
8,3

Snowking Mtn.
7,433 ft

Mt. Buckindy
7,320 ft

Green Mountain
Lookout
6,500 ft

FR 26 / Suiattle River Rd.

BUCK
CREEK

FR 2680

TH

Suiattle River

Suiattle River

MILES

0   1   2

N

Not
Shown

**GLACIER PEAK
WILDERNESS**

*Lake
Chelan*

PCNST

Kennedy Peak
8,384 ft

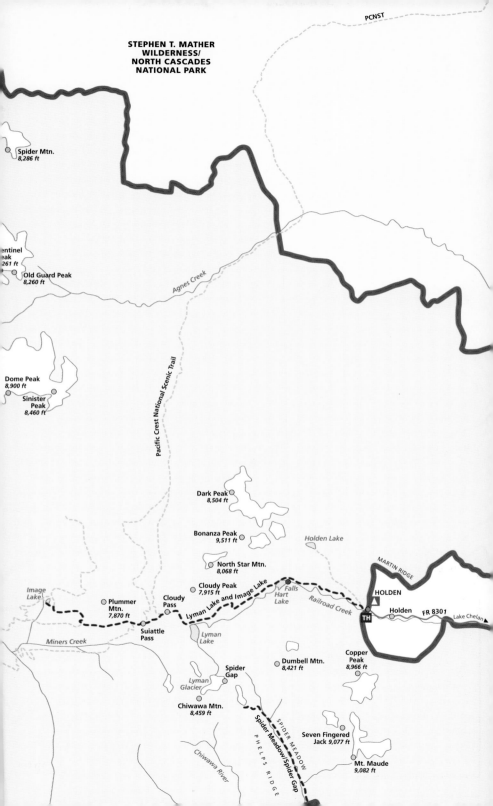

STEPHEN T. MATHER
WILDERNESS/
NORTH CASCADES
NATIONAL PARK

PCNST

Spider Mtn.
8,286 ft

entinel
eak
261 ft

Old Guard Peak
8,260 ft

Agnes Creek

Dome Peak
8,900 ft

Sinister
Peak
8,460 ft

Pacific Crest National Scenic Trail

Dark Peak
8,504 ft

Bonanza Peak
9,511 ft

Holden Lake

North Star Mtn.
8,068 ft

MARTIN RIDGE

Cloudy Peak
7,915 ft

Lyman Lake and Image Lake

Falls

Hart
Lake

HOLDEN

Image
Lake

Plummer
Mtn.
7,870 ft

Cloudy
Pass

Railroad Creek

Holden

FR 8301

Lake Chelan

TH

Miners Creek

Suiattle
Pass

Lyman
Lake

Dumbell Mtn.
8,421 ft

Copper
Peak
8,966 ft

Lyman
Glacier

Spider
Gap

SPIDER MEADOW

Chiwawa Mtn.
8,459 ft

Spider Meadow/Spider Gap

PHELPS RIDGE

Seven Fingered
Jack 9,077 ft

Chiwawa River

Mt. Maude
9,082 ft

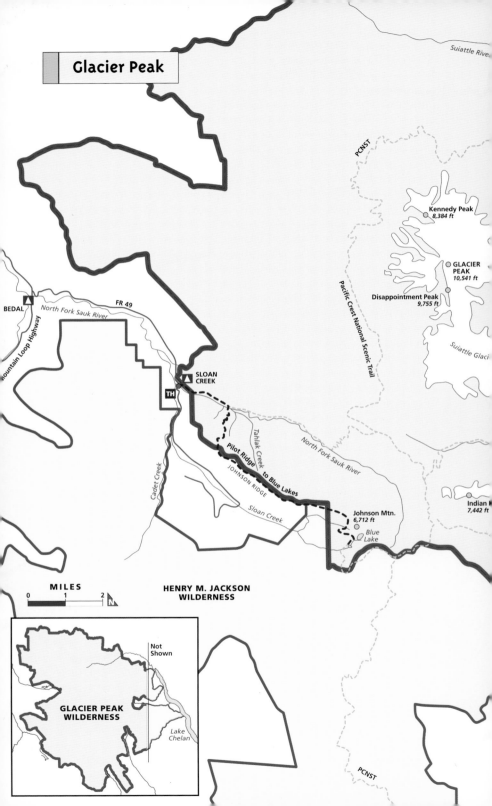

Glacier Peak

Suiattle River

PCNST

Kennedy Peak
8,384 ft

GLACIER PEAK
10,541 ft

Disappointment Peak
9,755 ft

Pacific Crest National Scenic Trail

Suiattle Glaci

BEDAL

FR 49

North Fork Sauk River

Mountain Loop Highway

SLOAN CREEK

TH

Tahlak Creek

North Fork Sauk River

Pilot Ridge to Blue Lakes

JOHNSON RIDGE

Sloan Creek

Cadet Creek

Johnson Mtn.
6,712 ft

Blue Lake

Indian
7,442 ft

MILES
0   1   2

**HENRY M. JACKSON
WILDERNESS**

Not Shown

**GLACIER PEAK
WILDERNESS**

Lake
Chelan

PCNST

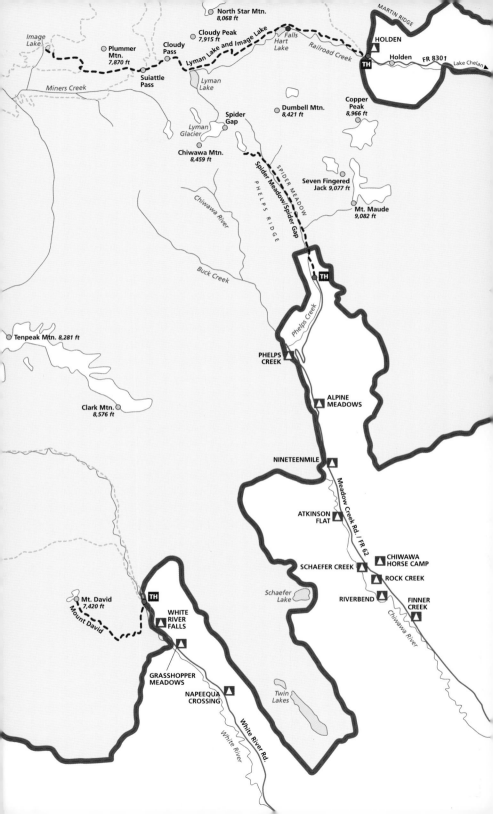

rocks lined with pink and white heather, paintbrush, bluebell, and nearly a dozen more wildflower varieties, and through sections of heart-pumping exposure.

You will reach the summit, site of a former lookout post, at mile 7.7 after nearly a vertical mile of climbing. It is a 360-degree visual feast from here: peaks like Sloan, Glacier, Clark, and Maude, along with dozens of glacially carved valleys, three times as many ridgelines, and enough dramatic peaks to keep you counting for days. Be advised that if the snowpack hasn't fully melted on the approach to the summit, the route can be difficult to travel upon—or find.

From the Leavenworth RD travel 15.6 miles west on US 2 to the turn for Lake Wenatchee and WA 207 (Lake Wenatchee Highway). The Lake Wenatchee RD is at 24.6 miles. Turn right onto White River Road at 26.4 miles. At 32.8 miles, just before a bridge crossing, the road surface changes from pavement to gravel. Make sure to go past the White River Falls Campground to reach the White River Trailhead at 37 miles.

> **OVERNIGHT HIKE: PILOT RIDGE TO BLUE LAKES**
> One-Way Distance: 10.5 miles
> Elevation Range: 2,100 to 5,700 feet
> Total Elevation Gain: 3,600 feet
> Difficulty: Strenuous
> Green Trails Maps: Sloan Peak No. 111, Glacier Peak No. 112,
> Benchmark Mtn. No. 144

The hike begins on the North Fork Sauk River Trail through a grand older-growth forest of cedar and fir, staying low along the river. At mile 1.5 the Pilot Ridge Trail heads to the right (south), crosses the river over a footlog, and begins a steep, long, switchbacking climb 3,000 vertical feet up a forested slope to the ridge. At mile 4.5 the trail begins its glorious 5-mile stretch along Johnson Ridge. The elevation ranges from 5,100 to 5,700 feet as the trail passes around and over knobs, through forested sections, and across small pocket meadows. If this weren't enough to keep you happily hiking along, views include dramatic takes on Glacier Peak to the north, the Monte Cristo Peaks close by to the south, and Cascade giant Mount Rainier farther south.

At mile 9.5 a spur trail leads to the summit of 6,712-foot Johnson Mountain, with the main trail heading west then southeast toward Blue Lake. At mile 10 you reach a fork: The left fork leads to the sizable Blue Lake and the right fork to the considerably smaller Little Blue Lake in another 0.5 mile. Camping is available at both lakes, but be aware that the lakes can be frozen into August.

From the Darrington RD take WA 530 south. At the intersection of WA 530 and FR 20 (Mountain Loop Highway) at 0.4 mile, continue straight. The pavement ends at 9.7 miles. At 16.7 miles turn left onto FR 49 (Sloan Creek Road) toward the North Fork Sauk Trailhead. At 23.5 miles bear to the left at the sign for North Fork Sauk Trailhead to reach Sloan Creek Campground and the trailhead at 23.7 miles.

Buck Creek, Glacier Peak Wilderness

MULTIDAY DESTINATION HIKE: LYMAN LAKE AND IMAGE LAKE
One-Way Distance: 15.8 miles
Elevation Range: 3,310 to 6,438 feet
Total Elevation Gain: 3,728 feet
Difficulty: Moderate
Green Trails Maps: Holden No. 113, Glacier Peak No. 112

NOTE: Plan your boat schedule ahead, before starting on this hike.

Start by hiking along the road about 0.6 mile to a sign marking the Glacier Peak Wilderness. The trail parallels Railroad Creek, staying flat or climbing slightly, with views of Martin Ridge to the north and Copper Peak to the south. You will pass the trail junction for Holden Lake at mile 1.4, cross over Holden Creek via a footlog, and go through a stand of lodgepole pine. The trail then enters a corridor of taller brush and climbs steeply up to the falls just before the outlet of Hart Lake.

   From the falls the trail climbs a bit more before dipping down at mile 4.7 along the north shore of Hart Lake and by some campsites. Past the lake the trail moves easily through another open, brushy area before climbing above Railroad

Creek with views of Dumbell Mountain to the south. At mile 6.2 a steep set of switchbacks climbs to a saddle, where the trail drops slightly into a treed-in basin, then ascends back out to reach Lyman Lake at mile 8.9.

Lyman Lake is wonderful—ringed by trees and backdropped to the south by Chiwawa Mountain, Spider Gap, and Lyman Glacier, which feeds first a series of small lakes and ponds situated above the lake, and eventually Lyman Lake and Railroad Creek. Campsites lie on the north, south, and west sides of the lake. For another beautiful camp setting, hike another 1.1 miles uphill through smaller pocket meadows to the spectacular grassland of Cloudy Pass at mile 10.

Numerous small creeks, overlooks of Lyman Lake, and views of spectacular peaks in all directions abound from here. Look for heather and for wildflowers including paintbrush, monkeyflower, buttercup, and bluebell. You can find campsites in the middle of Cloudy Pass as well as on the high point of the pass. The trail descends Cloudy Pass via slightly steeper switchbacks than the ascent from Lyman Lake, reaching a trail junction at mile 10.5. Take the left fork, with a sign for Suiattle Pass. This shortcut takes you across a rocky traverse, avoiding the descent then ascend up to Suiattle Pass. Note that this traverse, as well as both Cloudy and Suiattle Passes, can hold snow well into August, making the trail difficult to follow.

From Suiattle Pass at mile 10.8, the trail winds its way down to the junction with the Pacific Crest Trail at mile 12. Take the trail to the right, heading west on Miners Ridge Trail. The trail crosses a creek and passes a campsite, then moves below the ridgeline on a slope rising up from Miners Creek. At mile 14, just past an old miner's cabin, is the junction for Image Lake. The trail climbs up a series of switchbacks before straightening out and exiting the trees onto a meadow slope. Take the left fork here, working up to Lady Camp and on to Image Lake at mile 15.8. Many campsites dot this area, and with good reason. The open and rolling plateau is filled with heather and wildflowers, and Image Lake seems to snare within its banks the upper north face of Glacier Peak. It is a very tranquil place, well worth a few days' stay.

The only real access to this hike comes by way of boat or floatplane. The easiest and most economical route is to book passage on a boat operated by the Lake Chelan Boat Company. (Different schedules and rates apply depending on season, itinerary, and class of boat; contact the Lake Chelan Boat Company at 509-682-2224 or www.ladyofthelake.com.) Travel from Chelan (3 hours) or Field's Point Landing (2 hours) to Lucerne. Once in Lucerne, travel by bus (about $10 round-trip) another 12 miles to Holden Village. From Holden Village, hike along a road for less than a mile to the trailhead. Confirm bus schedules and costs by writing to Holden Village, HC00 Stop 2, Chelan, WA 98816-9769, or by visiting www.holdenvillage.org. Note that there is no phone service—or e-mail—at the village.

Henry M. Jackson Wilderness 17

Monte Cristo Peak

IN A FITTINGLY IRONIC TWIST, this wilderness—named in honor of a Washington senator and congressman of 42 years whose legacy remains in many bills protecting natural habitats—has one of the richest histories of interaction and exploitation by man. Preservation has prevailed, but not without the mark of private interests and human history. The wilderness' inkblot shape is a result of the private land that rings a healthy majority of the 100,337-acre wilderness. Luckily, the powers that be had the forethought to designate some 35,000 acres on various points of the wilderness boundary

LOCATION: In a diagonal line between Darrington and Stevens Pass, approximately 35 miles west of Leavenworth

SIZE: 100,337 acres

ELEVATION RANGE: 1,800 to 7,835 feet

MILES OF TRAIL: 49

TREES AND PLANTS: Alaska cedar, Douglas fir, mountain hemlock, Pacific yew, subalpine fir, avalanche lily, blueberry, devil's club, dwarf lupine, fern, heather, huckleberry, paintbrush

WILDLIFE: Black bear, black-tailed deer, cougar, lynx, marten, mountain goat, black-capped chickadee, northern flicker, red-tailed hawk, robin, Steller's jay

ADMINISTRATION: Mount Baker–Snoqualmie NF: Darrington RD, 360-436-1155; Skykomish RD, 360-677-2414. Wenatchee NF, Lake Wenatchee RD, 509-763-3103.

BEST SEASON: Summer through fall

as a roadless area with hope that it will someday become inclusive with the rest of the Henry M. Jackson Wilderness (a current wilderness proposal calls for additional land to be added).

The ironies continue with a hike along the Monte Cristo Road, formerly the railroad grade that hauled out tons of gold, silver, and copper ore bound for Everett. The old tracks lead into the once-bustling town of Monte Cristo in a section of the wilderness proudly boasting a spectacular concentration of 7,000-foot, fanglike peaks draped in glaciers. Perhaps ultimately it is apropos that this place bears the late senator's name, since he believed that the environment could be protected without harming the necessary functions of industry.

Prospectors Frank Peabody and Joseph Pearsall are credited with discovering the glint of the minerals gold and silver in Glacier Basin in 1889, after a hard-fought traverse from Sultan over densely forested mountains. As in Alaska and elsewhere in the American West, the fever took hold; claims were marked in Glacier Basin and Seventy-Six Gulch, among other sites, which soon became inhabited by hundreds of dream chasers. By 1893 the town of Monte Cristo—named for good luck after the rich count in the Dumas novel—was born. The boomtown boasted a 200-ton concentrator, saloons, hotels, private homes, and a daily train into Everett.

At its height, Monte Cristo had a population of 2,000. However, as in other present-day wilderness areas of Washington, mining eventually proved to be unprofitable. The millions of dollars of ore taken from the mountains via mines, tunnels, aerial tramways, and rail couldn't cover the cost it took to run these operations. By the 1920s, mining gave way to recreation, with Monte Cristo playing host to hunters, campers, and sightseers. But even before the balance sheet proved the uselessness of this region for financial profit, nature showed its distaste in some devastating ways.

Only four years after the boom that created Monte Cristo, severe floods and washouts closed the railroad, effectively halting the progress of the town. The will of the miners pushed ahead, though, and operations resumed in 1901 for a time, before a steady decline in mining started in 1904. Another huge blow was dealt in 1915, when heavy snows crushed most of the town's buildings. Fast-forward to 1973, when the ghost town's remaining tramway cable fell: Nature was apparently continuing her quest to erase human impacts on the area. However, the human history cannot be denied, nor should it be forgotten. This section of the wilderness is well worth a visit, both for what used to be here and what still remains. It is also satisfying to know that nature is bigger than us.

Nature's history is of course millions of years old; tectonic plate movement, volcanic activity, and the sculptor's hand of glacial action have left their traces in jagged arêtes (ridges) and steep-sided drainages. Relatively few trails access the northwestern part of the wilderness, but trails like the one to Blanca Lake are worth taking. A long set of switchbacks up, and then a short drop to the lake, offer fantastic views of the south faces of Columbia, Monte Cristo, and Kyes Peaks. In the southern and eastern portions of the Henry M. Jackson Wilderness, expect to find ridgeline meadows colored in the months of summer like sleeping rainbows with avalanche lily, phlox, paintbrush, and dwarf lupine, especially along the Pacific Crest Trail, which cuts through middle of the southern half of the wilderness.

Some 60 lakes dot the wilderness, including the deep blue Twin Lakes, shelved one over the other above the West Fork Troublesome Creek valley. Approaching the lakes involves a combination of hiking and scrambling, with a high amount of exhilarating exposure and overviews of all the big peaks surrounding the disappearing town site of Monte Cristo.

DAY HIKE: MINOTAUR LAKE
One-Way Length: 2 miles
Elevation Range: 3,700 to 5,600 feet
Total Elevation Gain: 1,900 feet
Difficulty: Strenuous
Green Trails Map: Benchmark Mtn. No. 144

A loose-surfaced trail climbs steeply for the first 1.4 miles. Be prepared for a good leg burn and multiple rest stops. Beyond this point the trail condition improves as it levels out, becoming much less intense but still continuing to climb toward Minotaur Lake. At mile 2 you reach Minotaur Lake. A trail crosses the creek at the lake's outlet to give access to Theseus Lake, which sits some 500 vertical feet below Minotaur Lake. By scrambling around Minotaur Lake and taking other side trails, you can enjoy views of Mount Rainier to the south and of Glacier Peak to the north. The water in August is a fine temperature for a swim on a hot day. The trail is well traveled and well maintained. Campsites are available.

Turn on FR 6700 off of US 2, just west of Stevens Pass Nordic Center. Look for the sign marking FR 6700 or a sign for Smithbrook. The road surface is dirt and loose gravel. At 4.2 miles the road crosses over a pass; head down the other side for 2.8 miles. At 7 miles, turn left onto FR 6704 and continue up the road for 0.8 mile to the trailhead at 7.8 miles.

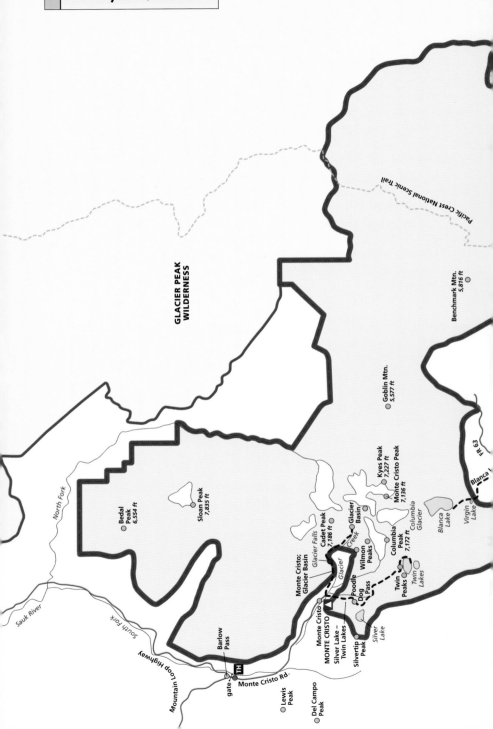

Henry M. Jackson

GLACIER PEAK
WILDERNESS

Pacific Crest National Scenic Trail

Benchmark Mtn.
5,816 ft

Goblin Mtn.
5,577 ft

FR 63

Bedal
Peak
6,554 ft

Sloan Peak
7,835 ft

Kyes Peak
7,227 ft
Monte Cristo Peak
7,136 ft

Blanca L

Cadet Peak
7,186 ft

Glacier
Basin

Columbia
Peak
7,172 ft

Columbia
Glacier

Virgin

Blanca
Lake

Monte Cristo;
Glacier Basin

Glacier Falls

Glacier

Wilmon
Peaks

Creek

Poodle

Dog
Pass

Twin
Peaks

Twin
Lakes

North Fork

Monte Cristo

MONTE CRISTO
Silver Lake –
Twin Lakes

Silver
Lake

Silvertip
Peak

Barlow
Pass

Sauk River

South Fork

Mountain Loop Highway

gate

Monte Cristo Rd.

Lewis
Peak

Del Campo
Peak

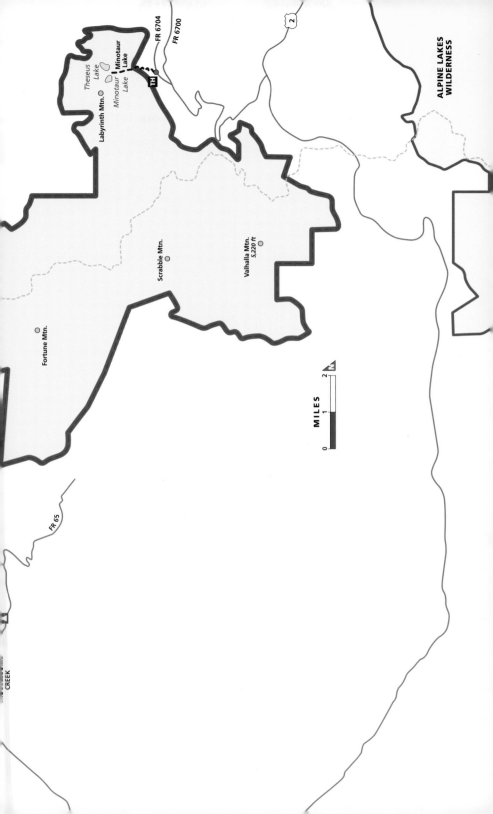

CREEK

FR 65

Fortune Mtn.

Scrabble Mtn.

Valhalla Mtn.
5,220 ft

Labyrinth Mtn.

Theseus
Lake

Minotaur
Lake

Minotaur
Lake

TH

FR 6704

FR 6700

2

ALPINE LAKES
WILDERNESS

MILES

0   1   2

N

DESTINATION OR DAY HIKE: BLANCA LAKE
One-Way Length: 3.3 miles
Elevation Range: 1,900 to 4,600 feet
Total Elevation Gain: 2,700 feet
Difficulty: Moderate
Green Trails Map: Monte Cristo No. 143

This trail is well traveled and comfortable to hike, which makes facing the 30 or more switchbacks that begin almost immediately and continue for 2.5 miles a bit more tolerable. At the end of the switchbacks the trail starts up a rib with views of Kyes Peak and Columbia Peak in the distance. Continue climbing the rib for another 0.4 mile.

At mile 2.9 and an elevation of 4,600 feet you cross the wilderness boundary and make a short descent to Virgin Lake. The last 0.4 mile to 179-acre Blanca Lake is somewhat steep, rocky, and loose in sections. Blanca Lake offers hikers a great setting in which to camp, rest, and gaze upon Columbia Glacier as well as (left to right) Columbia Peak, Monte Cristo Peak, and Kyes Peak.

Off of US 2 turn onto the North Fork Skykomish River Road (FR 63) toward the town of Index. Continue past Index toward Troublesome Creek Campground at 10 miles and San Juan Campground at 12 miles. At 12.6 miles take the left fork, heading uphill. The pavement ends at 13.5 miles, at the left turn for FR 63. Continue up a dirt and loose gravel road for 2.1 miles to the trailhead at 15.6 miles.

DAY OR OVERNIGHT HIKE: MONTE CRISTO; GLACIER BASIN;
SILVER LAKE–TWIN LAKES
One-way Distance: 4 miles (Monte Cristo); 2.1 miles (Glacier Basin);
4.8 miles (Silver Lake–Twin Lakes)
Elevation Range: 2,350 to 2,800 feet; 3,200 to 4,500 feet;
2,800 to 5,350 feet
Total elevation gain: 450 feet; 1,300 feet; 2,550 feet
Difficulty: Easy; Moderate; Strenuous
Green Trails Map: Monte Cristo No. 143

MONTE CRISTO

The hike into the old Monte Cristo town site is really a pleasant stroll down a backcountry road—except the road is now closed to vehicle traffic. Paralleling the South Fork Sauk River, the gravel Monte Cristo Road is actually the former railroad grade of the Everett & Monte Cristo Railroad that hauled ore out and visitors and townspeople into Monte Cristo. It is an easy walk, with the grade tilting slightly more upward after mile 2, but the sound of the river and the views of Cadet, Toad, Silvertip, Lewis, Del Campo, and Monte Cristo Peaks at various points along the way will make the 4-mile stretch go quickly. Many buildings, including the pump house, a garage, and some houses still stand from its time as a town of 2,000 people, and from its beginnings in the 1890s until its abandonment in the 1930s. Sites where buildings once stood are signed. The town site is well worth historical exploration.

GLACIER BASIN

From Monte Cristo, follow the trail over Glacier Creek, up to Dumas Street, and out of town along an old railroad grade to start out toward Glacier Basin. At approximately 0.5 mile the trail climbs steeply past Glacier Falls and around Mystery Hill. You will reach the bottom end of Glacier Basin at mile 2.1. Be careful not to damage the delicate meadows of the basin, which is ringed by a collection of fantastic peaks: Wilmon, Monte Cristo, and Cadet. The basin also holds interesting remnants of former mining operations.

SILVER LAKE–TWIN LAKES

From Monte Cristo, this section starts with a climb up to Poodle Dog Pass. As you head south, the first 0.5 mile is brushed in, and the trail becomes dramatically steeper as it approaches the pass at mile 2.2. From here a second trail descends 0.2 mile down to Silver Lake, which sits below Silvertip Peak. The lake can be frozen well into August, but campsites are available.

The route to Twin Lakes continues up through a stretch of pink and white heather and lots of huckleberry. It makes a slight descent down to a notch before contouring below a ridgeline. The trail is narrow and uneven. At mile 3.5 the trail climbs onto a ridge, or rib. From here enjoy the fantastic combination of hiking and scrambling up to the saddle between the Twin Peaks at mile 4. On the highly exposed ridge, take in incredible views of Wilmon Peaks and Columbia Peak, and of numerous ridgelines and steep, V-shaped valleys. From the saddle is an overlook of Twin Lakes, which are a deep, blue color and seemingly hang above the West Fork Troublesome Creek valley to the south. It is another 0.8 mile down to the larger Upper Twin Lake via a trail to the left (east) as you face the lake. A trail accesses the lower lake from the upper, and campsites are available at both.

From the Darrington RD take the Mountain Loop Highway 23.4 miles to the parking area at Barlow Pass. The road changes from pavement to gravel 7 miles up. Alternatively, from the Verlot Public Service Center take the Mountain Loop Highway 19.5 miles to the parking area at Barlow Pass.

South Cascades

The South Cascades region is a cluster of mountainous islands that contains three of the state's most recognized Cascade volcanoes, Mounts Rainier, Adams, and St. Helens. Artificially bordered by interstates and highways on three sides, the region terminates to the south at the natural boundary of the Columbia River. I use the word "bordered" merely to make it easier to understand what constitutes the South Cascades region and its location within the state, not to impose some naïve notion that the human hand could fully control any of the wildlands that make up this fabulous cross-section of nature.

There is a fascination, almost a hypnotizing sensation, when in the presence of the marvelously intimidating volcanoes of Rainier, Adams, and St. Helens, rising above the humbled lowlands like rounded white pyramids. Mount Rainier, the signature backdrop for the city of Seattle, could bury nearby towns under cataclysmic mudflows for tens of miles if it ever erupted. But in the same cool breath as her power to devastate, she beckons us to explore the lowlands surrounding her and the forests stretching up her slopes that break into magnificent, high-mountain parklands filled with wildflowers in summer. Places like Spray Park and Indian Henry's Hunting Ground seem even brighter set against the white tongues of glaciers that drape the upper third of the mountain.

Like cleaner fish who serve their host but also have singular qualities of their own, the wilderness areas of Glacier View, Tatoosh, Norse Peak, and Clearwater form a fabulous wall around Mount Rainier. Tatoosh Ridge is a spectacular high-mountain escape. Rewards await those who make the effort up its difficult approach: sweeping open hillsides, lit by wildflowers and green grass in the summer, that collide with the looming glacier-capped Mount Rainier directly to the north; and spilling southward, pulling the eye with it, views of the Goat Rocks and the other volcanic giants of the region, Adams and St. Helens.

Big basins line up next to each other in the Norse Peak Wilderness. Hikers and backpackers can move from the pale, craggy ridgelines and spectacular panoramic views gained from the summit of Norse Peak, down into the green and lush bottoms along tree-canopied drainages like Lost Creek and Greenwater River. The South Cascades region also contains wilderness areas like the William O. Douglas, which display features of both the wetter, more densely vegetated west side and the drier east-side life zones of the Cascades.

Comet Falls, Mount Rainier National Park

The unofficial link between the Mount Rainier zone and the Mount Adams–Mount St. Helens zone is the Goat Rocks Wilderness. Its dark band of pointed rock, with high points in Johnson Peak, Old Snowy Mountain, Tieton Peak, and Gilbert Peak, make up half the wilderness's namesake. The other of course is the sure-footed king of the rocky high ground, the mountain goat. Below these peaks, steep ridges and wildflower basins open up fantastic views. Jordan Basin on the way to Goat Lake is not so unlike basins in the Austrian or Italian Alps.

Mistaken for one another for hundreds of years, Mount Adams and Mount St. Helens gaze over the tops of trees and across the regal Columbia River at the northernmost of Oregon's volcanic splendors, Mount Hood. The three volcanoes have been part of Indian folklore, a "lover's triangle," for centuries. The Indian legend even hints at some of the geological history of this area, since geologists have hypothesized that a land bridge once existed here, linking the two states. From the perspective of legend, this land bridge more importantly joined Loo-wit (St. Helens) to her lover Wy-east (Hood). The tale tells of how the Great Spirit got so fed up at the petty jealousies of Loo-wit's two suitors, Pah-to (Adams) and Wy-east, that he turned them into mountains. He then encased the object of their affection, Loo-wit, in a cape of white, and destroyed the bridge between her and Wy-east.

Perhaps the heartache had been building over time, or the jealousy of the outcast Pah-to caused it, but on May 18, 1980, Mount St. Helens erupted, collapsing 1,300 feet of her top, devastating some 150 square miles, killing thousands of animals as well as 63 people, and capturing the attention of the world. Science continues to explain the ongoing story of Mount St. Helens as the eruption site rises with new life. The Mount St. Helens landscape captures the imagination even today, more than two decades on; visitors still marvel in the Mount Margaret Back-country at the devastation and regrowth that meet in stark contrast. In the southern reaches of the region, the Cascade Range seemingly fades into the ocean-bound waters of the Columbia River Gorge south of the Indian Heaven and Trapper Creek Wilderness Areas. But amazingly enough, the Cascades continue south of the mighty river, into Oregon and California.

Mount Adams at sunset, Mount Adams Wilderness

18 | Clearwater Wilderness

View of Mount Rainier and Summit Lake

LOCATION: North of the Carbon River and Mount Rainier National Park, and approximately 15 miles southeast of Enumclaw

SIZE: 14,374 acres

ELEVATION RANGE: 2,000 to 6,089 feet

MILES OF TRAIL: 27

TREES AND PLANTS: Douglas fir, western hemlock, western red cedar, blueberry, heather, huckleberry, lady fern, sword fern, wild ginger

WILDLIFE: Black bear, black-tailed deer, bobcat, cougar, marmot, raccoon, skunk, bluebird, Clark's nutcracker, golden eagle, goshawk, Steller's jay

ADMINISTRATION: Mount Baker–Snoqualmie NF, Enumclaw RD, 360-825-6585

BEST SEASON: Midsummer through fall

THE MOST POPULAR DESTINATION in the Clearwater Wilderness, because of its beauty, short distance from Seattle, and accessibility, has been Summit Lake. The bridge over the Carbon River, which accesses Summit Lake and the southern portion of the wilderness, was reopened in the summer of 2002 after being closed for repairs for several years. During that period, Summit Lake was something of a wilderness within a wilderness, accessible by trail only from farther to the north and east. Since the road access to these trailheads was inconvenient for most Seattleites, a much lower number of visitors came to the Summit Lake area and to the Clearwater Wilderness

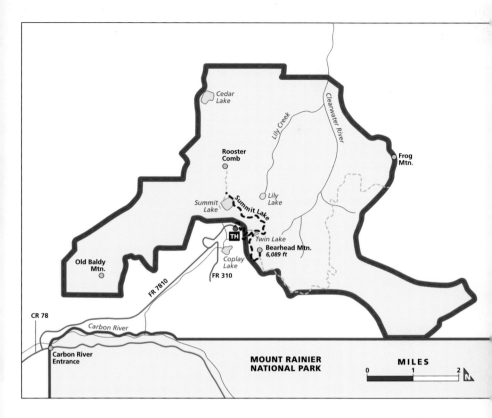

overall. Unintended, but nevertheless beneficial, the Summit Lake area's access cutoff effectively allowed it to recover from years of heavy traffic.

It's no surprise why the Summit Lake area is a choice Cascades destination. As with the Tatoosh Wilderness to the south, views of 14,411-foot Mount Rainier are dramatic. The wildflower meadow approach to Bearhead Mountain, and the sight of the Willis Wall features on Mount Rainier from the summit of Bearhead Mountain, make this a most worthwhile climb. Bearhead and Clear West Peak both held lookouts until their removal by the Forest Service in the 1960s.

The flora in the Clearwater is typical of the west Cascades, with hemlock, cedar, and fir creating the canopy, and an understory made up of such plants as lady fern, sword fern, deerfoot vanillaleaf, blueberry, huckleberry, heather, wild ginger, and moss. Eight lakes and numerous creeks like Canyon, Lily, and Viola, as well as the Clearwater River running into the White River to the north, provide the wilderness with good water sources for hikers. The middle of the wilderness, in excess of 4,000 acres, has been left trail-free. Only 27 miles of trail, originating from five trailheads, provide access to the remainder of the wilderness.

> **DAY HIKE: SUMMIT LAKE**
> One-Way Distance: 2.4 miles
> Elevation Range: 4,400 to 5,450 feet
> Total Elevation Gain: 1,050 feet
> Difficulty: Moderate
> Green Trails Map: Enumclaw No. 237

The trail switchbacks up from the parking area through an older clear-cut before climbing through old-growth to the Bearhead Mountain Trail junction at the west end of Twin Lake, at 0.8 mile. Follow the sign for Summit Lake. The trail moves around from the north to the east side of Twin Lake and climbs for 0.5 mile before starting a long, straight ascent to Summit Lake at mile 2.4. Shortly before the lake the trees give way to views of nearby Bearhead Mountain and the north-side Rainier features of Russell Glacier, Carbon Glacier, and the Willis Wall. Summit Lake is nicely lined by spruce and fir trees along with a healthy covering of heather and blueberry. Campsites are situated around the lake.

An equally rewarding trip from the Summit Lake Trailhead is to head east at the junction with the Carbon Trail at Twin Lakes for a nice hike to the top of the highest point in the wilderness, 6,089-foot Bearhead Mountain. An additional 2.2 miles each way, the trip to the top affords a higher and closer vantage point from which to take in Mount Rainier.

From the Enumclaw RD on WA 410, drive south about 4.5 miles to the junction with WA 165. Turn left (south) toward Wilkeson, drive through Wilkeson at 10.5 miles, then past Carbonado at 12.5 miles. At 16.5 miles the road forks; bear left toward the Carbon River Entrance of Mount Rainier National Park. At about 24 miles turn left onto a bridge over the Carbon River. Shortly past the bridge bear to the right onto FR 7810. At 32.1 miles bear left, continuing on FR 7810. (Note the sign, "Northwest Forest Pass Required Beyond This Point".) This section of the road is narrow and can be heavily brushed in. The parking area for Summit Lake is at 33.5 miles.

Glacier View Wilderness 19

View of Mount Rainier at sunset from Glacier View Wilderness

SWEPT INTO OFFICIAL WILDERNESS STATUS, the Glacier View Wilderness came to be during the congressional wilderness designations of 1984. It is small—just 3,123 acres—but noble in its position of having the finest elevated views of Tahoma, Puyallup, and South Mowich glaciers draping the west face of Mount Rainier. The wilderness is set between the most distinctive high points, Glacier View at 5,450 feet to the north and Mount Beljica at 5,475 feet to the south, and cradled between ridgelines located along its east and west sides. Glacier View contains a pleasant mix of ribbed, benched,

LOCATION: Adjacent to the southwest corner of Mount Rainier National Park and approximately 18 miles north of Randle

SIZE: 3,123 acres

ELEVATION RANGE: 3,320 to 5,507 feet

MILES OF TRAIL: 8.5

TREES AND PLANTS: Douglas fir, noble fir, Pacific silver fir, western red cedar, white pine, bead lily, blueberry, deerfoot vanillaleaf, dwarf blackberry, huckleberry, lady fern, queen's cup

WILDLIFE: Black bear, black-tailed deer, elk, marten, mountain goat, Clark's nutcracker, grouse, Steller's jay, Swainson's hawk

ADMINISTRATION: Gifford Pinchot NF, Cowlitz Valley RD, 360-497-1100

BEST SEASON: Midsummer through fall

cirqued, and meadowed terrain, housing nine lakes and summer herds of elk and mountain goat. Glacier View and Mount Beljica, both former lookout sites used by the Forest Service as part of the fire-suppression system, offer the clearest of the views of glaciated Mount Rainier and the surrounding area.

The handful of trails in the wilderness make their way through stands of Pacific silver fir, Douglas fir, noble fir, true fir, western hemlock, western red cedar, and white pine. Heavy snowfall reaching annual depths of 30 feet usually have fully retreated by mid-July, leaving behind a moist environment that facilitates the growth of oak fern, lady fern, devil's club, and moss. The berry production is also notable, with a variety of huckleberry, dwarf blackberry, and bunchberry dogwood.

Glacier View Wilderness is a peaceful place, whether spent high on a peak, down in the lush Beljica Meadows, or relaxing by a glacially formed lake. It also has the advantage of being flush against Mount Rainier National Park, making it quite tempting to pop into accessible locations like Gobblers Knob.

DAY HIKE: GOAT LAKE AND GOBBLERS KNOB
One-Way Distance: 3.7 miles
Elevation Range: 4,300 to 5,500 feet
Total Elevation Gain: 1,200 feet
Difficulty: Moderate
Green Trails Map: Mt. Rainier West No. 269

A short pop up the hill from the trailhead will bring you to the junction with Trails #267 and #248. Take Puyallup Trail #248 heading south along a ridge top for 0.2 mile before descending into Beljica Meadows. The trail continues past the meadows, with views of Mount Beljica, through an older stand of Douglas fir, and by plenty of huckleberry bushes. At the 1-mile point will be the junction with Lake Christine Trail #249. Trail #248 cuts to the north here, then rolls along and around a point. At mile 1.7 the trail begins a slightly steeper descent, marking the approach to Goat Lake at mile 2.1. The lake is small and skinny but quite pleasant,

Glacier View

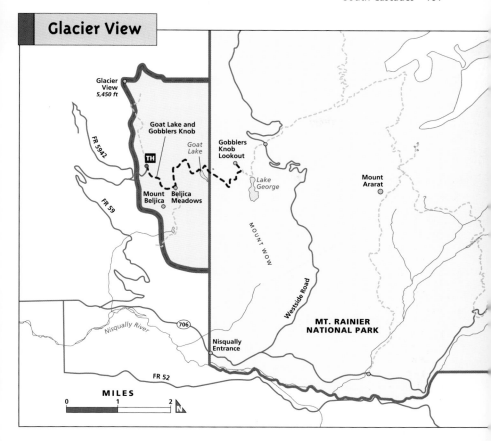

surrounded by trees and watched over by Mount Wow to the southeast. A few short switchbacks and then a long diagonal climb above the lake brings you to the boundary with Mount Rainier National Park at mile 2.6.

The trail continues to climb steeply until a bend at the mile 3.1, where the trail descends for about 0.2 mile to the junction with the trail to Gobblers Knob Lookout, a steep 0.4-mile climb. At mile 3.7 you reach Gobblers Knob Lookout, with awesome views of Mount Rainier and, most prominently, Tahoma Glacier. Please note that dogs and stock are not allowed on the portions of this hike that lie within Mount Rainier National Park.

From the Cowlitz Valley RD, take US 12 east about 16 miles to Packwood. Turn left onto Skate Creek Road (FR 52), go 23 miles to the junction with WA 706, and turn right (east). In another 0.6 mile turn left (north) onto FR 59. At 32.1 miles you will reach the trailhead for Glacier View Trail #267 and Puyallup Trail #248.

20 Goat Rocks Wilderness

Beautiful wildflower meadows

LOCATION: South of White Pass and north of Mount Adams, and about 40 miles west of Yakima

SIZE: 108,279 acres

ELEVATION RANGE: 2,200 to 8,201 feet

MILES OF TRAIL: 120

TREES AND PLANTS: Alaska yellow cedar, Douglas fir, mountain hemlock, noble fir, subalpine fir, whitebark pine, arnica, aster, avalanche lily, blueberry, cinquefoil, goldenrod, heather, huckleberry, lupine, marigold, paintbrush, phlox, sandwort

WILDLIFE: Black bear, black-tailed deer, coyote, elk, mountain goat, pine marten, Clark's nutcracker, mountain chickadee, ptarmigan, ruffed grouse

ADMINISTRATION: Gifford Pinchot NF, Cowlitz Valley RD, 360-497-1100; Wenatchee NF, Naches RD, 509-653-2205

BEST SEASON: Summer through fall

ALONG WITH THE BIG VOLCANOES of the southern Washington Cascades is a geologic feature that comes into view from many high points in this region: dark rocks with sharp ridgelines clustered together in distinguishable peaks, running in a line from the southeast to the northwest. These are the Goat Rocks, the center of the Goat Rocks Wilderness, reaching a high point in Gilbert Peak at 8,184 feet. Dramatic and daunting, these mountains command respect, deservedly so given the 25 feet of snow that falls onto them each season, sustaining the active glaciers on Gilbert, Ives, and Old Snowy—and given the fierce storms that can blast hikers and climbers even in midsummer.

The erosional effects of glaciers and streams have cut away the layers of older, softer rock into a collection of summits created from volcanic cones that once rose in excess of 12,000 feet. Much of the 120 miles of trail here follow along or below ridge-lines and above timberline, opening up a world of meadows and panoramic mountain vistas not so unlike the picturesque settings of the European Alps. When the snows have retreated into the shaded gullies and cirques of north- and east-facing slopes, and swelled the streams with their cold melt (which drains into places like Lily Basin, Packwood Lake, and the South Fork Tieton River Valley) the high-mountain meadows come alive with a show of wildflowers: prairie lupine, goldenrod, phlox, paintbrush, marigold, and avalanche lily.

The beauty seems to spill from these ominous peaks into the broad basins and meadows and through the pleasant forests of subalpine fir and whitebark pine that eventually give way, as the elevation drops, to Alaska yellow cedar and noble fir. Bookended by Packwood Lake to the north and Walupt Lake to the south, Goat Rocks contains dozens of lakes and streams, most of which are accessible by established trails. Cutthroat and rainbow trout are common, and Dolly Varden trout live in sections of the North Fork Tieton River. The namesake mountain goat is visible around Bear Creek Mountain, above Goat Lake, and in other exposed, high, rocky areas, at times in numbers in excess of 40 head. Goat Rocks also has healthy populations of black-tailed deer, elk, pika, and game birds like blue, ruffed, and spruce grouse.

Its dark and light elements of beauty brought both the Klickitat and Cowlitz Indians to the area for hunting and gathering. Elk Pass, north of Old Snowy Mountain, was also a trade route between tribes from the Columbia Plateau and Puget Sound. Goat Rocks' history with white Americans is linked more with preservation than exploration or exploitation. In 1931, 44,500 acres—the dark heart of the present-day wilderness— was already designated a primitive area. In 1935 and then again in 1940 more land was added, bringing the total to 82,860, its designation changing from "primitive" to "wild" area. Goat Rocks was then included in the Wilderness Act of 1964 and later benefited from the subsequent induction of numerous Washington wilderness areas in 1984, when it reached its current size of 108,279 acres.

DAY HIKE OR DESTINATION HIKE: BEAR CREEK MOUNTAIN

One-Way Distance: 3.5 miles
Elevation Range: 6,000 to 7,336 feet
Total Elevation Gain: 1,336 feet
Difficulty: Moderate
Green Trails Map: White Pass No. 303

Because of the high starting point, the hike begins in a subalpine setting of fir and whitebark pine, ascending on a moderate stair-stepping trail with views of the Goat Rocks. The trail passes pleasantly through the trees and into grassy, open areas. At mile 2.3 the trail climbs a bit steeper up to the junction with Bear Creek Mountain Lookout Trail #1130A. From here, Trail #1130A switchbacks up a ridge

continued on p. 166

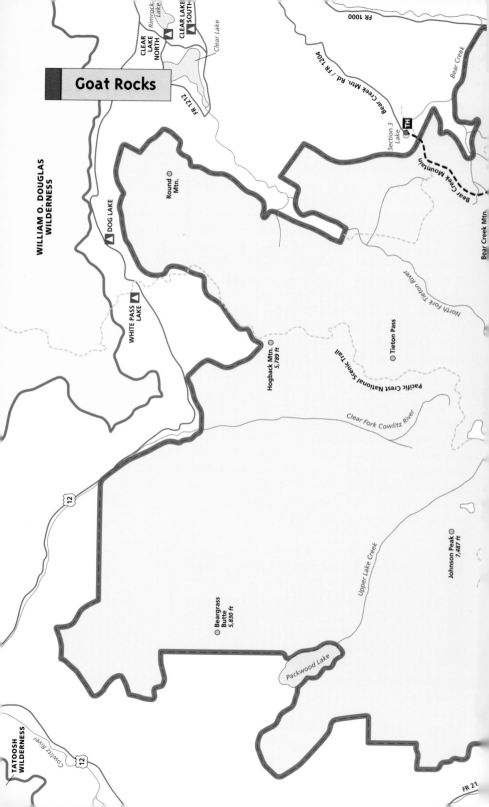

Goat Rocks

CLEAR LAKE NORTH
CLEAR LAKE SOUTH
Rimrock Lake
Clear Lake
FR 1212
FR 1000
Bear Creek
Bear Creek Mtn. Rd. / FR 1204
Section 3 Lake
Bear Creek Mountain
Bear Creek Mtn.

WILLIAM O. DOUGLAS WILDERNESS

DOG LAKE

Round Mtn.

WHITE PASS LAKE

North Fork Tieton River

Hogback Mtn.
5,789 ft

Tieton Pass

Pacific Crest National Scenic Trail

Clear Fork Cowlitz River

12

Upper Lake Creek

Johnson Peak
7,487 ft

Beargrass Butte
5,830 ft

Packwood Lake

TATOOSH WILDERNESS

Cowlitz River

12

FR 21

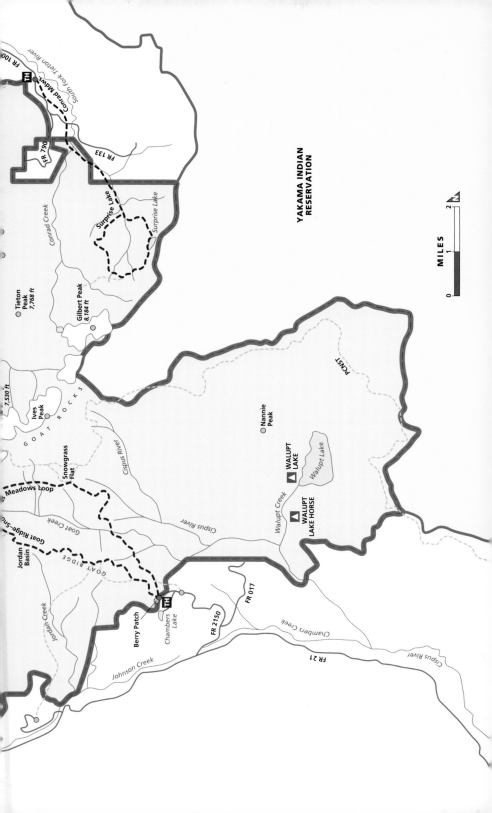

FR 100

South Fork Tieton River

Conrad Mdws

TH

FR 790

FR 133

Conrad Creek

Surprise Lake

Surprise Lake

Tieton Peak
7,768 ft

Gilbert Peak
8,184 ft

YAKAMA INDIAN
RESERVATION

7,530 ft

Ives Peak

G O A T   R O C K S

Snowgrass Flat

Cispus River

Nannie Peak

PCNST

WALUPT
LAKE

Walupt Lake

Walupt Creek

s Meadows Loop

Goat Ridge–Snow...

Goat Creek

Jordan Basin

G O A T   R I D G E

Cispus River

WALUPT
LAKE HORSE

Jordan Creek

Berry Patch

TH

Chambers Lake

Johnson Creek

FR 2150

FR 017

Chambers Creek

FR 21

Cispus River

MILES

0   1   2

through loose rock on the eastern face of Bear Creek Mountain. Treats abound from the site of the old lookout at mile 3.5, with grand views of Devils Horns, Tieton Peak, Gilbert Peak, and Old Snowy nearby; Mount Adams to the southwest; and Mount Rainier slightly farther to the northwest.

From Randle, head east about 44 miles on US 12 and turn right on Tieton Road, following signs for Clear Lake. At approximately 0.4 mile down Tieton Road turn left toward Clear Lake Campground (gravel road). At 2.4 miles is the junction with paved FR 12; turn left. At 5 miles turn onto gravel Bear Creek Mountain Road (FR 1204). At 12.5 miles the road surface changes to dirt and becomes more primitive. Reach the Bear Creek Mountain Trailhead #1130 and a parking area in 13.7 miles.

OVERNIGHT LOOP HIKE: GOAT RIDGE–SNOWGRASS FLAT LOOP
Total Distance: 13 miles
Elevation Range: 4,600 to 6,600 feet
Total Elevation Gain: 2,000 feet
Difficulty: Moderate
Green Trails Maps: Packwood No. 302, White Pass No. 303,
Blue Lake No. 334, Walupt Lake No. 335

Start hiking on Goat Ridge Trail #95 toward Jordan Basin. The trail climbs from the beginning through patchy woods of fir and western hemlock alongside huckleberry bushes. At mile 1.2 the trail pops in and out of small meadows, providing views of Mount Adams to the south and the Goat Rocks to the east. At mile 1.6 where Trail #95A meets back up with Trail #95, you will have a grand view of Mount Rainier to the north. Reach the junction with Jordan Creek Trail at mile 2.5. Continue on Goat Ridge Trail through more small meadows and up into a subalpine environment. At mile 3.5 you begin to work around the upper end of magnificent Jordan Basin. At the top of the basin near where the trail moves along Jordan Creek, look for a great camping spot behind a small stand of trees. A smaller basin above here, where the trail cuts through, also contains campsites.

Five miles into the hike is the junction with Lily Basin Trail #86. The loop continues along this trail, heading east up along the upper basin between Goat Ridge and Old Snowy Mountain. At mile 5.3 is an overlook into glacial-green Goat Lake, which you will reach in 0.2 mile. Campsites lie near the lake. The trail continues to wrap along the top of the basin before it slowly loses elevation, as the valley itself seemingly flows into Mount Adams to the south. At mile 7.5 the trail enters a more treed area with some meadows, leaving behind the broad expanse of the valley but not completely denying great views of Mount Adams to the south.

You will reach the junction with Snowgrass Trail #96 at mile 8.3. Keep heading in a southerly direction on the Snowgrass Trail. Snowgrass Flat is another preferred camping area. The trail continues its nice, gradual descent through a more wooded area of fir and hemlock. At mile 11.3 cross Goat Creek over a footbridge and begin to climb. At about mile 12.6, Mount Adams—which hasn't been visible for some time—gives hikers a last salute before exiting behind the trees. You will eventually arrive at a fork, where you can either take the short trail to the Snowgrass Trailhead or the feeder trail down to the Goat Ridge/Snowgrass Trailhead.

From Randle, take US 12 east 19.5 miles and turn right onto gravel FR 21. At 16.4 miles down FR 12, turn left onto FR 2150 toward Chambers Lake and Snowgrass Trail #96. At 19.4 miles is the junction with Chambers Lake; continue toward the Snowgrass Trailhead. At 19.8 miles is the trailhead for both Goat Ridge Trail #95 and Snowgrass Trail #96. You can also park at the Snowgrass Trailhead and take the short feeder trail back to the Goat Ridge/Snowgrass Trailhead.

OVERNIGHT LOOP HIKE: SURPRISE LAKE
Total Distance: 15.6 miles
Elevation Range: 4,000 to 5,500 feet
Total Elevation Gain: 1,500 feet
Difficulty: Moderate
Green Trails Map: Walupt Lake No. 335

Hike approximately 300 yards up the road to reach South Fork Tieton River Trail #1120. The trail sign is next to a road gate. Two creek crossings will follow, then follow the signed trail to the right (west). You will pass through a couple of large clearings before hiking along a narrower trail through some younger trees. After crossing over a gravel road you will reach the true trailhead and wilderness permit sign-in at mile 1.4. Continue through a more mature pine forest. At mile 2.1 the trail crosses over Conrad Creek via a footbridge.

At mile 4.4 is the junction with the Surprise Lake Loop. Take the left (south) fork. After crossing the South Fork Tieton River, the trail begins climbing up a series of switchbacks. At mile 6.9 you come to Surprise Lake, which is a good place to camp. After climbing above the lake, at about mile 7.2, you will have the best views of the top of Gilbert Peak and ridgelines along the southern end of the Goat Rocks. The trail contours around the basin in the open until mile 8.7, when it reenters the forest. At mile 9.7 the trail begins its descent into the bottom of the basin via switchbacks. At mile 11.2 is the junction with the South Fork Tieton River Trail and your return trip to the trailhead and parking area, to finish the 15.6-mile loop.

From Randle, head east about 44 miles on US 12 and turn right on Tieton Road, following signs for Clear Lake. At approximately 0.4 mile down Tieton Road turn left toward Clear Lake Campground (gravel road). At 2.4 miles is the junction with paved FR 12; turn left. At 9.7 miles is the junction with FR 1000; bear right at the bend in the road. You'll see a sign for Conrad Meadows about 150 feet in on FR 1000. Continue following signs. At 15.6 miles the pavement turns to gravel. You will reach Conrad Meadows and the starting point for this hike at 22.6 miles.

21 Indian Heaven Wilderness

Frost-covered fields

LOCATION: Southwest of Mount Adams and approximately 18 miles from Trout Lake

SIZE: 20,960 acres

ELEVATION RANGE: 3,020 to 5,927 feet

MILES OF TRAIL: Approximately 40

TREES AND PLANTS: Douglas fir, lodgepole pine, mountain hemlock, noble fir, subalpine fir, white pine, bog willow, camas, cotton-grass, huckleberry, marsh horsetail, northern starflower

WILDLIFE: Black bear, black-tailed deer, elk, blue grouse, Clark's nutcracker, gray jay, mountain chickadee, northern spotted owl

ADMINISTRATION: Gifford Pinchot NF, Mount Adams RD, 509-395-3400

BEST SEASON: Late spring through fall

THE YAKAMA TRIBE HAS ITS OWN creation myth, passed down the generations, about the huckleberry, in which the Creator donates his eyes so that the mountains can bring forth berries. The huckleberry has beckoned tribes of the Northwest for nearly 10,000 years into and around the present-day boundaries of the Indian Heaven Wilderness. As recently as a century ago, summer gatherings brought Northwest tribes together here from as far away as Montana and Wyoming to pick and dry huckleberries, carry out various communal tasks, fish, and have fun. Traces of a race track in the southern part of the wilderness are a testament to the horse races that were a part of these popular gatherings.

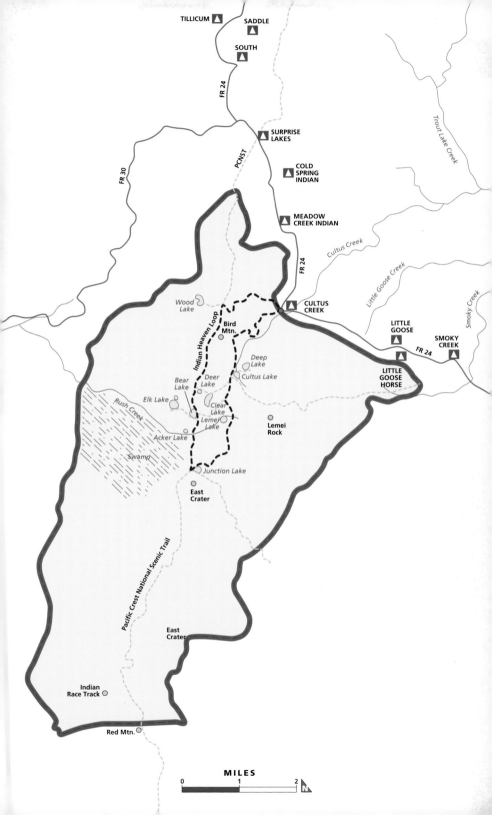

TILLICUM ▲ SADDLE ▲

SOUTH ▲

FR 24

SURPRISE ▲ LAKES

PCNST

COLD ▲ SPRING INDIAN

MEADOW ▲ CREEK INDIAN

FR 30

Cultus Creek

Trout Lake Creek

FR 24

Little Goose Creek

Smoky Creek

Wood Lake

Indian Heaven Loop

Bird Mtn.

CULTUS ▲ CREEK

LITTLE ▲ GOOSE

SMOKY ▲ CREEK

FR 24

LITTLE GOOSE HORSE ▲

Deep Lake

Cultus Lake

Bear Lake

Deer Lake

Rush Creek

Elk Lake

Clear Lake

Lemei Lake

Lemei Rock

Acker Lake

Swamp

Junction Lake

East Crater

Pacific Crest National Scenic Trail

East Crater

Indian Race Track

Red Mtn.

MILES

0   1   2

N

The native people continue the heritage today by picking berries from the blessed Sawtooth Berry Field. Huckleberries grow quite well in areas where there has been fire. The Sawtooth Berry Field has been subjected to many fires over the centuries, most by natural causes, including the great fires of 1902; accidental ones from out-of-control berry-drying fires; and ones that are believed to have been deliberately set. An agreement made between the Yakama Nation and the Forest Service in 1932, which still exists today, designated portions of the Sawtooth Berry Field exclusively for the local Indian people. Perhaps its significance relative to other agreements made between Native Americans and the U.S. government is minor, but remarkably it has existed without dispute for over 70 years—and was made official by merely a handshake.

A smaller wilderness, Indian Heaven sits upon a plateau whose surface rolls along with very little elevation gain. The high points running south to north through the heart of the wilderness—Red Mountain, Gifford Peak, East Crater, Bird Mountain, Sawtooth Mountain, and the tallest, 5,927-foot Lemei Rock—are the results of fairly recent volcanic activity. Small eruptions during the Pleistocene period formed cones like East Crater and Lemei Rock along with other high and knobby points within the wilderness. Despite the relatively consistent terrain, high points do offer fantastic views of the Cascades to the north. It is a pleasant environment, with meadows of cotton-grass, camas, and northern starflower; marshes of bog willow and marsh violet, home for bird species such as blue grouse, gray jay, and mountain chickadee; open forest made up of Douglas fir, mountain hemlock, and lodgepole pine; and over 150 lakes, many of which are stocked with rainbow and eastern brook trout.

With an average annual snowpack of 4 to 6 feet, Indian Heaven receives relatively little snow, but its moderately heavy rainfall accounts for an annual precipitation of up to 100 inches, keeping many of the small lakes and ponds full throughout the summer months. An unfortunate side effect of the retention of water, coupled with low elevation and warm summer temperatures, is a healthy population of mosquitoes, giving the area the unflattering nickname "Mosquito Heaven." Mid-August through October is the optimal time to visit, with the mosquitoes at tolerable levels, wildflower colors still glowing, good fishing, and huckleberry bushes plentiful.

> **DAY OR OVERNIGHT HIKE: INDIAN HEAVEN LOOP**
> Total Distance: 8.7 miles
> Elevation Range: 4,000 to 5,250 feet
> Total Elevation Gain: 1,500 feet
> Difficulty: Moderate
> Green Trails Map: Lone Butte No. 365

The Indian Heaven Loop begins on Indian Heaven Trail #33, climbing steadily but with only moderate difficulty. At mile 1.1 up the trail, a switchback offers a nice overlook of the forest below and of Mount Adams to the northeast. At mile 1.3 the trail flattens out, contouring along a hillside and working its way in and out of the trees. By mile 2, after 1,000 feet of elevation gain, you arrive at Deep Lake. For those who like to fish, the lake is stocked with trout. At mile 2.2 is the junction with Lemei Trail #34; continue on Trail #33 through a more wooded area of predominantly fir trees. At mile 2.7, leave Trail #33 and continue on Lemei Lake Trail #179.

After crossing through a large meadow at mile 3.3 you will pass by Lemei Lake. Be aware that along this portion of the trail there can be a fair amount of water to work through and around, primarily in the early season. At mile 4 the trail winds its way down to Junction Lake. In another 0.2 mile is the junction with Pacific Crest Trail #2000; head north on the PCT.

This portion of the loop is mostly within the trees on a pleasant trail. At mile 5.2 is the first of a string of lakes: Acker, Bear, Elk, Clear, and Deer. Most have trail access down to them—and campsites. Continue on the PCT, under the eastern slopes of Bird Mountain, to the junction with Cultus Creek Trail #108 at mile 7.2.

This section of the loop follows a narrower trail and descends steeply some 1,250 feet in 1.5 miles; however, there are plenty of huckleberry bushes, wildflowers in small pocket meadows, views of Mount Adams, and thick stands of spruce. You will reach Cultus Creek Campground again at mile 8.7.

From the Mount Adams RD take WA 141 north. At the junction with FR 88 (2 miles) continue on WA 141 toward Carson. At 5.6 miles WA 141 becomes FR 24; stay on FR 24. At mile 8.1 is the junction with FR 60; bear right to stay on now-gravel FR 24 toward Cultus Creek Campground. At 17.2 miles turn into the campground to reach the beginning of the hike on Indian Heaven Trail #33.

Black-tailed deer

22 Mount Adams Wilderness

Mount Rainier as seen from the Mount Adams Wilderness

MODERATE TO SMALL IN SIZE, the Mount Adams Wilderness still encircles the most massive and second tallest Cascade volcano in Washington. Decorated by ten active glaciers, Mount Adams is also the third tallest (after Rainier and Shasta) in the string of Cascade volcanoes running from southern British Columbia at Garibaldi to the terminus at Lassen in northern California. Mount Adams comprises approximately half of the wilderness acreage, and like its neighbors Rainier, St. Helens, and Hood, the stratovolcano utterly dominates the surrounding landscape. If not as picturesque as Glacier, Rainier, Hood, or Shasta, Adams is more than impressive in terms of statistics and should be easily distinguishable and recognizable.

LOCATION: Southeast of Mount St. Helens and approximately 15 miles north of Trout Lake

SIZE: 46,626 acres

ELEVATION RANGE: 3,300 to 12,276 feet

MILES OF TRAIL: 64

TREES AND PLANTS: Douglas fir, Engelmann spruce, grand fir, mountain hemlock, Pacific silver fir, western red cedar, whitebark pine, avalanche lily, beargrass, heather, huckleberry, lupine, monkeyflower, paintbrush, salal

WILDLIFE: Black-tailed deer, coyote, elk, hoary marmot, mountain goat, pika, blue grouse, Clark's nutcracker, mountain chickadee, ptarmigan, red-tailed hawk, ruffed grouse

ADMINISTRATION: Gifford Pinchot NF, Mount Adams RD, 509-395-3400

BEST SEASON: Midsummer to the end of October

Even so, the easternmost Washington volcano suffered an identity crisis among Euro-American explorers. From vantage points to the west and south, and long before the May 1980 eruption of Mount St. Helens 35 miles to the west, Mount Adams has been overlooked and mistaken for its neighboring peak. Measuring in at 12,276 feet, Mount Adams stands nearly 4,000 feet higher than Mount St. Helens today—and stood more than 2,500 feet above St. Helens's pre-1980 elevation. In his voyages of 1792 into Puget Sound, Captain George Vancouver does not make any record of seeing or "discovering" Mount Adams, though St. Helens is duly noted. The Lewis and Clark expedition often confused Mount Adams with Mount St. Helens. The unfortunate oversights and misidentifications continued in the year 1839, when Hall J. Kelly, known as the "Boston Schoolmaster," sought to rename the Cascades the "Presidents Range." Kelly hoped to rename British-identified Cascade peaks with the names of American presidents and did succeed in a few instances. So today in Oregon we have Mount Jefferson and Mount Washington; in Washington, "Mount St. Helens" was renamed "Mount Adams." Excuse me? Because of a 35-mile mistake, an unnamed peak was actually named "Mount Adams," instead of an already named peak, Mount St. Helens, being renamed.

Shepherds grazed sheep on the lower slopes and higher meadows of Mount Adams from the early 1900s until the expiration of permits in the 1970s. The Forest Service tried to take advantage of the mountain's height and constructed a lookout on the summit, but it was abandoned after a few years because of the often poor visibility and difficult access. The only other notable attempt to utilize the mountain for human gain was a sulphur mine, surprisingly claimed on the summit in 1929. After 30 years, test drilling of nearly 350 feet through ice and rock showed few valuable mineral deposits, and poor extraction quantities in other sections of the 210-acre summit plateau finally convinced yet another dreamer to abandon the mountain. Once again we must rely on the Indians for educational, entertaining, and perhaps more legitimate human and geological history of Mount Adams.

Generations of Yakama and Klickitat tribes have told a 9,000-year history of the land. In one myth, Pah-to (Adams) was a jealous wife of five belonging to Sun. Wahkshum (Simcoe Mountain) and Plash-Plash (Goat Rocks), two of the other wives,

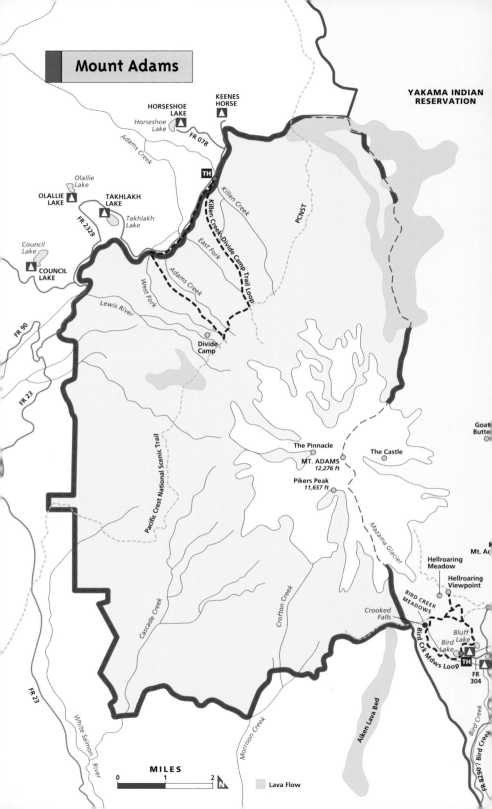

Mount Adams

YAKAMA INDIAN
RESERVATION

HORSESHOE
LAKE

KEENES
HORSE

*Horseshoe
Lake*

FR 078

Adams Creek

TH

*Olallie
Lake*

OLALLIE
LAKE

TAKHLAKH
LAKE

FR 2329

*Takhlakh
Lake*

Killen Creek

PCNST

Council
Lake

COUNCIL
LAKE

FR 90

Lewis River

West Fork

East Fork

Adams Creek

Killen Creek-Divide Camp Trail Loop

FR 23

*Divide
Camp*

Goat
Butte

The Pinnacle

The Castle

MT. ADAMS
12,276 ft

Pikers Peak
11,657 ft

Pacific Crest National Scenic Trail

Mazama Glacier

Mt. Ad

Hellroaring
Meadow

Hellroaring
Viewpoint

BIRD CREEK
MEADOWS

*Crooked
Falls*

*Bluff
Lake*

*Bird
Lake*

Bird Ck Mdws Loop

TH

FR 23

Cascade Creek

Crofton Creek

FR 304

FR-8290 / Bird Creek

Bird Creek

White Salmon River

Morrison Creek

Aiken Lava Bed

MILES

0   1   2

Lava Flow

always felt the tender touch of Sun before Pah-to. In a rage, Pah-to battled the two wives, breaking their heads off (the Goat Rocks once stood at an elevation above 12,000 feet). Pah-to then journeyed south of the Columbia River to bring back all the forest's plants and animals to live and multiply on her motherly slopes. This caused Klah-Klahnee (Three Sisters) to convince Wy-east (Mount Hood) to battle Pah-to. Wy-east managed to knock off the head of Pah-to, scattering it about. (Geologists believe eruptions as recently as 2,000 years ago created the Muddy Fork flow, one of the Cascades' largest lava fields.) The plants and animals migrated south, leaving the wounded Pah-to's slopes barren. But it is said that the Great Maker shaped her a new head and caused her slopes to once again teem with animals and plants to feed the Indians who relied on Pah-to.

At least two versions exist of another tale involving Mount Adams. Both stories revolve around a lovers' triangle. The first story talks of two chiefs, Wy-east and Pah-to (in this story a male), who were quarreling over the love of a lady, Loo-wit. The rivalry grew so fierce that villages and forests burned, and massive boulders were hurled by each at the other. The Great Spirit, Sahale, punished all three young lovers, striking them down and turning them into mountains. He wrapped Loo-wit (Mount St. Helens) in a gown of white snow. Wy-east (Mount Hood) is said to be holding his head high in pride to be able to gaze on her beauty. But Pah-to (Mount Adams) is said to have bowed his head and wept at the sight of the woman who is now a mountain.

In the second version, after Wy-east and Pah-to suffered their fates they continued battling by spewing fire and rocks at each other over the land bridge that spanned the Columbia River. (Geologists believe that lava layers from Washington's Table Mountain oozed into the gorge, forming a dam and creating both a bridge and a lake stretching some 70 miles to the east.) In the Indian legend the Great Spirit destroyed the bridge, turned Loo-wit into a mountain, and placed her by Pah-to's side. Geological research indicates that over time the Columbia River eventually breached the lava dam, wearing it down and submerging any other evidence of its existence.

Whether a matter of confusion and forgetfulness, human striving, geological analysis, or the glory of the oral tradition, the story of Mount Adams has been embroiled in unusual controversy. Still, the stratovolcano can and should be appreciated for its own beauty and for the treasures of the surrounding forest.

DAY HIKE: BIRD CREEK MEADOWS LOOP
Total Distance: 5 miles
Elevation Range: 5,585 to 6,500 feet
Total Elevation Gain: 915 feet
Difficulty: Easy to moderate
Green Trails Map: Mt. Adams No. 367S

The loop is equally enjoyable no matter where you choose to start, but for clarity the hike described begins at the Bluff Lake #105 Trailhead, in the campground area by Bird Lake. It is 0.8 mile to Bluff Lake. The trail moves through thin stands of pine and spruce, with the open areas offering beautiful artistry in the form of wildflowers that peak from mid-July to early August. Nestled among the trees at 5,600 feet, Bluff Lake is somewhat horseshoe-shaped. Continue on Trail #105 toward Trail #9. Approximately 0.1 mile past Bluff Lake the trail climbs steeply but only for a few hundred yards before leveling out onto a benched meadow area. Small in size but grand in its stature, a waterfall marks the junction of Trail #105 and Trail #9 at mile 1.5.

Take a right to enter Bird Creek Meadows and begin the loop trail that leads to Hellroaring Viewpoint. (Note that by continuing on Trail #9 you can reach Bench Lake in about 2.3 miles.) The trail winds through and above Bird Creek Meadows, which in summer bloom with aster, cinquefoil, paintbrush, and Sitka valerian. At mile 2.1 is the connecting trail to Hellroaring Viewpoint, just 0.5 mile round-trip. From the viewpoint at 6,500 feet you stand high above Hellroaring Meadow, with views across of Little Mount Adams and of a force of nature at work—the headwall of the Mazama Glacier on the southeastern slope of Mount Adams.

Return via the same trail to continue around the loop for another 0.4 mile to link back up with Trail #9 at mile 3. Head west on Trail #9 for 0.5 mile to the junction with Trail #100. The many small footbridges throughout this loop give the hike a quaint and protective feel, like being in a separate sanctuary from the rest of the forest. At 0.3 mile along Trail #100 the 25-foot-high Crooked Falls spill over a cliff, splitting into three rivulets, which work their way down and around small islands of trees and wildflowers. From this point at mile 3.8 you have another 1.2 miles back to Bird Lake.

Take the Mount Adams Recreation Highway north from Trout Lake. At 1.3 miles follow the right fork, at the sign for Bird Creek Meadows. The pavement ends at 4.6 miles. Follow FR 82 to the right. The road is gravel from here on out. At mile 11.5 bear to the left onto Road 8290, Bird Creek Road. Continue past Mirror Lake at 15.1 miles and turn left onto Road 304. Bird Lake and the trailhead are reached at 16.1 miles. Parking is available either by the Administrative Center or at the campground. Note that Bird Creek Meadows resides in land owned by the Yakama Nation and is leased to the Forest Service during the summer and fall.

DAY HIKE: KILLEN CREEK–DIVIDE CAMP TRAIL LOOP
Total Distance: 10 miles
Elevation Range: 4,584 to 6,200 feet
Total Elevation Gain: 1,616 feet
Difficulty: Moderate
Green Trails Map: Mt. Adams No. 367S

This hike takes you from Killen Creek Trailhead up to the Pacific Crest Trail across to the Divide Camp Trail and back down. If you hike the loop in this direction, the last 2.3 miles from the Divide Camp Trailhead to the Killen Creek Trailhead are along FR 2329. If a shuttle isn't possible, the walk along the road can still be quite enjoyable, as it passes numerous blueberry and huckleberry bushes.

The Killen Creek Trail begins on a wide, sandy pack-trail, climbing moderately from the start. When wet, the trail can be muddy and slick in the steeper sections. Huckleberry bushes line the way as you move through patchy stands of younger pine and fir trees. Mushroom hunters will enjoy identifying the different varieties of mushrooms including the fly agaric, made famous in children's books and in the movie *Snow White and the Seven Dwarfs*. At approximately mile 2 the trail enters a larger meadow, perfect for wildflower pictures, with the trees framing a nice view of the northwestern flank of Mount Adams at mile 2.5. You will reach the junction with the Pacific Crest Trail and High Camp Trail #10 at mile 3. As the name implies, High Camp Trail offers a slightly higher view for those interested in a side excursion of about 2 miles round-trip. The location of the trail junction is also a great example of the union between high-mountain meadows and the glacially shaped slopes of Mount Adams.

Head south on the PCT to continue the loop. At mile 4.3 is a creek crossing of the West Fork Adams Creek. Crossing difficulty will depend on the water level of the creek. Early in the season or after heavy rains it's likely to be high. Reach the junction with Divide Camp Trail #112 at mile 4.4, and turn right. Down the trail at approximately mile 4.9 is a large meadow. From here, the trail stair-steps nicely down the benched terrain. At mile 7, the stands of trees become thicker. The trees here are also noticeably older than those on Killen Creek Trail. Divide Camp Trail reaches its trailhead at mile 7.6. Follow FR 2329 north back to the Killen Creek Trailhead, at about mile 10.

From Trout Lake, drive north on the Mount Adams Recreation Highway 1.3 miles and turn left onto FR 23 toward Randle. At 20.7 miles is the junction with FR 90. Bear right and continue on FR 23 toward Randle. The pavement turns to gravel at 21 miles. At 25.1 miles turn onto FR 2329 toward Killen Creek and Takhlakh Lake. The pavement begins again. Keep following signs for Killen Creek. At 26.7 miles the pavement turns back to gravel. At 30.1 miles you will reach the Killen Creek Trailhead.

23 Mount Rainier National Park

Mount Rainier reflected in a tarn

LOCATION: About 40 miles southeast of Seattle

SIZE: 235,612 acres (228,480 acres designated wilderness)

ELEVATION RANGE: 1,950 to 14,410 feet

MILES OF TRAIL: Over 300

TREES AND PLANTS: Alaska cedar, cottonwood, Douglas fir, grand fir, mountain hemlock, western hemlock, western red cedar, whitebark pine, anemone, aster, avalanche lily, beargrass, cinquefoil, devil's club, fern, fireweed, golden-rod, heather, huckleberry, lupine, monkeyflower, phlox, shooting star

WILDLIFE: Beaver, black bear, black-tailed deer, cougar, golden-mantled ground squirrel, hoary marmot, mountain goat, pine marten, blue grouse, Clark's nutcracker, hummingbird, mountain chickadee, red-tailed hawk, Steller's jay

ADMINISTRATION: NPS, 360-569-2211; Longmire WIC, 360-569-4453 (seasonal); Wilkeson WIC, 360-829-5127

BEST SEASON: Late spring through fall

MOUNT RAINIER IS NOT ONLY the focal point of a famous national park and wilderness; it has been a center of life and reverence for thousands of years, reaching out over thousands of square miles. The volcano dominates views and horizons from every direction, rising incredibly some 9,000 feet above the surrounding meadows to the summit cone, 14,410-foot Columbia Crest, guarded by the sentries of 14,122-foot Liberty Cap to the north and 14,153-foot Point Success to the south. (Volcanoes often have "false summits" or prominent features on or near the true summit that have been given names.) Geologists speculate that as recently as 75,000 years ago the mountain may have stood somewhere closer to 16,000 feet before a St. Helens–like eruption helped create its current stature. Regardless, Rainier today is the tallest volcano in the contiguous United States, containing the largest single-mountain glacier system in the Lower 48 and attracting more than 2 million visitors a year.

The mountain, known as Tahoma or Takhoma ("White Mountain" or "The Mountain That Was God," depending on whom you ask) to the Yakama tribe and *Tacobet* ("Nourishing Breasts" or "The Place Where the Waters Begin") to the Nisqually, attracted the Klickitat, Muckleshoot, Puyallup, and Taidnapam (Upper Cowlitz) tribes for more than 8,000 years in annual pilgrimages to its various climate zones. The visiting tribes came for the berries, deer, fish, ritual dances, and mild weather of summer and early fall. The Yakama hunted on the north side of the mountain into the early twentieth century, just as their ancestors had for hundreds of years.

There's no denying the pure dominance of this volcano. Only one thing is out of place: the mountain's name. Mount Rainier bears the name of a Rear Admiral in the British navy, a gesture of gratitude bestowed by Captain George Vancouver in 1792. However, neither man ever set foot anywhere close to the mountain.

Indian heritage is not forgotten, though; a good portion of the 27 named glaciers bear Indian names, including Tahoma, Puyallup, Mowich, Cowlitz, and Nisqually. Other features also acknowledge this heritage, such as Mowich Lake, Yakima Park, Ipsut Creek, and Wauhaukaupauken Falls. Sluiskin Mountain is named for the Yakama Indian who guided the first successful ascent of Mount Rainier. (Sluiskin himself did not summit it, fearing he would anger the Great Spirit; he even pleaded with the two white men, Hazard Stevens and Philemon B. Van Trump, not to go.) Indian Henrys Hunting Ground was a once-secret location used by an expatriate of sorts from the Yakama tribe, Henry (So-to-lick), to provide for him and his wives. For generations, Indian tribes had come for the mountain's offerings, taken what they needed, and returned to their homelands. Visitors today do the same, but instead of taking berries and deer, they take with them the incredible visual wonders of the park in pictures and memories.

Early recognition of Mount Rainier as a national natural treasure led to its national park designation, the country's fifth, in 1899. Out of the mountain's life force the 235,612-acre park and 228,480-acre wilderness area (designated in 1988) contain 382 lakes and ponds; 470 miles of rivers, streams, and creeks; and 100 major waterfalls —including Fairy Falls, dropping some 700 feet, and Comet Falls, cling 250 feet from a hanging glacial valley. This abundance of water helps sustain 787 plant species, 54 varieties of mammals, 130 species of birds, and 17 species of reptiles and amphibians.

White settlement around Mount Rainier mirrors the history of other wilderness areas in Washington. Mills in Tacoma, and eventually in the more active hub of Grays Harbor, spurred a flourishing logging industry on the Olympic Peninsula and western edge of the Cascades. Connected to the growth in logging was the 1880s version of the superhighway, the railroad. The Northern Pacific established an east-west route over Stampede Pass in 1888 and the Great Northern Railway finished another six years later over Stevens Pass, opening up the rapid transport of resources, people, and capital investment to the cities of Tacoma and Seattle. Rail lines extended into areas of the Carbon River drainage and along the Nisqually River via towns like Buckley and Ashford for the transportation of both timber and coal.

Mining around and within the boundaries of the present-day park—mostly of coal and decent quantities of copper—followed the boom pattern of other regions of the state from the 1870s. At one time some 300 claims were filed within the borders of the present-day national park. In 1893, however, Mount Rainier and much of the current park were incorporated into the Pacific Forest Reserve, the forerunner to the national forest system. By 1897 the reserve was enlarged to the west and south and renamed Mount Rainier Forest Reserve. Because of the designation as a reserve, the Rainier forests were spared the logging roads that crisscrossed many nearby hillsides, scarring forested areas just outside the reserve boundary. Also, mining operations were shut down much sooner at Rainier than at some other present-day wilderness areas and so had less impact here. Nine years after the official formation of Mount Rainier National Park, a law was passed prohibiting the continuation of mining within the park's boundaries, in 1908.

Settlers in Tacoma, Seattle, and other towns radiating out from these metro-politan hubs quickly found an affinity with Mount Rainier and the forests and park-land ringing the mountain. Some roads were built, lodges at Longmire and Paradise were constructed in 1917, and the freedom of the automobile pulled people to this magical place from nearby towns and cities. The city of Tacoma, of course, took the Indian name for Mount Rainier. (The city even lobbied on three different occasions in the early twentieth century to change Rainier's name back to Tacoma in an effort to boost its association with the mightiest mountain in the Lower 48.)

Nearly 500,000 people visited the park in 1940. During World War II these numbers dropped considerably, and proposals were made to employ the park's protected natural resources in the war effort. However, in keeping with its mission to provide a natural sanctuary for generations to come, the park avoided renewing mining opera-tions and grazing—activities which proved to cause significant damage during and after the war in areas like Yakima Park. The park also blocked logging plans, like those proposed but never carried out in Olympic National Park for the logging of Sitka spruce, used in airplane manufacturing. The park still found ways to contribute to the war effort by hosting the 10th Mountain Infantry Division, 938th Aviation Engineers, and Army Signal Corps, each of which staged training, testing, and training-film operations in the harsh winter conditions.

Mount Rainier has also been a beacon for those for whom reaching its base, or craning the neck up to gaze at the summit from the terminus of a glacier, is not enough. Full satisfaction only comes for such people with climbing the giant to stand on its summit and reveling in the commanding views of the topography, which seems to flow outward from the mountain. Recorded attempts were made as early as 1857 by August Valentine Kautz, who left his climbing team behind only to turn back himself a mere 400 feet from the summit. Credit for the first successful ascent goes to Stevens and Van Trump in 1870. James Longmire successfully climbed the mountain in 1883 at the age of 63. One of Rainier's founding fathers, Longmire later built roadways and a lodge to spur tourism in the park. Following him were people like John Muir in 1888 and Fay Fuller in 1890, the first woman to summit Rainier. Today approximately

Fog below the Tatoosh Range, Mount Rainier National Park

9,000 people a year attempt the summit, and about half are successful. Many climbers make Mount Rainier a training ground for climbing larger peaks like Denali in Alaska or the 24,000-foot-plus Himalayan peaks, on account of Mount Rainier's vast and varied glacier system and the extreme weather that collides into it or is produced by it at higher elevations. Whiteouts and winds up to 100 mph can engulf the mountaintop in a matter of minutes.

Most of us will not reach the summit or even have the urge to do so. Our pull will be to the parklands of Summer Land, Indian Henry, and Spray. To stand among the heather, aster, cinquefoil, lupine, shooting star, and other brilliant plants growing beneath the tips of cold, thick tongues of glacial ice running from the pinnacle high above, will deliver an energy and worthiness equal to the thrill of reaching the mighty summit. It'll be hard not to feel the life force of Mount Rainier from any vantage point.

In his short essay "An Ascent of Mount Rainier," John Muir wrote: "The noble King Mountain was in full view from here, glorifying the bright, sunny day with his presence, rising in godlike majesty over the woods, with the magnificent prairie as a foreground." After reaching the summit and returning to the lowlands, however, Muir writes that, "apart from the acquisition of knowledge and the exhilaration of climbing, more pleasure is to be found at the foot of mountains than on their tops."

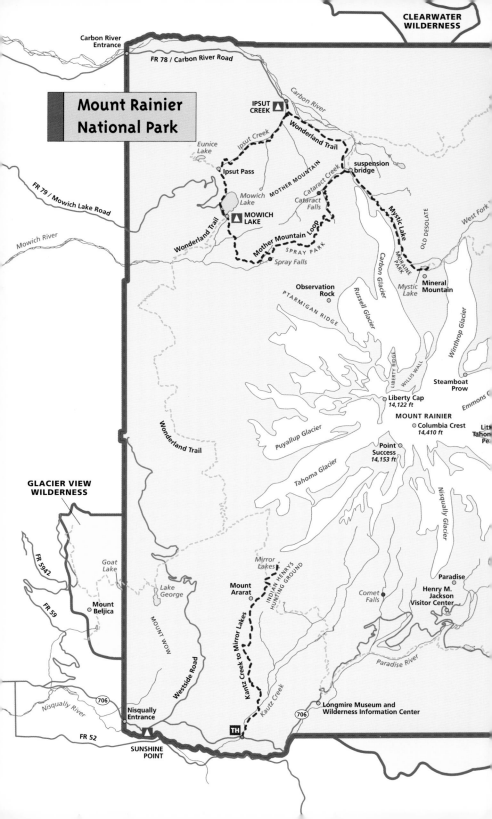

Mount Rainier National Park

CLEARWATER WILDERNESS

Carbon River Entrance

FR 78 / Carbon River Road

Carbon River

IPSUT CREEK

Wonderland Trail

Eunice Lake

Ipsut Creek

suspension bridge

Ipsut Pass

Cataract Creek

MOTHER MOUNTAIN

Mowich Lake

FR 79 / Mowich Lake Road

Cataract Falls

Mystic Lake

West Fork

MOWICH LAKE

Wonderland Trail

Mother Mountain Loop

OLD DESOLATE

MORAINE PARK

Mowich River

SPRAY PARK

Mystic Lake

Mineral Mountain

Spray Falls

Observation Rock

PTARMIGAN RIDGE

Russell Glacier

Carbon Glacier

LIBERTY RIDGE

WILLIS WALL

Winthrop Glacier

Steamboat Prow

Emmons G

Liberty Cap
14,122 ft

Puyallup Glacier

MOUNT RAINIER

Columbia Crest
14,410 ft

Litt
Tahor
Pe

Wonderland Trail

Point Success
14,153 ft

Tahoma Glacier

Nisqually Glacier

GLACIER VIEW WILDERNESS

FR 5942

Goat Lake

Mirror Lakes

INDIAN HENRY'S HUNTING GROUND

Paradise

FR 59

Lake George

Mount Ararat

Comet Falls

Henry M. Jackson Visitor Center

Mount Beljica

MOUNT WOW

Kantz Creek to Mirror Lakes

Wesside Road

706

Paradise River

Nisqually River

Nisqually Entrance

Kautz Creek

706

Longmire Museum and Wilderness Information Center

FR 52

TH

SUNSHINE POINT

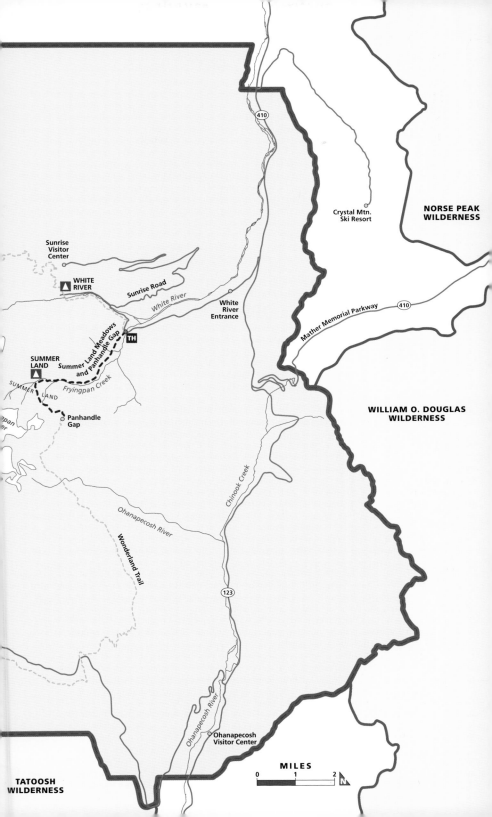

NORSE PEAK
WILDERNESS

Crystal Mtn.
Ski Resort

410

Mather Memorial Parkway

410

WILLIAM O. DOUGLAS
WILDERNESS

Sunrise
Visitor
Center

WHITE
RIVER

Sunrise Road

White River

White
River
Entrance

Summer Land Meadows
and Panhandle Gap

TH

SUMMER
LAND

Fryingpan Creek

SUMMER LAND

Panhandle
Gap

Chinook Creek

Ohanapecosh River

Wonderland Trail

123

Ohanapecosh River

Ohanapecosh
Visitor Center

TATOOSH
WILDERNESS

MILES

0   1   2

N

DESTINATION OR DAY HIKE: SUMMER LAND MEADOWS
AND PANHANDLE GAP
One-Way Distance: 5.6 miles
Elevation Range: 3,800 to 6,800 feet
Total Elevation Gain: 3,000 feet
Difficulty: Easy
Green Trails Map: Mt. Rainier East No. 270

From the trailhead near Fryingpan Creek Bridge, a short 0.1-mile connector trail links up with Mount Rainier National Park's well-known Wonderland Trail, which, in 93 miles, circles the entire mountain. A 5.6-mile hike along a portion of the Wonderland Trail will bring you to Summer Land Meadows and Panhandle Gap.

An easy walk through a mature forest along Fryingpan Creek begins this relaxed hike. At 0.7 mile the trail begins a moderate climb. The creek can still be heard nearby with the trail passing, at points, close enough for views. A stable foot-log at mile 2.8, suspended a mere foot above the roiling Fryingpan, gives passage across to a series of easy switchbacks ascending to Summer Land Camp and Summer Land Meadows. It is through this brushy valley of Fryingpan Creek that views of Mount Rainier and Little Tahoma appear in great splendor. You will reach a camp and meadows of wildflowers at mile 4.2. Campsites are available by permit only, available at the White River Ranger Station.

From the marvelous vantage of Summer Land you can spend hours studying such features of Rainier's east face as the Emmons and Winthrop Glaciers, the Steamboat Prow, and the impressive defense of the Willis Wall farther to the north. Equally intoxicating is Little Tahoma Peak with its jagged top and formidable face of rock and ice.

To reach Panhandle Gap, continue beyond the camp and through the meadows onto a gray rockscape. Through here you are treated to a handful of creek crossings and skirtings of small, glacial pools. Halfway to Panhandle Gap the rockscape changes from gray to red-and-tan rock, punctuated by compact, hardy green plants that thrive quite miraculously in this harsh environment. At mile 5.6 (1.4 miles from Summer Land) you reach Panhandle Gap. The gap is a nice high point on which to have lunch or from which to spend some time scrambling around the surrounding area. Despite its immense popularity, this easy, pleasant hike still offers hikers and backpackers an untrammeled feel. Be advised that, depending on the season or depth of snowpack, the trail out of Summer Land Meadows to Panhandle Gap may be difficult to follow. Be sure to check with the ranger station for current trail conditions.

From the White River Entrance of Mount Rainier National Park off WA 140, drive 3 miles to a parking area on the right-hand side of the roadway, just beyond the Fryingpan Creek Bridge. The trailhead is located across the road.

DAY HIKE: KAUTZ CREEK TO MIRROR LAKES
One-Way Distance: 6.5 miles
Elevation Range: 2,400 to 5,400 feet
Total Elevation Gain: 3,000 feet
Difficulty: Moderate to strenuous
Green Trails Map: Mt. Rainier West No. 269

A stroll along a flat, wide trail through a mix of alder, cedar, fir, and hemlock takes you the first 0.7 mile. Cross the creek via a footlog at this point; note that the crossing can be fairly precarious depending on the water level, so always check with the ranger station for current conditions. Once across, the trail enters a rainforest setting and begins climbing on a narrower trail. The climbing is sustained at a moderate incline for the next 3.3 miles, as the zone changes from rainforest to subalpine forest, with a greater mix of fir and spruce as you ascend.

At mile 4 the trail briefly offers relief by passing through an open area. Enjoy a nice view of Mount Rainier at mile 4.4. The view fades as you move more directly below Mount Ararat. The trail begins climbing, rolling along an open ridge, climbing up and across a hillside (on the way back, great views await of Goat Rocks, Mount Adams, and Mount St. Helens) before descending to the fabulously wide meadows of Indian Henrys Hunting Ground, backdropped by Mount Rainier. At mile 5.7 is the junction with the Wonderland Trail. Turn left to reach the trail junction with Mirror Lakes at mile 5.9. You reach these small, shallow lakes at mile 6.5. They offer a unique perspective of the massive volcano, seeming to hold within their banks an entire, shimmering face of Mount Rainier.

From the Nisqually Entrance of Mount Rainier National Park on WA 706, drive 3.2 miles to the parking area located across the bridge of Kautz Creek. The trailhead is located directly across the road from the parking area.

DESTINATION HIKE: MYSTIC LAKE
One-Way Distance: 7.6 miles
Elevation Range: 2,300 to 6,000 feet
Total Elevation Gain: 3,900 feet
Difficulty: Moderate
Green Trails Map: Mt. Rainier West No. 269

Mystic Lake received its name from park ranger J. B. Flett and a professor named H. H. Garretson, who reported seeing a mysterious whirlpool near the lake's outlet. At 0.3 mile the Wonderland Trail meets the Ipsut Creek Trail that goes to Mowich Lake. Continue on the Wonderland Trail toward Mystic Lake, ascending this easy, somewhat rolling section of the hike. Move from enclosed forest to a thin canopy of trees as you reach a tributary of the Carbon River and eventually break out into the open next to the main river. Brief views of Mount Rainier are possible through here.

You will pass Carbon River Camp and a small, pleasant waterfall of Cataract Creek, then cross a footbridge to the junction with the Spray Park Trail at mile 2.8. At 0.2 mile beyond the Spray Park Trail junction a suspension bridge spans the Carbon River. If the bridge is under repair, a series of footlogs will provide passage across.

A steep and rocky trail climbs above the Carbon River as well as the northernmost tip of the Carbon Glacier, the lowest-elevation glacier in the contiguous 48 states. The trail eventually reenters the trees and makes its way up a series of longer switchbacks, relaxing upon entry into the narrow subalpine valley of lower Moraine Park. The valley widens further along into the broader meadow of Moraine Park. Take in stellar views of the upper end of the Carbon Glacier, Liberty Ridge, and the Willis Wall on Mount Rainier. A steep 0.3-mile climb leads up and out of the meadow and to the sign for Mystic Lake at mile 6.8.

The trail dips down, up, and then down again, reaching at mile 7.6 the charming Mystic Lake, ringed by an open, grassy area and flanked by Mineral Mountain and Old Desolate. By-permit campsites lie at the east end of the lake. Obtain a permit at the Wilkeson Wilderness Information Center.

From Wilkeson on WA 165, travel 17 miles to the Carbon River Entrance of Mount Rainier National Park. Follow the road 5 miles to its end at the Ipsut Creek Campground and the trailhead.

OVERNIGHT LOOP HIKE: MOTHER MOUNTAIN LOOP
Total Distance: 16.6 miles
Elevation Range: 2,300 to 6,400 feet
Total Elevation Gain: 5,200 feet
Difficulty: Moderate
Green Trails Map: Mt. Rainier West No. 269

At the end of the hiker/backpacker parking lot the trail starts into the trees and crosses a creek before reaching the junction with the Wonderland Trail at 0.3 mile. Follow the signs for Mowich Lake, continuing on the Ipsut Creek Trail. A moderate climb through the trees takes you to mile 2.3 where a hard 1.5-mile push begins, leaving the comfort of the woods to head up a rocky trail lined with thick brush to Ipsut Pass. From the 5,100-foot pass—the first and lower of the two high points of this loop—the trail descends along the Wonderland Trail to Mowich Lake under trees. At mile 5.3 you will reach the lake and have your first views of Mount Rainier.

The trail follows the west side of the lake, passing through Mowich Lake Camp; 0.4 mile beyond this point, take the Spray Park Trail. You will drop still lower in elevation to Eagles Roost Camp at mile 7.1. A short side trail to a view of Spray Falls lies 0.2 mile beyond Eagles Roost, while the main trail begins a short climb up a series of switchbacks into the west-side entry of Spray Park at mile 7.9.

A pleasant ramping uphill allows the opportunity to leisurely take in the colors and contrast of the spongy green meadows set against the dramatic features of Mount Rainier, such as Ptarmigan Ridge, Observation Rock, and the Russell Glacier. You reach the high point, 6,400 feet, at mile 10, where you have an even closer vantage point of the northwestern side of what the local tribes call Tahoma.

From here you also have the extra treat of views to the north of Mount Stuart and Glacier Peak, and, into the horizon farther northwest, a view of Mount Baker.

From here the trail crosses through a boulder field (fairly well cairned if the snow hasn't fully retreated) before entering an open, forested area, all the while losing elevation under the watchful eye of Mother Mountain. At mile 11.8 the trail is contained more in the trees, passing by the spur trail for Cataract Camp and continuing its descent to the junction with the Wonderland Trail at mile 13.8. Head north (left) at the junction, crossing a bridge and passing a small, pleasant waterfall of Cataract Creek. The trail parallels the Carbon River in the open; by turning about-face through this section you can take in the last views of Mount Rainier. The trail continues under a thin canopy of trees, gradually descending along the main flow and tributaries of the Carbon River. At 0.8 mile before the end of the loop, the forest becomes more enclosed as the trail approaches the junction with the Ipsut Creek Trail and the final 0.3 mile back to the trailhead. Camping at Eagles Roost, Cataract, and Carbon River Camps are by permit only; permits can be obtained at the Wilkeson Wilderness Information Center.

From Wilkeson on WA 165, travel 17 miles to the Carbon River Entrance of Mount Rainier National Park. Follow the road 5 miles to its end at the Ipsut Creek Campground and the trailhead for the Mother Mountain Loop.

Martha Falls, Mount Rainier National Park

24 Mount St. Helens National Volcanic Monument

Mount St. Helens rises above the fog

LOCATION: About 35 miles east of Longview and 35 miles west of Mount Adams

SIZE: 113,151 acres

ELEVATION RANGE: 800 to 8,365 feet

MILES OF TRAIL: Approximately 110

TREES AND PLANTS: Alder, Douglas fir, lodgepole pine, noble fir, Pacific silver fir, western hemlock, beargrass, fireweed, huckleberry, kinnikinnick, lupine, salmonberry

WILDLIFE: Beaver, black bear, black-tailed deer, coyote, elk, bald eagle, bluebird, finch, flicker, goshawk, red-tailed hawk, spotted owl

ADMINISTRATION: Mount St. Helens NVM Headquarters, 360-449-7800

BEST SEASON: Summer through fall

LOO-WIT IS WHAT THE YAKAMA tribe called her. The affections of Pah-to (Mount Adams) and Wy-east (Mount Hood) toward Loo-wit became fierce enough that the Great Spirit, Sahale, transformed the three into mountains and broke apart the land bridge that spanned the Columbia, separating the lovesick Wy-east from Pah-to, his rival, and Loo-wit, his love. Sahale cloaked Loo-wit in a beautiful cape of snow and ice for the two lovers, and the local people, to gaze upon.

This Indian myth may be about the sometimes destructive pursuit of love; the fair maiden is left, in all her natural splendor, merely to be seen but never touched. However, the Indian tribes understood, in their appropriate naming of the mountain, the force that lay beneath the splendor.

Loo-wit means "Smoking Mountain"; this is the mountain that the people of the Northwest and the rest of the world know as Mount St. Helens.

The mountain is the youngest of the Cascade volcanoes, and even before the historic eruption of 1980 it was also one of the shortest. Its initial formation began some 40,000 years ago, its pre-1980 dimensions the result of alternating active and dormant periods of andesite and pyroclastic flows. Geologists and volcanologists believe that since the 1600s Mount St. Helens had been active on seven occasions, with explosions, pyroclastic flows, lava extrusions, lava dome formation, and mudflows.

Spirit Lake, which sits to the north of the mountain, had been for years a favorite destination for Pacific Northwesterners. Canoe trips, boat outings, fishing trips, weekends at the Spirit Lake Lodge, or summer camp at the YMCA property on the south side of the lake all took place with the backdrop of what was called the "Mount Fuji of America." From 1917 until 1927 a lookout was manned in summers on the top of the mountain. As part of the public works program of the Civilian Conservation Corps, trails were constructed in the 1930s along the bottom of the north slope and farther to the north. But the Smoking Mountain was still restless.

By 1975 predictions were made about the potential of the mountain erupting, followed in 1978 by an eerily accurate forecast of the mountain's gathering forces. The date clearly etched in the minds of people, "The Day That Became Night," was May 18, 1980. However, more than two months prior to that date Mount St. Helens had given warning of her intentions through a series of small earthquakes, capped by one registering 4.2 on the Richter scale on March 20. Over the next several weeks there were hundreds of earthquakes; steam and ash explosions; a plume rising some 6,000 feet above the volcano and ripping open a 250-foot crater on the summit; several avalanches; and an unsettling feeling of worse to come. Despite this, it came as a terrifying shock to many people when Mount St. Helens let loose on that pleasant morning in May.

Firsthand accounts and nearly second-by-second and minute-by-minute photographic evidence leave very little unknown about the eruption. Shortly after 8:32 A.M. on May 18, a shallow, 5.1-magnitude earthquake struck beneath the mountain, triggering a three-part slide of the north face, each of massive proportions. Seconds later, both the vertical and lateral eruption columns began to poke through. A minute later—60 short seconds—the mountain was raging, blasting projectiles upward and outward, far outpacing the avalanche of debris rushing out to the north. This landslide, or debris avalanche, was the largest in recorded history and hurtled toward Spirit Lake and the Toutle River Valley at speeds nearing 180 mph. It covered an area of some 24 square miles, filling the valley to an average depth of 150 feet, raising the bottom of Spirit Lake nearly 300 feet and its water level by 200 feet, and sending a 200-foot-high water wave crashing into the ridgeline beyond the south end of the lake. Pictures show trees flattened like wheat stalks—trees in excess of 100 feet tall, some with diameters of 4 feet, ripped from the ground by a blast of superheated air and volcanic debris reaching speeds of 670 miles per hour. This lateral blast changed a landscape of old-growth forests into a 230-square-mile desert of destruction.

The apocalyptic reversal of day to night was the result of the ash column reaching a height of 12 miles in the atmosphere and drifting to the east, depositing ash more than 2 feet deep as far as 195 miles away, with measurable traces recorded as far away as Minnesota and Oklahoma. Joining these debris slides and projectiles, other elements that reshaped the landscape included pyroclastic flows, hot magma, and rock, which poured onto the area below the lateral blast's epicenter; and mudflows and floods, which clogged streams and rivers, wiped out bridges, and buried houses.

A report assembled by the Department of the Interior and the U.S. Geological Survey, entitled *Eruptions of Mount St. Helens: Past, Present, and Future,* shows two high-altitude infrared photographs, before and after. The "before" picture shows live zones in red ringing the bluish (little to no vegetation) top of Mount St. Helens. The "after" picture is a cold blue color, with the altered north face of Mount St. Helens scattered apart and mangled as if from a shotgun blast. Plants, trees, 5,000 black-tailed deer; 1,500 elk, some 200 black bears, and countless fish, amphibians, reptiles, and insects—all were wiped out.

Mount St. Helens continued to pop and gurgle for months and years after the May 18, 1980 eruption, and even today the mountain is still classified as an active volcano. The composite dome in the bottom of the 1,300-foot-deep crater continues to build on itself. It is not certain but possible that the dome could grow large enough to fill the summit crater and return the mountain to its pre–May 1980 stature.

The surrounding area was left barren, inactive, and in some portions sterilized. But just as the volcano remains active, rebuilding or at least reshaping itself, so too does the landscape. The area closest to the crater, which was devastated by pyroclastic flows reaching temperatures of 1,100 degrees Fahrenheit, snuffed out all local organisms. Today, however, a striking contrast can be seen: Lupine, like a purple blanket, lies across the gray moonscape—a phoenix rising from the ashes.

The lupine does two important things besides providing beauty. First, it helps build the nitrogen content of the nutrient-poor soil, preparing it for the growth of other plants. Second, the lupine lures insects and herbivores like elk to venture out onto the pumice plain, where they deposit pollen and the seeds of grasses and other plants, which then begin to reestablish and diversify the living landscape.

Farther to the north, plants like fireweed and pearly everlasting actually survived the eruption and worked their way through the layers of ash to help revive those barren areas. Trees like red alder, black cottonwood, and bitter cherry were the first to sprout and grow. The old-growth forest of Pacific silver fir and mountain hemlock that were eradicated are expected to return within 200 years but will take on a slightly different mix with more noble fir, western hemlock, lodgepole pine, and Douglas fir. Some trees like mountain hemlock survived; salmonberry and huckleberry shrubs on north slopes that were still buried under snow when the ash hit also reemerged. You can find an abundance of life, as plants and trees, and a greater display of wildflowers than pre-eruption, prove their resiliency. Insect populations have increased, and fish in ponds that were still covered with ice survived and are thriving. Trout have even been pulled from Spirit Lake, which scientists believe to be a possible sign of the recovery of the area's most devastated lake.

Wildlife like elk (three times the pre-eruption population) have returned in force, because of the greater amount of open area, fewer predators, and hunting restrictions within the National Volcanic Monument. In fact, except for the creation of a drainage outlet for the swollen Spirit Lake and the cordoning off a few small study areas for research purposes, the whole monument has been left to its own devices to recover. Hikers thus have an amazing opportunity to immerse themselves in a world of beautiful contrasts, and volcanologists have had a lucky chance to see how such volcanoes behave, and how surrounding areas recover from such an eruption.

Walk onto a pumice plain beneath the breach of the volcano and try to imagine the forces that roared from the depths of the earth and out over hundreds and thousands of square miles. Hike along the ridgelines of the Mount Margaret Backcountry to see below the thousands of trees logjammed at the southern end of Spirit Lake, or merely look beside the trail at the vigorous growth of salmonberry, alder, and various young conifers sprouting from the rocky slopes. From whereever you may stand while exploring it, Mount St. Helens National Volcanic Monument is perhaps more of a jewel now than it was before the morning of May 18, 1980.

DAY HIKE: APE CAVE
One-Way Distance: 0.8 mile (Lower Cave);
1.5 miles (Upper Cave)
Difficulty: Easy to Moderate

NOTE: This is a fee area. The cave is accessible anytime, but guided day tours are available from the end of June to the beginning of September.

First discovered by Lawrence Johnson of Amboy in 1946, the cave comes by its unusual name from a youth group self-styled the St. Helens Apes who conducted extensive explorations of the cave in subsequent years. The cave (actually two, Lower and Upper) formed when an eruption more than 1,900 years ago created a lava tube. A stairway at the main (lower) entrance will bring explorers down into the Lower Cave. The floor surface is a combination of sand and rock and for the most part level. The dimensions of the cave stay consistent except for a few narrow spots and at the end, where the ceiling and walls come to an impassable point. In those narrower or constricted sections you can feel the wind speed increase, much like water in a river moving through slot canyons.

The cave throughout is cool—maintaining a temperature of around 42 degrees. The air is also damp because of the water dripping from the walls. Be sure to wear sturdy shoes, preferably hiking boots, and carry two or three light sources, such as flashlight, headlamp, propane lantern, or glow sticks. Artificial light, of course, is the only light there will be. The end of the Lower Cave requires a bit of crawling. The ceiling drops before rising slightly into a small chamber at the cave's end.

The Upper Cave is accessible from either the main (lower) or upper entrance. Unlike the level surface of the Lower Cave, the Upper Cave slopes upward and has

continued on p. 194

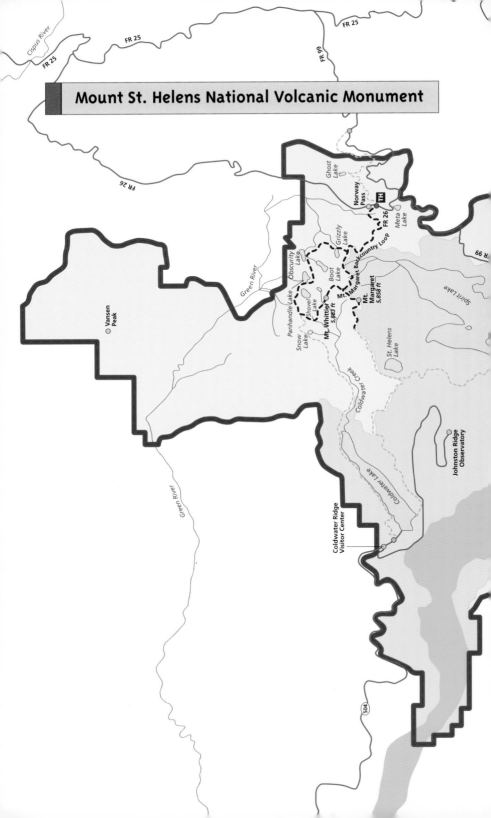

Mount St. Helens National Volcanic Monument

numerous rock piles that must be negotiated. The exploring is easier if you start at the main entrance. The piles of rock, called breakdown, which you must clamber over have collapsed off of the walls and ceiling. Somewhere near three-quarters of the way up is a small wall (8 feet tall) that you must scale. It is not overly difficult, but if rated on a rock-climbing scale would probably be a 5.4. Close to the end is a visible opening in the ceiling; continue past this to the next opening, which is equipped with a fixed ladder. The cave does continue on for a short distance past the upper entrance/exit for those still wanting to explore. The trail back to the parking lot is about 1.4 miles long.

From Mount St. Helens National Volcanic Monument Headquarters 4 miles north of Amboy, travel 6 miles on WA 503. Take the WA 503 spur east toward Cougar. At 14.6 miles the 503 spur turns into FR 90. At about 22 miles take the WA 503 spur toward Ape Cave. The route to the cave is very well signed. At 31 miles the WA 503 spur turns into FR 90. Turn left on FR 83 at 34 miles. Take another left at 36 miles onto FR 8303, and proceed 1 mile to the trailhead.

> **DAY HIKE: TRUMAN TRAIL LOOP**
> Total Distance: 7.5 miles
> Elevation Range: 4,000 to 5,038 feet
> Total Elevation Gain: 1,038 feet
> Difficulty: Easy
> Green Trails Map: Mt. St. Helens NW No. 364S

The loop begins from the lot at the Windy Ridge Viewpoint. During peak season (end of June to early September) a park ranger gives a short lecture on the 1980 eruption several times during the day. The start of Truman Trail #207 was formerly a road. The surface is primarily pumice—small, porous, light-colored rock that rained down on this area during the big eruption. Alder, small plants, wildflowers, and a few stands of small conifers are beginning to occupy this completely open, barren landscape some 23 years later. It is quite beautiful in its starkness, especially with the mouth of the crater ahead, Mount Adams looming nearby, and wildlife encounters. I once saw here a stringless mobile of red-tailed hawks riding the thermals above the graveyard of trees downslope from the road and trail.

At mile 1.8 is the junction with Abraham Trail #216D; continue past and downhill on the Truman Trail. Take Windy Trail #216E toward Loowit Trail at mile 2. The surroundings remain open but take on a more desolate or otherworldly feel because of the reduced amount of vegetation and increased level of grayness. Hiking through here and looking to the north you can see down into Spirit Lake, which became deeper and bigger as a result of the eruption. At mile 3 is the junction with Loowit Trail #216. Take this trail, heading southeast, toward Abraham Trail #216D. If time allows, from this junction you can head west to the Loowit Falls Viewpoint (1.5 miles one-way) and then double back to continue the loop. This section of the loop hike offers an incredible view into the mouth of the crater and of other geological features like Sugar Bowl and Dogs Head on the lower east rim of the crater.

At mile 4.3 the trail works its way up a ravine surprisingly covered with vegetation. At mile 4.5 is Windy Pass. Continue straight to reach Abraham Trail #216D, or scramble up the small knob of pumice on your left to be treated to a marvelous view of the surrounding landscape, including a nice take on Mount Rainier farther to the north. From the top of the knob, pick your way down the ridgeline toward the visible Abraham Trail and make your way over a narrower part of the ridge slightly to the north. It is approximately 0.3 mile from the knob to the trail. At mile 5.5 is the junction of the Abraham and Truman Trails. Return back along the Truman Trail.

From Mount St. Helens National Volcanic Monument Headquarters 4 miles north of Amboy, travel 6 miles on WA 503. Take the WA 503 spur east toward Cougar. At 14.6 miles the 503 spur turns into FR 90. At 30.2 miles, just past the Pine Creek Information Center, turn left onto FR 25 and head north toward Windy Ridge. At 55.6 miles turn left onto FR 99. You will reach the Windy Ridge Viewpoint and trailhead at 71.9 miles.

OVERNIGHT OR MULTIDAY HIKE:
MOUNT MARGARET BACKCOUNTRY LOOP
Total Distance: 15.5 to 19.1 miles
Elevation Range: 4,200 to 5,883 feet
Total Elevation Gain: 2,383 feet
Difficulty: Moderate to strenuous
Green Trails Map: Spirit Lake No. 332

The hike begins by climbing on Boundary Trail #1 heading toward Mount Margaret. At mile 1.2 is the junction with Trail #227A and a last view of Meta Lake below and to the southeast. Continue on the Boundary Trail. At mile 2.2 is the junction with Independence Pass Trail #227 and a stunning view into the logjammed Spirit Lake and the mouth of St. Helens. Continue climbing on the Boundary Trail in a northerly direction, wrapping around and above a basin. The Lakes Trail #211 junction comes at mile 3.2. Continue climbing on the Boundary Trail, now in a westerly direction. You won't mind the uphill, with huckleberries and salmonberries to snack on and the constant companionship of Helens, Rainier, Adams, Hood, and even Jefferson farther to the south.

At mile 4 the trail begins working along a fantastic ridgeline with a nice blend of up and down. At mile 4.6 you will come to Bear Camp. This is the first and nicer of the two camps (the other is Margaret Camp) along the ridge for this variation of the Mount Margaret loop. (Note that all of the campsites in the Mount Margaret Backcountry are by permit only; obtain one at the headquarters in Amboy.) At mile 5 you reach the junction with Mount Whittier Trail #214. Margaret Camp is 1.8 miles past this junction. Up to this point, the trail is quite nice, working its way across a soft volcanic ash surface. The ridgeline does have some new-growth conifers. Water is available by way of natural springs at both Bear Camp and Margaret Camp. Be sure to treat all drinking water.

The loop continues on Mount Whittier Trail #214. This trail is as exhilarating as a roller-coaster ride. It works across a knife-edge ridge, falling away hundreds of feet in both directions, giving hikers high exposure with high thrills, a place normally reserved for the birds. This trail may also take some route-finding skills, especially at the north end because of frequent washouts of that part of the trail. Don't let the warnings keep you from hiking this, though, because overall it is safe, if strenuous in sections, and truly a unique hiker's pathway.

If the trail does not make itself apparent on the north end near the junction with Lakes Trail #211, make sure to stay on the east side of the ridge toward Shovel Lake (don't lose too much elevation) and not the west side toward Snow Lake. At mile 7 (add 3.6 miles if you have camped at Margaret Camp) is the junction with Lakes Trail #211.

The scenery changes here to rugged and mountainous, as the trail works its way along a lower ridgeline to the north of the Boundary Trail ridgeline, which blocks views of Helens, Hood, and Jefferson. After passing by a handful of delightful lakes, by mile 9.5 the trail has worked down to Panhandle Lake. Farther on, the trail passes a beautiful stair-stepped waterfall running over blocky, rust-colored rocks, welcoming hikers to Obscurity Lake. The trail from here begins to contour around three or four drainages, gaining elevation the whole time. At mile 11.4 you will come to Grizzly Lake and begin a rapid, steep ascent for 0.6 mile, gaining 700 feet in elevation up to Bear Pass. At mile 12.1 is the junction with Boundary Trail #1 and the return to the Norway Pass Trailhead. You could also spend at least two nights on this loop, making another camp along the Lakes Trail at one of four sites: Snow, Shovel, Panhandle, or Obscurity Lakes.

From Mount St. Helens National Volcanic Monument Headquarters 4 miles north of Amboy, travel 6 miles on WA 503. Take the WA 503 spur east toward Cougar. At 14.6 miles the WA 503 spur turns into FR 90. At 30.2 miles, just past the Pine Creek Information Center, turn left onto FR 25 and head north toward Windy Ridge. At 55.6 miles turn left onto FR 99. At 64.7 miles turn right onto FR 26 for the Norway Pass Trailhead, at 65.7 miles.

Norse Peak Wilderness

Fifes Peaks

THIS PLACE IS MERELY the rocky high point along a ridgeline. A grassy northern slope slides into the broad, treeless Big Crow Basin below, where a small wooden shelter is visible. As your eyes climb out of the basin they will fall upon a rocky ridge jutting out toward the east-northeast, another to the north doing the same near Little Crow Basin, and two others to the south running out from Cement Basin and Pickhandle Gap.

To the east are Fifes Peaks and Fifes Ridge, to the north and northeast other crusted, blocky rock peaks like Mutton Mountain, Arch Rock, and Raven Roost. As you look above and past the

LOCATION: East of Mount Rainier National Park, north of the William O. Douglas Wilderness, and approximately 35 miles east-southeast of Enumclaw

SIZE: 52,180 acres

ELEVATION RANGE: 3,200 to 6,856 feet

MILES OF TRAIL: Approximately 90

TREES AND PLANTS: Douglas fir, Engelmann spruce, lodgepole pine, larch, mountain hemlock, subalpine fir, western hemlock, western red cedar, cinquefoil, deerfoot vanillaleaf, devil's club, huckleberry, lupine, moss, paintbrush

WILDLIFE: Black bear, black-tailed deer, cougar, lynx, mountain goat, bald eagle, golden eagle, grouse, Steller's jay

ADMINISTRATION: Mount Baker–Snoqualmie NF, Enumclaw RD, 360-825-6585; Wenatchee NF, Naches RD, 509-653-2205

BEST SEASON: Summer to mid-autumn

Norse Peak

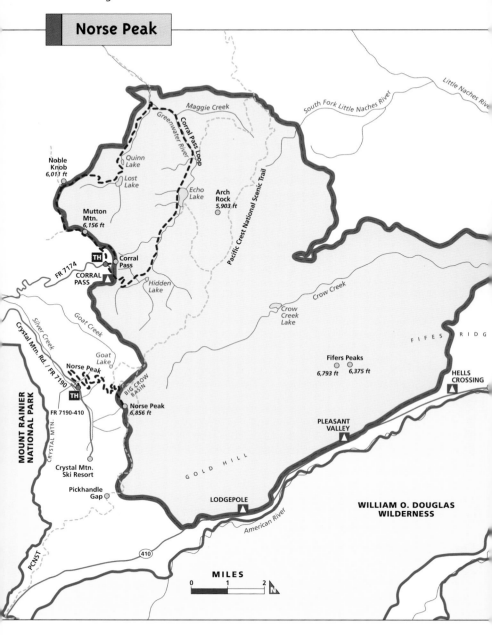

boundaries of the Norse Peak Wilderness, the explosion of panoramas begins: Mount Baker to the north with Canada standing close by; Mount Stuart and the spectacular Goat Rocks; Mount Adams; Mount St. Helens, like the back of a bluish elephant lying down; and finally Mount Rainier, close enough that it seems possible to feel the icy chill of Emmons Glacier. These are the highlights of the mind-spinning vistas taken in from the unassuming rocky summit of Norse Peak.

Rows of ridgelines, such as Fifes Ridge and Dalles Ridge, extend like point-ing fingers. Numerous blocky rock summits and the flaring, dinosaur-like armor-plate formations of Fifes Peaks are visible from various trails in the wilderness. Grassy wild-flower basins, like Bullion, Lake, and Cement, are sunk deep in the trees below, while drainages such as Lost Creek, Greenwater River, and Little Naches River make their way out of the maze of mountainous terrain. The appearance of the wilderness is primarily the result of volcanic activity some 25 million years ago. But a much more recent human legacy remains in the names of features like Gold Hill, Bullion Basin, Pickhandle Gap, and Placer Lake.

The Summit Mining District, located in and around the Morse Creek drainage just outside the wilderness boundary, attracted prospectors with the glint of gold. The mining activity lasted from 1885 to 1920, but the mining legacy remains only in the old cabins, mine shafts, and place names today, not in the scant amount of gold nuggets mined from the area. The only other noteworthy human activity that utilized the nat-ural resources of Norse Peak was grazing, which was heavy from 1890 up until 1950. But as with the miners, the only trace left of the shepherds are the names of the geo-graphic features that remain: Mutton Mountain, Corral Pass, and Sheepherder Lake.

Two dozen or so lakes dot the wilderness, some perched up high in places like George and Goat Basins, others down in the densely treed valleys, like Lost Lake fed by Lost Creek, and Echo Lake fed by the Greenwater River. Even though Norse Peak sits in the large rain shadow of Mount Rainier, parts of the wilderness receive upwards of 100 inches of annual precipitation, providing the water to sustain the western Cascade forest of Douglas fir, western hemlock, western red cedar, sword fern, deer fern, devil's club, and a collection of mosses.

Go ahead and stand on the top of Norse Peak and spin, very slowly, around for an hour. Try to name all the incredible landscape features that lie within and beyond the Norse Peak Wilderness. You won't be able to.

DAY HIKE: NORSE PEAK
One-Way Distance: 4.7 miles
Elevation Range: 3,855 to 6,856 feet
Total Elevation Gain: 3,001 feet
Difficulty: Strenuous
Green Trails Map: Bumping Lake No. 271

The trailhead for Norse Peak Trail #1191 is 0.2 mile up FR 7190-410. Long, sustained switchbacks through the trees begin the hike, which nevertheless offers frequent views of Crystal Mountain across to the west as well as the namesake ski resort up valley. At mile 2.6 the trail enters an open slope, which marks the begin-ning of vistas of Mount Rainier as it rises up from the west.

After climbing back into and out of the trees the trail reaches a ridge top at mile 4.3. From here Mount Rainier looks absolutely massive. Perched over Big Crow Basin, look to the northeast to take in views over and into the heart of the

Norse Peak Wilderness. Follow Trail #1191A (there is no sign for the former lookout) up and to the right, climbing over to the west side of the ridge, back along the ridgeline through some trees, and then over to the east side, where the trail curls up to the site of the old lookout on the summit of Norse Peak at mile 4.7.

You could go dizzy trying to take in all the views from here: the mesmerizing glaciers on Mount Rainier's east side; the Goat Rocks lined up as in a jagged wall of defense of Mount Adams to the south; Mount St. Helens to the southwest; an uncountable number of Cascade peaks around and beyond Mount Stuart to the north; and even a good glimpse of Mount Baker perched near the Canadian border. There are places to camp on Norse Peak. Either pack in water or retrieve it from the basin below.

From Enumclaw drive 33.1 miles east on WA 410. Turn left onto Crystal Mountain Road (FR 7190). At mile 37.3 park in a small lot located on the right side of the road, diagonally across from FR 7190-410.

OVERNIGHT HIKE: CORRAL PASS LOOP
Total Distance: 15.9 miles
Elevation Range: 3,000 to 5,700 feet
Total Elevation Gain: 2,800 feet
Difficulty: Moderate
Green Trails Map: Lester No. 239

Choose from two options to start this hike: (1) begin where the road is blocked by boulders and hike through the trees below the ridgeline; or (2) take the trail heading up a sidehill and rolling across the ridgeline along an old roadbed. I recommend the second option for the views of Mount Rainier and the Cascade peaks to the north. These trails merge at approximately 1 mile on Noble Knob Trail #1184.

At mile 1.6 is the junction with Deep Creek Trail #1196. Continue rolling along on Trail #1184 with constant views of Mount Rainier and even the top of Mount Adams behind you. The trail then heads into the trees for a short distance before dropping out and around the opposite side of the ridge and down to the junction at mile 2.5 with Lost Lake Trail #1185.

To gain a higher vantage point, you can hike another 0.4 mile to the top of Noble Knob. The hike continues, though, on Lost Lake Trail #1185, which stays dramatically high, contouring the Lost Lake basin before the descent at mile 2.8. Begin descending on short, steep switchbacks before reaching a slightly more gradual decline. By the time you reach Lost Lake, however, you will have lost 2,000 feet of elevation.

Lost Lake at mile 4.5 makes for a good campsite. The trail continues to lose elevation past the lake, alternating at first between darker groves and open, rocky areas and passing Quinn Lake before settling into a steady rhythm in the moist world of cedars, moss, mushrooms, and devil's club. At mile 7.5 you reach the junction with Greenwater Trail #1176, which at 3,000 feet marks both the low point and the looping-back point for the hike. A sign will indicate the way toward Echo Lake.

Climb from here in a similar environment until you reach the Maggie Creek Trail #1186 junction at mile 10, where the tree and understory mix changes and the trail climbs a more bit steeply until it reaches a short, flat section and descends to Echo Lake at mile 11.4. You will find good campsites and even backcountry toilets at Echo Lake. The lake is medium size and although surrounded by trees it offers a nice view of Arch Rock, east and slightly to the south.

The climbing continues moderately, reaching the vicinity of Hidden Lake at mile 13.9. At mile 14.7 is the junction with Trail #1188. From here you have 1.2 miles back up to Corral Pass.

From Enumclaw drive 31.6 miles east on WA 410 and turn left onto Corral Pass Road (FR 7174); Silver Springs Campground will be on the right. This road is narrow, rough, and steep with a gravel-dirt surface. At 37.9 miles bear to the left past the sign for Noble Knob #1184 and park in the small parking lot by the trailhead. Additional parking is available by staying to the right at the pass and driving another 100 yards to a circular parking area.

Endless views from the Norse Peak Wilderness

26 Tatoosh Wilderness

Mount Rainier looms above the Tatoosh Range

THE PROXIMITY OF THE TATOOSH WILDERNESS to Mount Rainier is such that its entire northern border makes it look as if it is merely an extension, an appendage, living off of the incredible vistas of the giant volcano. Surely, "Mount Rainier's a good chaperone, looking down like a nice big papa," as Martha Hardy wrote in her book *Tatoosh,* about her experiences as a fire finder in the summer of 1943 at Tatoosh Ridge Lookout. But as far as the Taidnapam (Upper Cowlitz) Indian history is concerned, the Tatoosh Range is *Neq'u't* (Nuk-koot) which means "breast" or "milk." The Tatoosh still

LOCATION: Borders the southern boundary of Mount Rainier National Park, approximately 5 miles north of Packwood

SIZE: 15,750 acres

ELEVATION RANGE: 1,230 to 6,310 feet

MILES OF TRAIL: 12.5

TREES AND PLANTS: Douglas fir, mountain hemlock, noble fir, Pacific silver fir, western hemlock, western red cedar, arnica, beargrass, bluebell, dwarf blackberry, huckleberry, lupine, paintbrush

WILDLIFE: Black bear, black-tailed deer, bobcat, cougar, elk, mountain goats, pika, marmots, golden eagles, Swainson's hawk white-tailed ptarmigan

ADMINISTRATION: Gifford Pinchot NF, Cowlitz Valley RD, 360-497-1100

BEST SEASON: Summer to early fall

provides for humans, mainly for the benefit of robust backpackers passing through today, as it did for the Taidnapam, for whom it provided materials for basket making and huckleberries for drying to use as a food source in winter months.

One primary trail works strenuously up from the lowland creek bottoms of Hinkle Tinkle Creek to the south and Butter Creek to the west. The trail climbs through hemlock and Douglas fir into an amazing parkland expanse full of wildflowers, "[b]eds of flowers blooming with their first fresh vigor where the snows had faded," as Hardy wrote. All the while you can take in views of the southern Cascade peaks. What is sometimes called "Tatoosh Mountain" is really just the highest point (6,310 feet) along Tatoosh Ridge and where the lookout once stood. The explosion of colors in wildflowers is short, starting most years in mid-July and fading by August.

The Tatoosh receives on average 100 inches of precipitation a year, most of which comes from the hammering winter months that can unleash snows swelling to levels of nearly 40 feet in the highest elevations. Because of its steep ridgelines, water runs quickly away into the surrounding creeks of Johnson, Butter, and Hinkle Tinkle, as well as into the Muddy Fork Cowlitz and Cowlitz Rivers. There are only a half dozen lakes in the wilderness with available water, making late summer and early fall pushes along the ridge dry. A side trip up and down to the Tatoosh Lakes is worth the spectacle of observing these tiny lakes balanced between tall rock walls and releasing a stream of water into a thickly forested basin en route to Taos Creek, which joins the Muddy Fork Cowlitz River, which in turn joins the Cowlitz River, eventually feeding the Pacific-bound Columbia River.

The 15,750 acres of the Tatoosh can seem bigger due to the degree of solitude earned in the effort to reach the spectacles on the high ground. A variety of wildlife, though, do call the Tatoosh home. Black bear feed on huckleberries; deer graze on the lush grasses; cougar hunt game big and small, like pika and snowshoe rabbit; and Swainson's hawks soar above the ridge, backdropped by Mount Rainier. When visiting the Tatoosh Wilderness, expect splendors on the ground, in the air, and across the deep horizon.

DAY OR DESTINATION HIKE: TATOOSH RIDGE LOOKOUT
One-Way Distance: 5.1 miles
Elevation Range: 2,900 to 6,310 feet
Total Eevation Gain: 3,410 feet
Difficulty: Strenuous
Green Trails Map: Packwood No. 302

The trail climbs immediately through a mixed stand of fir and deciduous trees. At mile 0.2 the trail begins a series of 15 switchbacks up a steep slope for 1.2 miles, with views of Mount Rainier sifting through the trees along the way. The trail eventually leaves the trees, working along a hillside through colorful wildflowers that bloom from mid-July to August. At mile 2.3 take the switchback to the left; the trail straight ahead has been abandoned. Approximately 0.1 mile farther, the trail reaches another switchback to the left. This unmarked trail brings you up and over a ridge and into another basin area with an unmaintained trail heading to the north. It is worth exploring if you have time, but at the very least take the trail up to the ridge for a spectacular "in-your-face" view of Mount Rainier. The main trail continues to the right up a small section of steps toward Tatoosh Lake and the former lookout on Tatoosh Ridge.

You will reach the junction with Tatoosh Lake Trail #161B at mile 2.6. Hike 0.5 mile to the lake, which sits beautifully on a small shelf wedged between rock walls. Note that camping is not allowed by the lake. Approximately 0.2 mile past the junction is a point where you can set up camp, with a view of Mount Adams to the south and Mount Rainier to the north—although this site does not have a water source. The trail continues to move up and down while contouring along open, flower-laden hillsides. At mile 4.3, just before reaching a saddle, the lookout trail cuts back to the left and uphill. The trail is not marked. Before heading up to the former lookout site, hike the short distance to the saddle in order to look down onto the green benched area below, and take in the rows and rows of peaks surrounding the wilderness, including a spectacular view of Goat Rocks.

Following the lookout trail, you will summit the high point of Tatoosh Ridge, the old lookout site, at mile 5.1. Mount Rainier dominates the horizon to the north from this vantage point. This also makes for an excellent campsite, for both the amazing views and the presence of a water source—a small lake just below the lookout site. The Tatoosh Wilderness may be small and equipped with only one major trail, but its formidable geography and incredible vistas surely make it worthy of a visit.

From Cowlitz Valley RD, take US 12 east about 16 miles to Packwood. Turn left onto Skate River Road (FR 52), drive north 4.2 miles, and turn right onto gravel FR 5270. At 11.5 miles is the trailhead for Tatoosh Trail #161.

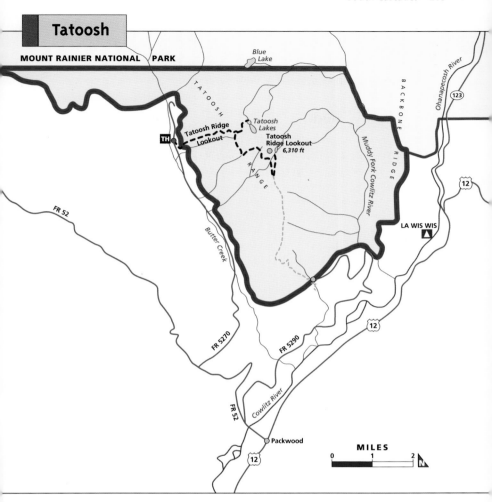

Tatoosh

MOUNT RAINIER NATIONAL PARK

27 Trapper Creek Wilderness

Ferns fill the understory in the Trapper Creek Wilderness

TRAPPER CREEK IS THE ONLY WILDERNESS in Washington that can credit industry for its existence. It is true that Trapper Creek did not receive its official wilderness designation until 1984, making it unavailable for mining, logging, or any other activity, for profit or not, that would destroy its natural habitat and cycles. But a flourishing resort in the early twentieth century deserves substantial credit for saving Trapper Creek's natural attributes. Star Brewing Company of Portland, Oregon, constructed a hotel and resort in 1909 at Government Mineral Springs, near the confluence of Trapper Creek

LOCATION: About halfway between Mount St. Helens and the Columbia River, and approximately 35 miles northeast of Vancouver, Washington

SIZE: 5,970 acres

ELEVATION RANGE: 1,200 to 4,268 feet

MILES OF TRAIL: Approximately 23

TREES AND PLANTS: Douglas fir, mountain hemlock, noble fir, Pacific silver fir, subalpine fir, western hemlock, western red cedar, whitebark pine, bunchberry dogwood, huckleberry, rhododendron, salal

WILDLIFE: Black bear, black-tailed deer, bobcat, cougar, elk, pine marten, barred owl, Clark's nutcracker, goshawk, gray jay, grouse, northern spotted owl, pileated woodpecker

ADMINISTRATION: Gifford Pinchot NF, Mount Adams RD, 509-395-3400

BEST SEASON: Late spring through fall

and Wind River. A regal outpost in the wild woods, the resort was decorated with flower gardens and offered guests a dance pavilion, horseback riding, and the soothing if not curative benefit of mineral baths.

A popular mineral water was bottled here for decades, but legend holds that the attractiveness of Trapper Creek as a retreat increased during the Prohibition era because of the availability of illegal alcohol. Prohibition was repealed in 1933, and the hotel burned down in 1935, never to be rebuilt. However, a popular campground constructed east of the resort, which was improved by Civilian Conservation Corps workers after the resort closed, continued to attract families to the area.

Now what does this history of recreation and self-indulgence have to do with Trapper Creek? Forest plans of the early twentieth century had a stipulation that buffer zones—areas not to be logged—must exist beside roadways and around establishments like the Government Mineral Springs Hotel. The size and location of the resort and the Forest Service's buffer zone around it effectively blocked access into the forests of Trapper Creek, leaving forested areas far beyond the buffer zones inaccessible to logging. Today only a few private homes, under permits issued by the Forest Service, exist northwest of Government Mineral Springs Campground along the boundary of the wilderness.

Very few trails access one of the state's smallest wildernesses. The 4,268-foot high point, Sister Rocks, is not intimidating to most visitors. The low point, at 1,200 feet, suggests that the elevation gain also wouldn't appear to be very challenging. However, since Trapper Creek runs nearly the full length of the small wilderness and mainly inside a horseshoe-shaped basin, trails like the Trapper Creek Trail tend to make steep pushes, such as up the basin's headwall to the 100-foot Trapper Falls. The remaining trails are generally found up other drainages and across ridgelines along the northeastern portion of the wilderness. The Soda Peaks Lake Trail makes the sole diversion into the southern portion of Trapper Creek, leading to the only lake.

The terrain is heavily forested, blessed with old-growth rainforests of Douglas fir and a marvelous array of plant and tree life such as rhododendron, prince's pine, twinflower, bunchberry dogwood, western red cedar, and western hemlock. The subalpine zone hosts beargrass, huckleberry, rainbow-blasts of wildflowers in hidden

Trapper Creek

meadows, and such trees as whitebark pine, mountain hemlock, and subalpine fir. Crystal water fills the creeks, and large game like Roosevelt elk thrive in this wilderness. The main trails are the work of the Forest Service and were built for the function of fire suppression, providing access to the former lookout sites on Observation Peak and Sister Rocks. The more primitive, and what I think the more exciting, trails are the work of the Mazamas, a mountaineering group out of Portland. I think you will find that the Trapper Creek Wilderness is a friendly, quiet cousin to the giants—Mount Hood, Mount St. Helens, and Mount Adams—that surround it.

DAY HIKE: TRAPPER CREEK LOOP
Total Distance: 9.7 miles (add 3.5 to 5 miles for variations)
Elevation Range: 1,200 to 3,200 feet
Total Elevation Gain: 2,000 feet
Difficulty: Moderate to strenuous
Green Trails Map: Lookout Mtn. No. 396

Trapper Creek Loop begins on Trapper Creek Trail #192 in a Pacific Northwest rainforest setting of fern, moss, and mixed deciduous–Douglas fir forest. At mile 0.7 is the junction with Observation Trail #132. Take the footbridge across the creek and continue on Trail #192; do not take the trail to the left at this junction, which leads to a road. At mile 1.4 the trail dips down to a creek crossing and passes by Soda Peaks Lake Trail #133. At mile 2.5 the trail passes by Big Slide Trail #195. In a few yards you will have the option to stay on Trail #192 or take Deer Cutoff Trail #209. The loop described here is along Deer Cutoff.

The trail works its way down to a crossing of Trapper Creek at mile 2.9, where the clear water rushes over black, smooth rock. Deer Cutoff rejoins Trail #192 at mile 3.3. At the junction at mile 3.5 take Sunshine Trail #198. At this point, you have the option of continuing on Trail #192, choosing an out-and-back or one of a couple of other loop options (refer to your Green Trails Map). These variations will add anywhere from 3.5 to 5 miles to the hike, but the reward of coming upon 100-foot Trapper Falls might be enough enticement.

The Sunshine Trail is less maintained and may take some sniffing out at a few points, but you will quickly fall into its natural meandering without much trouble; for those less confident, the trees are marked at frequent intervals with metal, diamond-shaped tags. The nice part about this trail is that it is less used, allowing you to feel more in tune with the environment. At mile 4.2 the trail turns up a ridge steeply, continuing this way for 0.3 mile. Higher up, the trail gives a nice view across the Trapper Creek drainage. At mile 5.2 continue past the junction with Rim Rock Trail #202. At mile 5.7 take Observation Trail #132 heading southeast. This trail is a nice, gentle descent along a hillside, wrapping its way down to the creek drainages below. Observation Trail joins back with Trapper Creek Trail at mile 9 for the return stretch to the trailhead.

From Carson, travel 13 miles up the Wind River Highway (FR 30) and turn left onto Government Mineral Springs Road. At 13.5 miles turn right onto FR 5401. Take this gravel road 0.4 mile to the trailhead, at 13.9 miles.

28 William O. Douglas Wilderness

Lupine and alpine tarn

LOCATION: Between Norse Peak Wilderness and Goat Rocks Wilderness, west of Mount Rainier and approximately 25 miles west-northwest of Yakima

SIZE: 168,157 acres

ELEVATION RANGE: 3,200 to 7,766 feet

MILES OF TRAIL: Over 250

TREES AND PLANTS: Alaska cedar, Douglas fir, Engelmann spruce, mountain hemlock, ponderosa pine, western hemlock, western red cedar, whitebark pine, avalanche lily, beargrass, buttercup, cinquefoil, heather, paintbrush

WILDLIFE: Cougar, elk, fisher, lynx, mountain goat, mule deer, wolverine, blue grouse, red-shafted flicker, pileated woodpecker, ptarmigan, ruffed grouse, western grosbeak

ADMINISTRATION: Gifford Pinchot NF, Cowlitz Valley RD, 360-497-1100; Wenatchee NF, Naches RD, 509-653-2205

BEST SEASON: Summer through fall

SUPREME COURT JUSTICE William Orville Douglas began a chapter of his memoir *Go East, Young Man* by describing a "driving force" that drew him to the mountains west of his childhood home in Yakima—a force he did not recognize or understand until years later. Often when we enter the wilderness we are doing so to face adversity: adversity of the land, of everyday life in all its challenges, perhaps of something in our past that we have yet to make peace with or overcome. Douglas was a sickly child who yearned to overcome his frailties. Pushed both by the ridicule of his peers for his scrawny appearance, and by his own need to match his physical achievements with his scholastic ones, Douglas eventually built strength in his legs and heart. By his teens he had started hiking the terrain that some 70 years later would bear his name.

The William O. Douglas Wilderness reflects the character of the late justice; it is a place of diversity and adversity where he found both solace and energy for many years of his life. Douglas made numerous treks into the area from the home he built in Goose Prairie in the early 1920s, complete with views of Old Scab and Little Bald Mountains. Goose Prairie lies along the Bumping River, which flows from Bumping Lake a short distance to the southwest. Neither the lake nor Goose Prairie is actually part of the official wilderness area, but both are among the half-dozen access points along the valley and farther south to the heart of the wilderness. The William O. Douglas Wilderness is also accessible by way of trailheads originating off of Highways 123, 410, and 12, as well as number of Forest Service roads reached via these highways.

From the air, the wilderness appears to be split into two relatively even halves linked together by the lake-heavy southwestern section, which seemingly spills into the Goat Rocks Wilderness. The real division of these 168,157 acres is not in what lies to the west and east of Goose Prairie but in the distinctive characteristics west and east of the Cascade divide. Of the 59 named and 250 unnamed lakes, ponds, and puddles, the vast majority lie west of the divide in an 18-mile-long strip along the west side of the wilderness, from White Pass in the south to Chinook Pass in the north. Bumping River originates from Fish Lake, north of Fryingpan Mountain; Ohanapecosh River runs to the west; and American River flows along the northwest border of the wilderness. All are fed by numerous creeks branching out from the west side of the wilderness. The majority of annual moisture falls in the form of snow, and precipitation totals for the year are nearly 100 inches more than those east of the divide.

The western half is covered in thick forest. Numerous old-growth forests here consist of the typical west-side mix of Douglas fir, western hemlock, and western red cedar. Climbing higher you will pass through stands of Pacific silver fir, Engelmann spruce, and western white pine. At the highest elevations live Alaska cedar, mountain hemlock, and subalpine fir. The meadows and parklands contain heather, huckleberry, and wildflowers. Most peaks here are under 6,300 feet, with highpoints like Spiral Butte, Crag Mountain, and Tumac Mountain lifting their chins above the treetops.

Across the divide, especially farther to the east toward Nelson Ridge, the terrain is dramatically different. Much taller, bare, and craggy peaks rise distinctly above the steep-sided creek drainages. Arid and rugged, this region is still attractive, covered in ponderosa pine in the lower elevations and whitebark pine in the upper, and well worth the effort needed to explore it.

The tallest mountain in the William O. Douglas is 7,766-foot Mount Aix in the far eastern half of the wilderness, and views are grandest from its peak (or any of the ridgelines surrounding it). Aix provides a wonderful show of the Stuart Range to the north, Rainier to the west, Mount Adams and Goat Rocks to the south, and the beginnings of the vast Columbia Plateau of central Washington to the east. Significant herds of elk and mule deer live here, along with cougar, lynx, wolverine, mountain goat, and ruffed grouse. Other birds that may be seen in either region of the wilderness include ptarmigan, Steller's jay, red-shafted flicker, western grosbeak, and the pileated woodpecker.

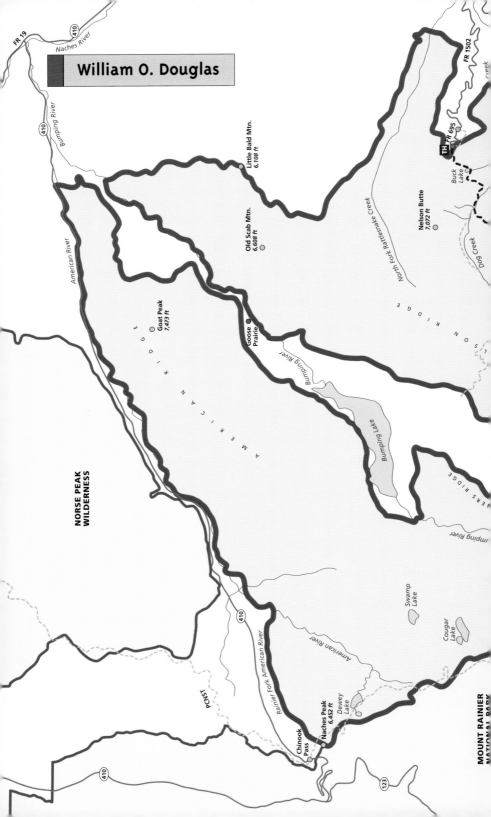

William O. Douglas

FR 19
410 Naches River

Bumping River

410

FR 1502
Creek

FR 695
TH
Buck Lake

Little Bald Mtn.
6,108 ft

Old Scab Mtn.
6,608 ft

North Fork Rattlesnake Creek

Nelson Butte
7,072 ft

Dog Creek

NELSON RIDGE

Goat Peak
7,473 ft

Goose Prairie

Bumping River

AMERICAN RIDGE

Bumping Lake

NORSE PEAK
WILDERNESS

Bumping River

RIDGE

Swamp Lake

Cougar Lake

American River

410

Rainier Fork American River

PCNST

Chinook Pass

Naches Peak
6,452 ft

Dewey Lake

MOUNT RAINIER
NATIONAL PARK

410

123

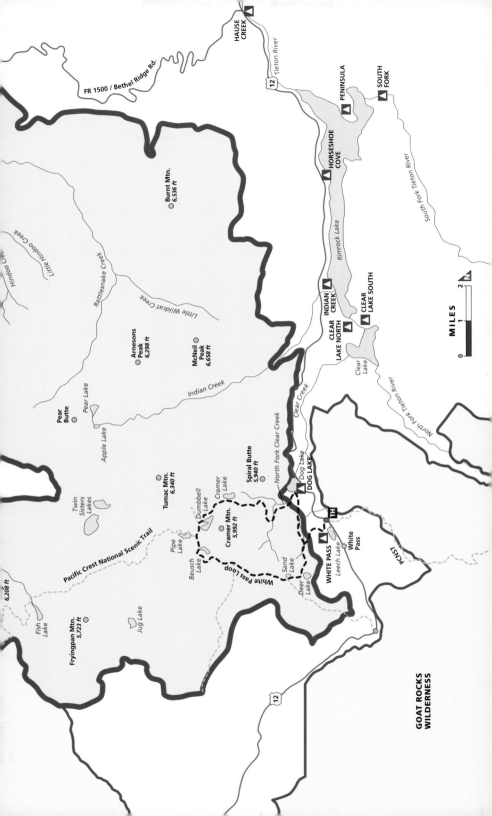

HAUSE
CREEK

Tieton River

FR 1500 / Bethel Ridge Rd.

12

PENINSULA

SOUTH
FORK

HORSESHOE
COVE

South Fork Tieton River

Burnt Mtn.
6,536 ft

Rimrock Lake

Little Hindoo Creek

Hindoo Creek

Rattlesnake Creek

Little Wildcat Creek

CLEAR
LAKE NORTH

INDIAN
CREEK

CLEAR
LAKE SOUTH

Arnesons
Peak
6,298 ft

McNeil
Peak
6,658 ft

Indian Creek

Clear Lake

North Fork Tieton River

Clear Creek

Pear Lake

Pear
Butte

Apple Lake

Dog Lake

DOG LAKE

12

MILES

0   1   2

Twin
Sisters
Lakes

Tumac Mtn.
6,340 ft

Spiral Butte
5,940 ft

North Fork Clear Creek

Dumbbell
Lake

Cramer
Lake

Pipe
Lake

Cramer Mtn.
5,992 ft

Pacific Crest National Scenic Trail

Beusch
Lake

White Pass Loop

Sand
Lake

WHITE PASS

Leech Lake

White
Pass

PCNST

6,208 ft

Fish
Lake

Jug Lake

Fryingpan Mtn.
5,723 ft

Deer
Lake

**GOAT ROCKS
WILDERNESS**

The author of the 1965 *A Wilderness Bill of Rights,* William O. Douglas was known for his conservation both as a Supreme Court justice and as an appreciative citizen, but this was something he came to learn. The land that now bears his name first gave him his physical strength and in time also gave him his spiritual strength. He lived at a time when nature or wilderness was seen as something to conquer and take. But Douglas learned through self-discovery, along with teachings from the East, that humanity was only a part of this cycle, a part that needed to be respected but also to show respect. Such teachings inspire love rather than fear of the wild. Eastern philosophy taught him that, rather than having evil connotations, wilderness can be an expression of universal harmony and unity. I believe all of us need to be reminded of this from time to time, and a visit to the William O. Douglas Wilderness will surely help you to do so.

> ### OVERNIGHT LOOP HIKE: WHITE PASS LOOP
> Total Distance: 12.9 miles
> Elevation Range: 4,400 to 5,700 feet
> Total Elevation Gain: 1,600 feet
> Difficulty: Easy
> Green Trails Map: White Pass No. 303

The hike begins on Pacific Crest Trail #2000, which heads up a few gradual switchbacks here before leveling out. Although the trail is under a canopy of trees, they are widely spaced and the understory is sparse, so the hike has an open feel. At the junction with Dark Meadows Trail #1107 at mile 1.2, the trail begins to climb moderately up to Deer Lake and on to Sand Lake at mile 2.6. At the Sand Lake Trail #60 junction the trail comes through a broad, open area around Sand Lake itself. The trail climbs from here a short distance, offering a view of Spiral Butte and Dog Lake before gradually descending into the Beusch, Pipe, and Dumbbell Lakes area. At mile 6.2 is the junction with Dumbbell Lake Trail #1156. Dumbbell Lake makes for a good overnight camp.

At mile 7.5 you reach the junction with Cramer Lake Trail #1106; continue on Trail #1106, an easy section of trail that leads through the trees before a descent at mile 8. You will have another overlook of Dog Lake, and will cross the North Fork Clear Creek. At mile 10.3 you reach Dark Meadows Trail #1107, as well as trail access to Dog Lake.

Dark Meadows Trail is neither dark nor lined with meadows, but it does maintain the pleasant, open forest feel with a few moderate uphill sections along the way. Rejoin the PCT at mile 11.7 for the final stretch back to White Pass Campground. Note that the trail sees heavy use from both hikers and equestrians given its accessibility, ease of hiking, and pleasant surroundings.

The trail begins from the White Pass Campground at Leech Lake off of US 12. The distance from Packwood is approximately 19 miles, the distance from Naches about 38 miles.

OVERNIGHT HIKE: MOUNT AIX
One-Way Distance: 7.1 miles
Elevation Range: 4,400 to 7,800 feet
Total Elevation Gain: 3,400 feet
Difficulty: Moderate to Strenuous
Green Trails Maps: Bumping Lake No. 271, Old Scab Mountain No. 272

As you face the registration box for this hike, the trail lies to the left. There is a sign for Mount Aix Trail #982, but it is mounted to a tree parallel to the trail, making it difficult to see when walking up to register. In any case, do *not* take the trail to the right that begins beyond the boulders that block the road. After 1.8 miles of hiking through a large stand of ponderosa pine, the trail loops around a point before descending to a crossing of Dog Creek at mile 2.3. The trail climbs steeply for 1.4 miles through a mix of fir and spruce. At mile 3.7, just before coming to and around another point, you will have the option of taking the trail that cuts uphill.

Following the lower trail, be sure to take the right fork at mile 4.8, just past an established hunters' camp. This section will seem faint, passing over rock and grass, but it will soon rejoin the upper trail, bearing to the left. At mile 5.5 you come to the junction with Lookout Trail #981A; continue to the right on the Mount Aix Trail. The trail will continue to climb out in the open for another 1.2 miles before reaching a benched area shielded with stands of whitebark pine. You can still take in beautiful views of Mount Stuart and other Cascade peaks to the north.

After another 0.4 mile up a rockslide from the benched area, you will pop out onto a ridge at mile 7.1 for marvelous views of peaks within the William O. Douglas and Goat Rocks Wilderness Areas, as well as Mount Adams to the south and the bluish, hump-shaped Mount St. Helens to the southwest. If energy abounds, push on another 0.4 mile to the next higher ridge (below Mount Aix) for the added bonus of views of Mount Rainier. The benched area below the rockslide makes for an excellent high camp, but you will need to pack water in the months after the snowpack has melted. This is a beautiful, arid, rocky, and rugged environment, offering a completely different experience than that on the west side of the wilderness area.

From Naches RD take US 12 west to WA 410, travel east 12.6 miles, then turn left onto signed Nile Road. At 14.1 miles turn left onto Bethel Ridge Road (FR 1500). At 21.9 miles continue straight on gravel FR 1502 toward McDaniel Lake. At 28.9 miles turn onto FR 695 for last, rocky 0.3 mile to the Mount Aix Trailhead.

Eastern Washington

The Eastern Washington region makes up more than 50 percent of the land in Washington but contains only 8 percent of the acreage of the state's official wilderness areas. The region lies east of the Cascade divide, framed by the Canada, Idaho, and Oregon borders and the Columbia River. The enormous heart of this region, edged by the Spokane, Snake, and Columbia Rivers, is a channeled scabland called the Columbia Plateau or Columbia Basin. Its topography is the result of volcanic basalt flows and deep cat-claw gouging from cataclysmic floods during the Ice Age.

The Eastern Washington region is farm country, a place where apple, apricot, cherry, and pear orchards in the Wenatchee Valley contrast with golden fields of wheat in every direction, from Ritzville to Pullman to the Tri-Cities. Hops, asparagus, and wine grapes grow from the Yakima Valley to the Walla Walla Valley, and pea and lentil farms thrive in the rich, loess hill country of the Palouse. The agrarian culture is still very much alive, vital, and necessary to sustaining the hundreds of small communities scattered north to south from Republic to Kennewick and west to east from Ellensburg to Pullman.

Much of the land in this region is private, occupied by the production of food for local consumption, statewide and interstate distribution, and export to Asia and Europe. National Forest land and the wilderness areas within them are concentrated in just a few areas here: in the eastern Cascades between Lake Chelan and the Twisp River Valley (Lake Chelan–Sawtooth Wilderness), managed primarily by the Wenatchee National Forest; in the southeastern corner of the state on the Oregon border in the Umatilla National Forest (Wenaha-Tucannon Wilderness); and in the northeastern corner near the Idaho and Canada borders in the Colville National Forest (Salmo-Priest Wilderness). The relatively limited amount of National Forest land in this region has kept the current number of wilderness areas to just four, although initial efforts are underway to protect a portion of the Kettle Range near Colville.

The fourth wilderness, Juniper Dunes, is the only one in the state, aside from the island areas, not located on National Forest land but instead administered by the Bureau of Land Management. It also is the odd duck of the state in that it contains only small concentrations of forest—entirely made up of western juniper trees—and its peaks and high points are windblown, grass- and flower-speckled sand dunes, not rocky ridges and mountaintops.

View of the Blue Mountains, Wenaha-Tucannon Wilderness

Water in the form of floods did its part to both sculpt and nourish the Eastern Washington region. The Ice Age floods from Lake Missoula carved away at the thick basalt flows with nearly unfathomably forceful blasts of water, leaving behind a channeled scabland and depositing finer sediments in a journey via the Columbia River to the Pacific Ocean. It was slack water backed up behind Wallula Gap, near present-day Pasco, that set the foundation for the formation of the Juniper Dunes.

The humpbacked Blue Mountains are bunched together and rise distinctly above the southeastern corner of the Walla Walla valley. Here you can hike open plateaus at 4,500 feet in the Wenaha-Tucannon Wilderness and gaze down into the steep-walled drainages, where dozens of creeks rush to their confluence with the Wenaha River to the south or the Tucannon to the north.

The proximity of the mountains east of Lake Chelan to the Central and North Cascade regions might warrant the inclusion of the Lake Chelan–Sawtooth Wilderness in one or the other of those regions. However, as it contains a forest mix consistent with wilderness areas east of the Cascade divide, receives considerably less precipitation than western Washington wilderness areas, and toes into the northern end of the Columbia Basin, Lake Chelan–Sawtooth can qualify for inclusion with in Eastern Washington. This wilderness area contains the tallest peaks in the region; a grand collection of high-mountain lakes, including Oval Lakes and the 51-mile-long Lake Chelan; and a spectacular high-line ridge run on the Summit Trail, complete with views of taller mountains in the Glacier Peak Wilderness to the west and in the Stephen T. Mather Wilderness to the north.

The Selkirk Mountains, like the Columbia River, originate in Canada. They are the first of the half-dozen Rocky Mountain–related ranges running in rows eastward, eventually reaching the run of the Canadian Rockies into Glacier National Park and continuing southward through Idaho, Montana, Wyoming, Colorado, and New Mexico. Unlike the Colorado Rockies, the Selkirks do not reach heights of 14,000 feet or draw thousands of visitors from around the world to hike summer meadows or ski winter slopes. But the Selkirks—built upon 500-million-year-old rock, some of the oldest in the state—offer solitude, brilliant meadows, open, grassy ridgelines like Crowell Ridge, and undisturbed forests over thousands of acres within the Salmo-Priest Wilderness.

Eastern Washington's wilderness areas are noticeably spread out, linked more by backroads than multilane highways. The adventurer in the east is afforded more frequent opportunities to commune with the landscape in greater solitude than is possible west of the Cascade divide.

Juniper Dunes Wilderness 29

Sand dunes

JUNIPER DUNES IS UNIQUE among wilderness areas in Washington, and one of the least visited. Located in a region of the state known more for wheat fields and a flourishing wine industry, Juniper Dunes Wilderness is a pleasant geologic and wildlife surprise. Water is responsible for its formation—in this case, the force of floods. As the continental ice sheet began to shrink some 12,000 to 10,000 years ago, ice dams formed along the Bitterroot Range, running north to south in the states of Idaho and Montana, more than 150 miles to the northeast of Juniper Dunes. Behind these ice dams formed massive lakes thousands of feet deep, including the well-known

LOCATION: Approximately 18 miles northeast of Pasco

SIZE: 7,140 acres

ELEVATION RANGE: 750 to 1,130 feet

MILES OF TRAIL: None designated

TREES AND PLANTS: Western juniper, aster, balsamroot, blue flax, knotweed, larkspur, prairie star, Russian thistle, wheatgrass, wild rye

WILDLIFE: Badger, bobcat, coyote, mule deer, kangaroo rat, porcupine, blackbird, bunting, ferruginous hawk, goshawk, great horned owl, Lewis's woodpecker, merlin, oriole, partridge, pheasant, quail, red-tailed hawk, Townsend's warbler

ADMINISTRATION: Bureau of Land Management, Spokane District, 509-536-1200

BEST SEASON: March 1 to May 31 (private land restrictions all other times)

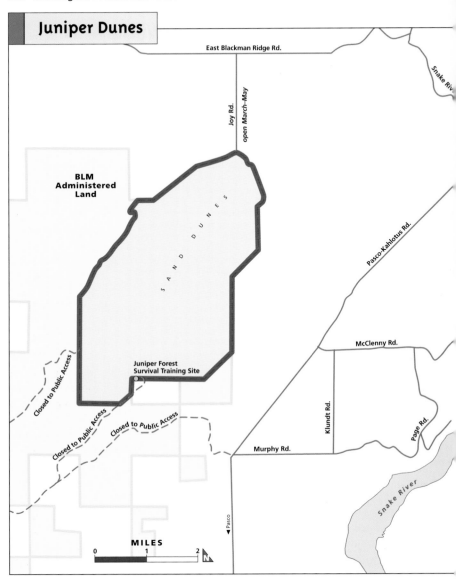

Lake Missoula, which covered an area of 500 cubic miles (equivalent to Lakes Erie and Ontario combined).

Standing today on a 100-foot-high dune at Juniper Dunes and looking northeast, a person can scarcely fathom the release of 500 cubic miles of water spread over the Columbia Plateau in a super-tsunami blast 2,000 feet high. The water backed up after trying to squeeze through Wallula Gap south of Juniper Dunes, creating floodplains thousands of square acres wide. Over a two-week period the water receded, running eventually via rivers such as the Snake into the Pacific-bound Columbia River.

During the fierce impact of the initial flooding the water tore away at the surface soil for hundreds of square miles, depositing it farther along in its course. These finer sediments were dumped into the present-day Juniper Dunes Wilderness. By the action of wind over time, the 7,100-acre dune environment—the feature that most defines this wilderness area—came to be. The second of many unique attributes of this wonderful place is the groves of western juniper trees, which represent the largest concentration in the state. The densest stand of these trees, which reach heights of 30 feet, can be found in the east-central portion of the wilderness.

Exposed to lashings by the elements, and containing no designated trails, Juniper Dunes is by no means sterile or capable of only supporting one species of flora like the western juniper tree. Numerous plants such as balsamroot, Russian thistle, blue flax, wild rye, phlox, and larkspur grow in healthy numbers in a climate that sees on average a meager 7 to 8 inches of rain annually, and a winter snowpack of barely 12 inches. You may also be surprised to know, and hopefully discover, the abundance of wildlife. Small creatures, including the pocket gopher, harvest mouse, deer mouse, and kangaroo rat, live with larger animals like mule deer, coyote, bobcat, badger, weasel, and skunk.

If Juniper Dunes had not been designated a wilderness area in 1984, it could have easily been proposed for bird-refuge status. Raptors such as the red-tailed hawk, Swainson's hawk, merlin, long-eared owl, and great horned owl make their home here. Game birds and year-round birds include quail, partridge, pheasant, magpie, and horned lark. Migratory and seasonal birds range from oriole to blue-bird, song sparrow to goshawk, Lewis's woodpecker to hummingbird. Juniper Dunes is also on the short list of wilderness areas in Washington that have significant reptile populations: skink, four species of lizard, and six species of snake, including rattlesnake.

The final unique aspect of Juniper Dunes is that it has no public access. But this is not because of wildlife-sanctuary status, as is the case with the Washington Islands off the west coast of the Olympic Peninsula; it just so happens that the two access roads leading to Juniper Dunes travel across private property. Fortunately, from March 1 to May 31 hikers have authorization to travel the roadway and park vehicles at the road's end on the northern access (Joy Road). From the parking area, pass through a gate and follow a 150-yard-long trail that cuts across a field and through another set of gates. A trail leads up a short hill into the wilderness area. The southern access, off of the Pasco-Kahlotus Road, is closed indefinitely to public access. Negotiations are currently underway between the BLM and the landowner to secure public access.

It may take some planning to get to Juniper Dunes, but it is not a wilderness to be denied. It should be celebrated for its beauty and uniqueness among its mountainous and forested siblings in the rest of Washington.

30 Lake Chelan–Sawtooth Wilderness

Kangaroo Ridge

FORMING THE WESTERN BOUNDARY of the Lake Chelan–Sawtooth Wilderness, Lake Chelan stretches for more than 50 miles at a maximum width of just 3 miles and a depth of some 1,500 feet, nearly a third of which is below sea level. Seemingly pressed along its entire shoreline are dramatically rugged mountains—a setting like no other lake in the Lower 48 in its diversity of climate and vegetation. The lake is also said to have some of the world's clearest and purest water because of its remoteness: Only a handful of people live beside it, mostly on a short stretch of its southern end. In fact the only access up Lake Chelan and into portions of the Lake Chelan–Sawtooth Wilderness is by boat, floatplane, or foot.

LOCATION: Between Lake Chelan and the Twisp River valley, and approximately 20 miles north-northwest of Chelan

SIZE: 151,435 acres

ELEVATION RANGE: 1,098 to 8,974 feet

MILES OF TRAIL: Approximately 194

TREES AND PLANTS: Douglas fir, Engelmann spruce, lodgepole pine, ponderosa pine, western larch, whitebark pine, anemone, arnica, baldhip rose, balsamroot, beargrass, huckleberry, snowberry, wheatgrass

WILDLIFE: Black bear, cougar, mountain goat, mule deer, bald eagle, goshawk, raven, red-shafted flicker, western grosbeak

ADMINISTRATION: Wenatchee NF, Chelan RD, 509-682-2576; Okanogan NF, Methow Valley RD, 509-996-4003; Methow Valley Visitor Center, 509-996-4000 (seasonal)

BEST SEASON: Summer through fall

Running southeast from Battle Mountain (northwest of Eagle Pass) into the southeast portion of the Sawtooth Roadless Area, Sawtooth Ridge is the backbone and host of the premier scenic path in the wilderness, the Summit Trail. Views here are as numerous as the drainages spilling down to Lake Chelan and the Twisp River valley. You can see nearby Martin Peak, Mount Bigelow, Oval Peak, and Sun Mountain; peaks in the Stephen T. Mather and Glacier Peak Wilderness Areas; as well as high-elevation overlooks of Lake Chelan.

The Summit Trail runs below Sawtooth Ridge, alternating between runs up to lower, open ridgelines above 7,000 feet and back into grass and wildflower basins. The southwestern slopes of the ridge pour down to the east shore of Lake Chelan through a range of life zones, from the highest points of beargrass, whitebark pine, and Engelmann spruce; through wild ginger, huckleberry, and mountain hemlock; and finally to the east Cascade dry-zone mix of balsamroot and ponderosa pine along the shoreline of Lake Chelan.

East of Sawtooth Ridge the slopes take a more lazy, swooping path but pass through similar life zones down to the U-shaped Twisp River valley, carved and sculpted by alpine glaciers over the last 2 million years. Running parallel to Sawtooth Ridge on the east side of the Twisp River valley are Abernathy and Canyon Creek Ridges. These constitute the western wall of the Wolf Creek drainage, whose head-waters originate in the vicinity of the near-9,000-foot peaks of North Gardner and Gardner Mountains in the far northeastern corner of the wilderness. The Wolf Creek trails, which terminate in the broad expanse of Gardner Meadows, are part of a collection of trails in the northern and northeastern portion of the Lake Chelan–Sawtooth Wilderness. The majority of the 194 miles of trail are concentrated in the southern portion, however. Access to the west side of Sawtooth Ridge is best by boat, and to the east side by FR 44, which runs up the Twisp River valley.

The lake's Euro-American history begins in 1870, when railroad engineer D. C. Linsley employed an Indian guide to paddle him in a canoe along the length of Lake Chelan. Looking for military routes over the Cascades, the U.S. Army began exploring the lake region by the 1880s, discovering gold and silver and creating a mining rush, as had happened in much of central and north-central Washington. This swelled the town of Stehekin (current population 72) to 2,000 people, who arrived to prospect, trade, and log. For over 30 years the Hotel Field, one of the grandest in the Pacific Northwest, operated at the head of the lake (see pp. 103–104).

A few years after the historic expedition of Lewis and Clark along the Columbia River to the south, an employee of the British North West Company, Alexander Ross, surveyed with the help of Indian guides the area at the north end of the Twisp River in 1814. This area would be the site of mining operations some 70 years later. Following Ross, various expeditions were undertaken to find road and railway routes across this formidable northern region of Washington, all unsuccessful. Even so, by the mid-1880s Abernathy Peak, Crescent Mountain, Gilbert Mountain, and Twisp Pass were all busy mining areas and remained so for the next 25 years.

The Purple Point Visitor Center in Stehekin offers information on hiking conditions for not only the Lake Chelan–Sawtooth Wilderness but also the Lake Chelan National Recreation Area and North Cascades National Park Complex. Tourist boats today on Lake Chelan are supplied by the Lake Chelan Boat Company, which has been in business since 1929. Tom Hackenmiller's book *Ladies of the Lake* recalls Lake Chelan's rich history of boating, including the use of steamboats to ferry tourists and hikers to the Hotel Field and Moore's Inn (flooded in 1948; burned in 1957) at Moore Point.

Moore Point and Prince Creek are two major stops that the ferry makes for hiker drop-offs, besides its regular stops at Field's Point, Lucerne, and Stehekin. Moore Point and Prince Creek drop-offs both lie along the 18-mile Lakeshore Trail.

DAY OR DESTINATION HIKE: SCATTER LAKE
One-Way Distance: 4.5 miles
Elevation Range: 3,250 to 7,047 feet
Total Elevation Gain: 3,797 feet
Difficulty: Moderate
Green Trails Map: Stehekin No. 82

From the parking area, follow the trail leaving from the east end by the sign-in box for 0.1 mile to reach Trail #427 to Scatter Lake. For the next 0.2 mile the trail follows an old roadbed before switchbacks head to the left onto a narrowing hiker's trail. The trail climbs up an arid slope of pine and fir, which years ago was subjected to fire. Across to the west is a prominent range that in the early fall hosts stands of yellowing larch near the ridgeline. Higher up, after a series of shorter then longer switchbacks, the trail begins at mile 2 to move above the Scatter Creek drainage into a denser forest setting.

At approximately mile 2.7 the trail comes closer to the creek, previously shielded by dense alder growth, in a subalpine zone of spruce and occasional aspen. The trail climbs steeply from here, working its way through a larch-filled basin at mile 4, then above the basin into a higher one at mile 4.5 that contains Scatter Lake.

The contrast of the gray and cinnamon talus slopes of the basin and Abernathy Peak to the north-northwest, combined with green conifers and yellowing larch trees in mid-September, all help to make Scatter Lake a fabulous lunch spot or overnight stay.

From Winthrop, take WA 20 south for about 8.5 miles toward Twisp, then turn right onto Twisp River Road (FR 44). The pavement comes to an end at 18.6 miles. Turn right at the sign for Scatter Creek Trailhead at 24.1 miles. The trailhead and parking area are about 0.1 mile up the road.

DESTINATION HIKE: OVAL LAKES

One-Way Distance: 9.4 miles

Elevation Range: 3,000 to 7,500 feet

Total Elevation Gain: 4,500 feet

Difficulty: Moderate

Green Trails Map: Buttermilk Butte No. 83

Eagle Creek Trail starts out on a wide swath, going from gentle to moderate as it climbs through an arid forest of predominantly ponderosa pine with an understory of thimbleberry and fireweed. The trail crosses over Eagle Creek at mile 1.7, working up a rib to a fork in the trail at mile 2.1; the left branch is Oval Lakes Trail #410A. The trail continues to climb steadily on gentle terrain alongside Oval Creek for 4 miles. At mile 6.1 the trail begins climbing more steeply up a series of alternating short and long switchbacks before reaching a subalpine setting of whitebark pine and larch, and the spur trail down to West Oval Lake at mile 7.4. It is 0.2 mile down to the beautiful, deep-green lake, which makes for a fantastic place to either lunch or overnight.

The trail to Middle and East Oval Lakes continues up a rocky gully and into a basin beneath the northeast, talus slope of Gray Peak. The trail continues through a grassy section and up a small rib decorated with larch trees before cutting across the talus slope toward a notch at mile 8.4 off the shoulder of Gray Peak to the east-southeast. From this point Middle and East Oval Lakes are visible below, surrounded by more larch trees and backdropped by Courtney Peak and Buttermilk Ridge. The trail down to the lakes is approximately 1 mile. You will find campsites by both lakes and plenty of exploring to do. Be sure to pop up to Sawtooth Ridge for an overlook of the western half of the Lake Chelan–Sawtooth Wilderness and, to the west, the mountain-congested Glacier Peak Wilderness.

From Winthrop, take WA 20 south for about 8.5 miles toward Twisp, then turn right onto Twisp River Road (FR 44). Drive another 16.5 miles to FR 4430; turn left toward War and Eagle Creeks. Approximately 0.4 mile from the last intersection turn left onto FR 4420 for Eagle Creek. Turn right onto FR 080 at 18.6 miles to reach the Eagle Creek Trailhead at 20 miles.

MULTIDAY HIKE: SUMMIT TRAIL (PRINCE CREEK TO STEHEKIN)
One-Way Distance: 33 miles
Elevation Range: 1,128 to 7,300 feet
Total Elevation Gain: 6,000 feet
Difficulty: Strenuous
Green Trails Maps: Stehekin No. 82, Buttermilk Butte No. 83,
Prince Creek No. 115

NOTE: Plan your boat schedule ahead, before starting on this hike.

The Prince Creek landing is just beyond a rocky floodplain less than 0.2 mile north of Prince Creek Trail #1255. The beginning of the hike is quite dry and moves through a recent burn. The trail climbs up a series of switchbacks alongside but above the north side of the Prince Creek drainage. Make sure to carry plenty of water later in the hiking season. It continues to climb beyond this section of switchbacks, contouring along the drainage in a dry, open environment with some nice vantage points of Lake Chelan as you gain higher ground.

At mile 3.3 the trail descends to a bridge crossing of Prince Creek, at mile 3.6. The trail then switchbacks before contouring along the south side of the drainage but not as high above Prince Creek. At mile 5.8 the trail crosses the Middle Fork Prince Creek and meets the junction with Trail #1254. Continue hiking on Trail #1254 toward Summit Trail. The trail crosses a creek at mile 6.2, climbs up a section of switchbacks with views back down the drainage, then reaches the junction with Summit Trail at mile 7.7. Head north (left) on Summit Trail toward Surprise Lake. The trail stays mostly in the trees, in a more subalpine setting, and crosses a good number of small creeks. Water is much more accessible here than in the section up Prince Creek. At mile 9.4 you reach the Surprise Lake junction, which is the most suitable area for the first night's camp, with ample campsites and water access.

To reach Surprise Lake, continue through a benched area into a grassy and boulder-strewn basin with some fantastic views of peaks to the southeast, then climb to an overlook of the lake. You will descend along the north side of the Surprise Lake basin, away from the lake, before reaching a junction. Bear left where the trail cuts back and makes a steep descent, passing through a camping area at the upper end of the basin and eventually reaching the west end of Surprise Lake, with more campsites, at 2.5 miles from the Summit Trail junction.

After returning up to the Surprise Lake–Summit Trail junction, continue on the Summit Trail as it winds and climbs through the trees in a northerly direction, reaching a small meadow-filled basin and ridgeline at mile 15.4 (this mileage includes the 5-mile Surprise Lake round-trip) with great views of Courtney, Gray, and Oval Peaks, among others, to the north and east. The trail descends into a basin, edging around and through a recent burn, wrapping around a point and down to a campsite at mile 17.6 before climbing to another ridgeline with incredible views again of the mountains and Lake Chelan. The trail stays on a

Continued on p. 230

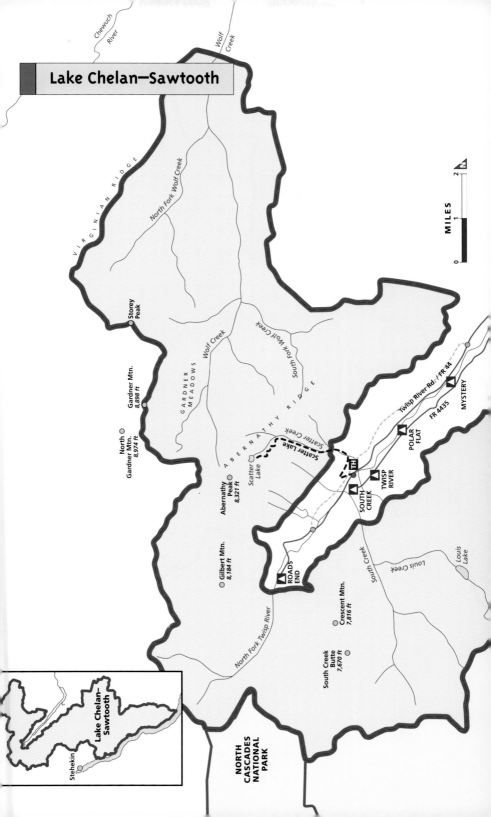

Lake Chelan–Sawtooth

Chewuch River

Wolf Creek

VIRGINIA RIDGE

North Fork Wolf Creek

Storey Peak

Gardner Mtn. 8,898 ft

North Gardner Mtn. 8,974 ft

GARDNER MEADOWS

Wolf Creek

South Fork Wolf Creek

ABERNATHY RIDGE

Scatter Creek

Abernathy Peak 8,321 ft

Scatter Lake

Scatter Creek

Gilbert Mtn. 8,184 ft

Twisp River Rd. / FR 44

FR 4435

MYSTERY

POLAR FLAT

TWISP RIVER

SOUTH CREEK

TH

ROADS END

North Fork Twisp River

Crescent Mtn. 7,816 ft

South Creek

Louis Creek

Louis Lake

South Creek Butte 7,670 ft

NORTH CASCADES NATIONAL PARK

MILES
0   1   2

Lake Chelan–Sawtooth

Stehekin

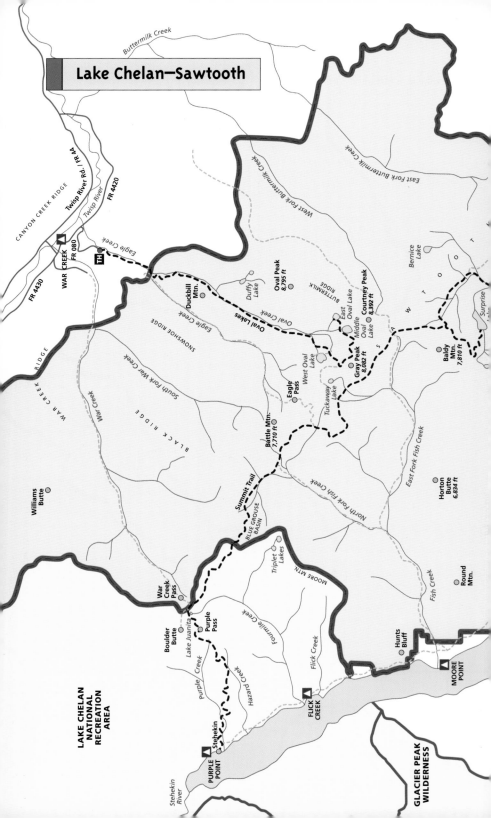

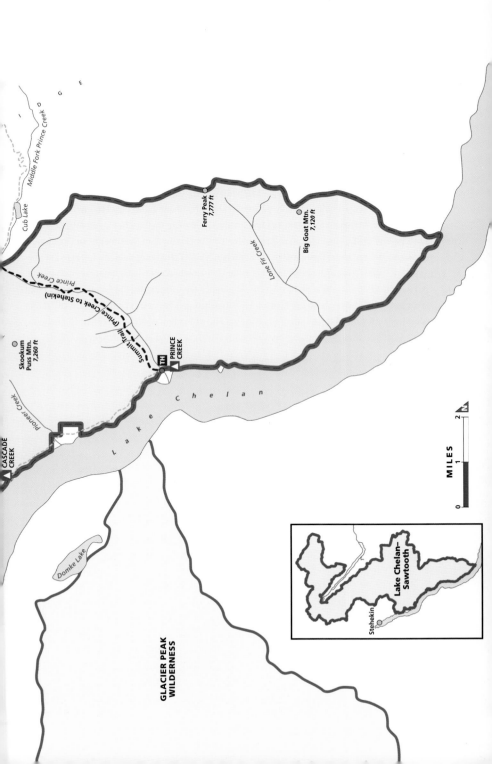

Middle Fork Prince Creek

Cub Lake

I D G E

Ferry Peak
7,777 ft

Big Goat Mtn.
7,120 ft

Lone Fir Creek

Prince Creek

Summit Trail (Prince Creek to Stehekin)

Skookum
Pass Mtn.
7,260 ft

PRINCE
CREEK

Pioneer Creek

L a k e   C h e l a n

CASCADE
CREEK

Domke Lake

GLACIER PEAK
WILDERNESS

MILES

0   1   2

Lake Chelan–
Sawtooth

Stehekin

high-line route for a short distance before dipping into another basin to meet the trail to Eagle Pass at mile 19.5, where you will find more campsites.

Beyond the Eagle Pass junction the trail continues to descend through the trees, reaching the Fish Creek Trail #1248 junction before beginning to climb at mile 21. The trail eventually moves out of the trees into an open, benched area, past another campsite, and onto a wide ridge. You will reach the entry into the Lake Chelan Recreation Area at mile 23.5. The views from the high points are again spectacular, including the peaks of the Glacier Peak Wilderness to the west, and McGregor Mountain and other massive and formidable peaks to the north in the Stephen T. Mather Wilderness.

The trail drops from the ridge onto an open slope, working its way across and then up to Lake Juanita, where there are campsites. You will reach the Purple Creek Trail junction at mile 25.5. The trail climbs easily up to Purple Pass before it begins its steep, corkscrewlike plunge to the shores of Lake Chelan and the town of Stehekin at mile 33. The descent is both a blessing and a curse, for with each switchback you come tantalizingly closer to the lake—but seemingly never close enough. When you finally arrive in Stehekin, catch the boat back to Chelan.

Leave the car behind for this hike; your only access is by boat or float-plane. An easy and economical way is to book passage on a boat via the Lake Chelan Boat Company for drop-off at the Prince Creek landing. The boat company has different schedules and costs depending on the season, itinerary, and class of boat. Contact Lake Chelan Boat Company at 509-682-2224 or www.ladyofthelake.com.

Sunset over Lake Chelan, Lake Chelan–Sawtooth Wilderness

Salmo-Priest Wilderness · 3I

Beargrass in bloom on Crowell Ridge

THE SHAPE OF THE Salmo-Priest Wilderness resembles two long lobes or, perhaps more appropriately, inverted spikes, falling between private land, national forest, roadless area, and the Canadian border. I don't mean railroad spikes used to fasten down steel rails, like those you may see leaving the old cement-manufacturing town of Metaline Falls, near the southwestern point of the wilderness. I mean the spikes you may be lucky enough to see on the antlers of the rare woodland caribou (less than 40 head) who make the Salmo-Priest their home. The Salmo-Priest is also one of the wettest regions in eastern Washington, with a rainforest-like environment that has fostered the growth of western red cedar trees for thousands of years. A

LOCATION: Far northeastern corner of Washington, at the Canada and Idaho borders and approximately 10 miles northeast of Metaline Falls

SIZE: 50,775 acres

ELEVATION RANGE: 2,600 to 7,309 feet

MILES OF TRAIL: 40 miles

TREES AND PLANTS: Douglas fir, Engelmann spruce, grand fir, larch, western hemlock, western red cedar, beargrass, bunchberry dogwood, fireweed, paintbrush, pearly everlasting, queen's cup bead lily, showy aster

WILDLIFE: Badger, bighorn sheep, black bear, bobcat, cougar, elk, gray wolf, grizzly bear, moose, mule deer, white-tailed deer, woodland caribou, goshawk, pileated woodpecker

ADMINISTRATION: Colville NF, Sullivan Lake RD, 509-446-7500

BEST SEASON: Summer through fall

Salmo-Priest

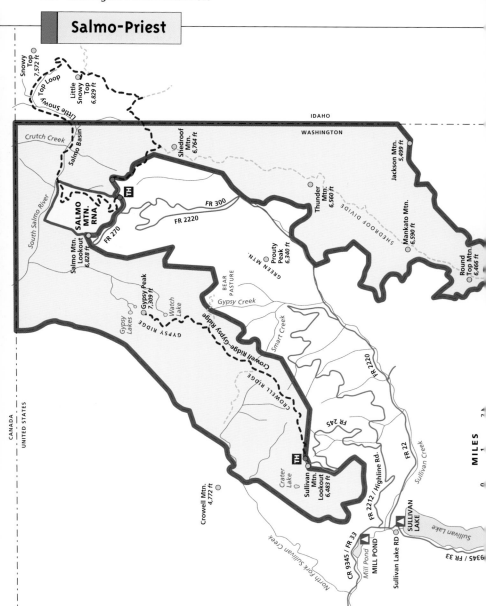

marsh in a roadless area just beyond the southwestern boundary contains common plants like wetland grasses and sedges but also nurtures sensitive plant species like crested shield fern, hoary willow, and black snake-root. Running northeast to southwest in both the western and eastern spikes you can find open, meadowed ridgelines, thoroughfares for still other rare creatures like the gray wolf and grizzly.

Crowell Ridge on the west side is more rock-encrusted and steep-sided than the shorter Shedroof Divide on the east side. With more rounded, wooded terrain, and punctuated with such distinctive mountains as Round Top, Thunder, and Shedroof, the east ridge also lies on some of the geologically oldest rock in Washington. Lateral creek drainages cut both sides of each ridge, feeding bigger creeks like Sullivan Creek and the Pend Oreille River to the west and Priest River to the east. The spikes, or ridgelines, are connected at the north end by an east-west ridgeline whose endpoints are the lookouts of Salmo Mountain in Washington and Little Snowy Top in Idaho.

Salmo-Priest contains just 40 miles of maintained trails, though many do cross into Idaho, adding additional miles. The most enjoyable and scenic paths include the high trails atop Crowell Ridge and Shedroof Divide, and a loop hike around Little Snowy Top in Idaho. At quite a distance from major population centers, the location of the wilderness has kept the number of visitors minimal. The benefits have been virgin forests of western red cedar, western hemlock, larch, and grand fir, which provide homes for rare species like woodland caribou, grizzly, and gray wolf, and more common animals like mule deer, cougar, badger, bighorn sheep, and moose. Elevations range between 2,600 feet and 7,309 feet at Gypsy Peak, along the north end of Crowell Ridge. Most prominent peaks measure between 6,500 and 6,800 feet. These mountains are part of the Selkirk Range that extends alongside Idaho's Purcells and into the more rugged summits of southern British Columbia. Don't be fooled into thinking that water is plentiful in this wet zone of eastern Washington—summers can be hot and dry. The Salmo-Priest is a place of both strength and fragility that has survived because people cared to preserve it for the sake of the natural cycles of life.

OVERNIGHT LOOP HIKE: SALMO BASIN–LITTLE SNOWY TOP LOOP
One-Way Distance: 13.8 miles
Elevation Range: 4,070 to 6,829 feet
Total Elevation Gain: 2,900 feet
Difficulty: Easy to moderate
USGS Maps: Salmo Mountain, WA; Continental Mountain, ID

Below and southeast of the Salmo Mountain Lookout, begin the hike by dropping into the Salmo Basin on Trail #506. Work through the trees, with a few glimpses of the Salmo Mountain Lookout early on, before losing 1,850 feet in elevation via switchbacks by the time you reach the crossing of the South Salmo River at mile 2.5. Campsites are available on both sides of the crossing.

Following along the river's north bank, the trail gains elevation gradually, crossing over Crutch Creek at mile 3.3 and coming to a trail junction with signs indicating directions for the Salmo River and Snowy Top. Follow the sign for Snowy Top, where the trail bends to the north and crosses into Idaho. The elevation gain continues to be gradual.

The trail crosses a creek shortly past the junction and stays in the trees before entering an open area at mile 5.3 beneath the southwestern slope of 7,572-foot Snowy Top. A short climb to a gap at mile 6.2 affords you a closer view of Snowy Top, as well as views of the mountainous geography unfolding to the east and north in Idaho, Montana, and British Columbia.

At mile 6.8, after a nice hike along a narrow, open ridge of beargrass and huckleberry, Trail #506 junctions with the Little Snowy Top Trail. A somewhat steep ascent of 0.4 mile will bring you to the summit and lookout. Enjoy higher views of the geography seen earlier, as well as Shedroof Divide, Crowell Ridge, and 7,309-foot Gypsy Peak, the high point of the wilderness, to the west-southwest.

The loop continues from the Little Snowy Top junction and past the junction with Trail #349 along a very pleasant, open slope just below the ridge. Enjoy more views to the east before you reach the Trail #315 junction at mile 9.1. Note that after passing Trail #349, Trail #506 has become Trail #512; be sure to take #512 toward Shedroof Mountain. From here the trail drops into a benched area and past a campsite with a water source, climbs out onto an open slope, and meets the junction with Trail #535 at mile 11.3.

Take Trail #535, which climbs above the junction onto a splendid open slope with views down both prominent ridgelines (Crowell and Shedroof) and the Sullivan Creek drainage separating the two, before entering the trees, passing by a trail junction, and dropping onto an abandoned Forest Service road that leads back to the trailhead at mile 13.8. Campsites exist along the South Salmo River, on the summit of Little Snowy Top (pack in water after the snowpack has melted), and in the benched area below the junction of Trails #512 and #315.

From Sullivan Lake RD, take FR 33 north 0.4 mile to FR 22 and turn right (east), following the sign for Salmo Mountain. At about 6 miles the road splits; follow the left fork, now FR 2220, still in the direction of Salmo Mountain. The road climbs up to Salmo Pass and bends to the right (east) to reach the Salmo Basin Trail junction at 19 miles (a left at the pass would take you to the Salmo Mountain Lookout).

DAY OR DESTINATION HIKE: CROWELL RIDGE–GYPSY RIDGE
One-Way Distance: 7.8 miles
Elevation Range: 6,200 to 6,800 feet
Total Elevation Gain: 800 feet
Difficulty: Moderate
USGS Map: Gypsy Peak

This hike is a bit of a roller-coaster ride at the start as the trail scoots around, over, and between various high points along the southern end of Crowell Ridge in a mixed environment of open forest and open ridge or slope. Be sure to pack enough water on this hike; there are no easily accessible water sources until Watch Lake.

The up-and-down course lasts for 2.3 miles before the trail eases up to take a more level route for 0.5 mile. From here it climbs moderately to the North Fork Sullivan Creek Trail junction at mile 3.3. You can find campsites at the junction, but the only accessible water source is from a spring or from Smart Creek, in a basin to the east some 400 vertical feet below.

Continue on Crowell Ridge Trail toward Bear Pasture in a more open and rocky environment but still in the company of plenty of beargrass, huckleberry, and whortleberry. Enjoy great views to the west and east, including views of Round Top, Thunder, Shedroof, and Little Snowy Top along the Shedroof Divide. At mile 5.5, just before the trail turns to the east and begins the descent to the Bear Pasture trailhead (if you reach a switchback after descending about 0.1 mile from the ridge, you have gone too far), you have the option of continuing cross-country on to Watch Lake and Gypsy Peak along Gypsy Ridge. For those not continuing on, this is a good turnaround point. The cross-country route isn't strenuous or difficult to follow, however a more detailed map (USGS Gypsy Peak) and compass are highly recommended.

Leave the trail heading northwest and hike along the natural incline of the ridge up to its high point at 6,617 feet. Descend its somewhat steep north slope to an open saddle. Keep an eye out for the boot path. Follow the saddle up a ridge toward another high point at 6,853 feet. Just as the ridge begins to climb more steeply up to the high point, contour to the right (northeast), rounding the high point back to the north and onto another open saddle.

From the saddle you will see a 7,177-foot high point nearby, directly to the north, and a farther 7,033-foot high point to the north-northwest approximately 0.5 mile away. Follow the saddle toward the near high point; before the trail begins to climb more steeply, angle cross-slope toward the distant high point. Pick as straight a line as possible, never losing or gaining much elevation. If you need to err, do it high. Another good habit to develop when hiking cross-country is to turn around frequently to see where you've come from and in this case to see if you're keeping a straight line.

This route will lead to yet another saddle, one containing trees, and an overlook of Watch Lake in a basin below. The big mountain to the north is Gypsy Peak. To reach Watch Lake, continue a short distance to the north on Gypsy Ridge to reach an easy descent to the lake, where you will find campsites. Gypsy Peak as well as the Gypsy Lakes are easily reached from here. The route to Watch Lake is approximately 2.3 miles from the point where you left the Crowell Ridge Trail.

This cross-country route basically follows the same patterns as does the trail along Crowell Ridge. A helpful thing to keep in mind when following this route is the order of the directions with regard to each of the four high points: over the 6,617, right of the 6,853, left of the 7,177, and right of the 7,033.

From the Sullivan Lake RD drive 0.8 mile on FR 33, cross a bridge, and turn right (east) onto Highline Road (FR 2212). At 4.3 miles turn left (north) by the sign for Sullivan Mountain Lookout onto FR 245. Follow the rough and bumpy road (with no less than 63 water bars) 7.3 miles to the trailhead at 11.6 miles. The road to the lookout is closed.

32 | Wenaha-Tucannon Wilderness

Buckwheat in bloom, Wenaha-Tucannon Wilderness

STACKED TOGETHER IN ROW AFTER ROW OF RIDGELINES, the Blue
Mountains seem to emit a heat-induced haze across the horizon in summer.
Forests of ponderosa pine rise from the deep and sheer canyons cutting
through the high plateau in a mazelike pattern, giving way to stands of
lodgepole pine, western larch, and Douglas fir at the 4,500-foot level, and
to subalpine fir at the highest points (5,000 to 6,400 feet). Summer hikes
through the Wenaha-Tucannon Wilderness can be unbearably hot. Many
trails follow the open, rounded, grassy ridges running mainly north to south,
which bake nicely in the near 90-degree daily highs, and there is not a single

LOCATION: Straddling the Washington and Oregon border south of Pomeroy and approximately 30 miles east-northeast of Walla Walla

SIZE: 177,465 acres (111,048 Washington; 66,417 Oregon)

ELEVATION RANGE: 1,700 to 6,387 feet

MILES OF TRAIL: 200

TREES AND PLANTS: Douglas fir, Engelmann spruce, grand fir, lodgepole pine, ponderosa pine, western white pine, balsamroot, bitterbrush, bluegrass, heartleaf arnica, sagebrush, scarlet paintbrush

WILDLIFE: Black bear, bobcat, cougar, coyote, elk, mule deer, snowshoe hare, white-tailed deer, blue grouse, chukar, downy woodpecker, golden eagle, quail, three-toed woodpecker

ADMINISTRATION: Umatilla NF, Pomeroy RD, 509-843-1891

BEST SEASON: Late spring through fall

lake or pond in the whole wilderness. Yet it is a landscape created in part by water and that thrives because of the life force of water.

The Wenaha-Tucannon Wilderness in the Umatilla National Forest comprises the majority of the northern Blue Mountains, which range from southeastern Washington into northeastern Oregon. The area is actually a high, volcanic plateau built up by layers of basalt that reach a thickness, at points, of nearly 5,000 feet. Over some 10 million years, water in the form of streams carved and sculpted the basalt, creating steep-walled drainages and canyons that differentiate the Wenaha-Tucannon from any other wilderness in Washington. Indeed, *umatilla* means "water rippling over sand."

The winter snowpack feeds more than 40 creeks and springs here, which flow through the canyons and then into two major rivers, the Tucannon in the north and the much wilder Wenaha to the south (on the Oregon side). As dry as the wilderness may seem in summer, there is enough water to support hundreds of species of plants, trees, fish, and wildlife. Groundcover varies with elevation and aspect but includes such species as bluebunch wheatgrass, lupine, queen's cup bead lily, sagebrush, and scarlet paintbrush. Forests are made up of ponderosa pine, western larch, grand fir, white fir, Engelmann spruce, western white pine, Douglas fir, and subalpine fir.

In fact, the wilderness is something of a sportsman's paradise. Fishing has grown in popularity in the Wenaha-Tucannon, and anglers will find spring Chinook salmon, steelhead, rainbow trout, bull trout, Kokanee, and whitefish. White-tailed deer, black bear, mountain lion, Rocky Mountain bighorn sheep, turkey, ruffed grouse, and chukar are the most common mammals and birds of the wilderness.

Introduced into the area in the early twentieth century, Rocky Mountain elk continue to thrive in the Blue Mountains, and this population has become one of the largest concentrations of the species in the United States. Throughout the area's brief recorded human history, hunters have been the most frequent and abundant users of the Wenaha-Tucannon. This has especially been the case since the introduction and growth of the elk population. But with 200 miles of trails and a limited fall hunting season, hikers and backpackers have also discovered a diverse and deserving landscape in the remote Wenaha-Tucannon Wilderness.

Wenaha-Tucannon

Dayton

North Fork Touchet River

North Fork Touchet River Rd./CR 9115

FR 64

FR 46

GODMAN

FR 300

TWIN BUTTES
5,674 ft

TH

TH
Slick Ear

WASHINGTON
OREGON

INDIAN

DEXTER RIDGE

Slick Ear Creek

Slick Ear-Grizzly Bear Ridge Loop

GRIZZLY BEAR

Rock Creek

FR 64

North Fork Wenaha River

Wenaha River

Wenaha
Forks

FR 65

FR 290

SQUAW
SPRING

South Fork Wenaha River

FR 62

FR 64

FR 6415

FR 6413

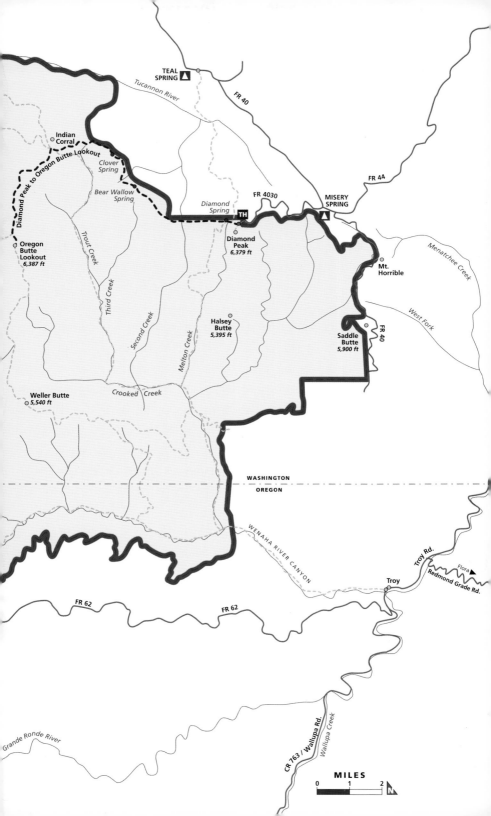

TEAL
SPRING

Tucannon River

FR 40

FR 44

Indian
Corral

Diamond Peak to Oregon Butte Lookout

Clover
Spring

Bear Wallow
Spring

Diamond
Spring

FR 4030

MISERY
SPRING

Oregon
Butte
Lookout
6,387 ft

TH

Diamond
Peak
6,379 ft

Menatchee Creek

Trout Creek

Third Creek

Second Creek

Melton Creek

Mt.
Horrible

West Fork

Halsey
Butte
5,395 ft

Saddle
Butte
5,900 ft

FR 40

Weller Butte
5,540 ft

Crooked Creek

WASHINGTON

OREGON

WENAHA RIVER CANYON

Troy Rd.

Flora

Troy

Redmond Grade Rd.

FR 62

FR 62

Grande Ronde River

CR 763 / Wallupa Rd.

Wallupa Creek

MILES

0   1   2

> **DESTINATION HIKE:** DIAMOND PEAK TO
> OREGON BUTTE LOOKOUT
> One-Way distance: 9.6 miles
> Elevation Range: 5,700 to 6,387 feet
> Total Elevation Gain: 700 feet
> Difficulty: Easy
> USGS Maps: Diamond Peak, Oregon Butte

Saddle Butte and Halsey Butte are visible to the south and southwest, respectively, from the parking area of the Mount Misery Trailhead, the starting point for this hike. Head uphill from the parking lot, passing a spur trail to 6,379-foot Diamond Peak at 0.4 mile. At 0.6 mile the trail breaks from the trees into a dry, open section at a trail junction. Continue straight as the trail dips down into the trees to another junction at Diamond Spring. Bear to the right toward Teepee, making a short climb to reach another open area that marks the beginning of the easy glide around the rim of numerous drainages on the way to Oregon Butte.

For the next few miles the trail alternates between dry meadows stippled with wildflowers and sections of forest. Enjoy great views across the Wenaha-Tucannon of numerous drainages and eventually of the 6,387-foot Oregon Butte Lookout. At mile 3.9 you will reach Bear Wallow Spring, where there is a campsite. At mile 4.6 you come to Clover Spring, distinguishable by the water trough cut from a log. At this point you begin a nearly 2-mile stretch through an open corridor with just a few short sections of trees. The combination of wind and poor soil moisture retention prevents significant growth of trees here.

From the trough bear left; the trail heading up and into the trees goes to a campsite. Begin a pleasant stroll through the grass corridor. At mile 6.2 is the Indian Corral Trail junction; take the trail that cuts hard to the left toward Teepee. At mile 6.4 the trail splits around an island of trees. Take the right fork, which reaches another section of trees in 0.2 mile.

At mile 8 the trail begins a moderate climb to the Weller Butte Trail junction at mile 9.1. Head uphill toward Weller Butte, passing a campsite en route. Continue onto a lovely open ridge leading to the Oregon Butte Lookout at mile 9.6. Built in 1931, the lookout is still active, and views from it include Twin Buttes to the southwest, Diamond Peak to the east, Kamiak and Steptoe Buttes way to the north, and—if visibility is clear and the lighting is right—Mounts Adams and Rainier far to the west. Be prepared for exposure to sun, rain, wind, and snow given the large amount of time you will spend in open areas.

From Pomeroy RD travel east on US 12 for 1 mile, then turn right onto 15th Street at the sign for Umatilla National Forest. The road is paved for the next 15.8 miles before turning to gravel; now you are officially on FR 40. At 32.6 miles turn right onto rough FR 4030 toward Mount Misery Trail #3113. You will reach the trailhead at 38.2 miles.

DAY OR OVERNIGHT HIKE: SLICK EAR–GRIZZLY BEAR RIDGE LOOP

Total Distance: 15.9 miles
Elevation Range: 2,520 to 5,400 feet
Total Elevation Gain: 2,880 feet
Difficulty: Moderate
USGS Map: Wenaha Forks

This hike begins at one trailhead and ends at another, so be prepared to arrange a vehicle or bicycle shuttle for the 2-mile difference, or just walk it. Starting from Slick Ear Trailhead, the hike passes through a gateway of trees before reaching the crest of a ridge in the classic open, dry meadows of the Wenaha-Tucannon. The trail drops gradually through here, passing ponderosa pine and even some western juniper, and crosses into the state of Oregon before reaching a short series of switchbacks that wind into the Slick Ear drainage. The trail follows the course of Slick Ear Creek through a predominantly fir forest along a brushed-in trail, crossing the creek five separate times. After the fifth crossing the trail meets the Dexter Ridge Trail in less than 0.1 mile. Turn left and hike less than 0.2 mile to the trail junction with the Wenaha River Trail at mile 5.2; head east (left), which is downriver. Campsites lie at various points over the next 0.7 mile.

At mile 5.9 the trail climbs above the river, occasionally dipping even with the river but never edging close to it. This high route is very pleasant, offering views of a ridge across the river and of the river itself. This rocky 2.5-mile stretch passes through some brushed-in sections.

At mile 8.4 the loop hike turns uphill (north), now on the Grizzly Bear Ridge Trail. The first section stays along Rock Creek before climbing a series of long, swinging switchbacks high above the Wenaha River. At the final switchback the trail climbs a steep slope through a grassy section before the grade lessens. From here it passes through the trees and up a grassy corridor before looping over a ridgetop onto its west slope, with views of Dexter Ridge to the west. The last 2 miles stay mainly in the trees, with a couple breaks into open, dry meadows. The last mile, back under the cover of trees, follows an old roadbed to the Grizzly Bear Ridge Trailhead at mile 15.9.

From Dayton on US 12, turn onto the North Fork Touchet River Road (CR 9115) at the sign for Bluewood Ski Resort. At 14 miles the road surface changes to gravel. The road will also have changed to FR 64. At 24.2 miles turn left (east) onto FR 46. Travel approximately 4 miles to FR 300 and turn right (the sign for FR 300 is in 20 yards and faded). At 4.9 miles the road splits, Grizzly Bear Ridge Trailhead to the left and Slick Ear Trailhead to the right. It is 0.3 mile to the Grizzly Bear Ridge and 1.7 miles to Slick Ear. On the way to the Slick Ear Trailhead, make sure to take the road to the left at the junction 1.4 miles up.

Appendix A: Wilderness Area Facts

Total Wilderness Areas in Washington: 4,324,182 acres (9.5 percent of state)

Bureau of Land Management Wilderness Areas

NAME	ACREAGE	YEAR DESIGNATED
Juniper Dunes	7,140	1984

Fish and Wildlife Service Wilderness Areas

NAME	ACREAGE	YEAR DESIGNATED
San Juan	353	1976
Washington Islands	485	1970

National Forest Wilderness Areas

NAME	ACREAGE	YEAR DESIGNATED
Alpine Lakes	362,670	1976
Boulder River	48,674	1984
The Brothers	17,239	1984
Buckhorn	44,258	1984
Clearwater	14,374	1984
Colonel Bob	11,961	1984
Glacier Peak	572,338	1964, 1984
Glacier View	3,123	1984
Goat Rocks	108,279	1964, 1984
Henry M. Jackson	100,337	1984
Indian Heaven	20,960	1984
Lake Chelan–Sawtooth	151,435	1984
Mount Adams	46,626	1964, 1984
Mount Baker	117,528	1984
Mount St. Helens *	113,151	1982
Mount Skokomish	15,686	1984
Noisy-Diobsud	14,133	1984
Norse Peak	52,180	1984
Pasayten	530,031	1968, 1984
Salmo-Priest	50,775	1984
Tatoosh	15,750	1984
Trapper Creek	5,970	1984
Wenaha-Tucannon	177,465	1978
William O. Douglas	168,157	1984
Wonder Mountain	2,349	1984

National Park Service Wilderness Areas

NAME	ACREAGE	YEAR DESIGNATED
Mount Rainier †	235,612	1899
Olympic ‡	913,043	1938, 1953
Stephen T. Mather/North Cascades §	684,600	1968

* Mount St. Helens is officially a national volcanic monument, not a wilderness area, but does have wildland qualities.

† Mount Rainier National Park was established in 1899; 228,480 acres of the park were designated wilderness in 1988.

‡ Olympic National Park was established in 1938, and the coastal section was added in 1953; 865,066 acres were designated wilderness in 1988.

§ North Cascades National Park was established in 1968; the acreage listed is the total for the North Cascades National Park Complex, including non-wilderness acreage within the Lake Chelan and Ross Lake National Recreation Areas. In 1984, 634,614 acres of the complex were designated the Stephen T. Mather Wilderness.

Appendix B: Proposed and Prospective Wilderness Areas

PROPOSED WILDERNESS AREA

Current Name: **Wild Sky**
Location: North and east of Index, near Stevens Pass
Potential Acreage: 106,000 acres
Highlights: Includes four major, distinct regions:

1) **Ragged Ridge:** forests of western hemlock and silver fir, high lakes, and ridges.

2) **Lower North Fork Skykomish Valley:** lowland environment; thick older-growth forest, and healthy salmon spawning grounds.

3) **Eagle Rock:** rugged mountains like Gunn, Merchant, and Baring; high-mountain lakes like Eagle and Sunset; rarely visited by humans.

4) **Kelly Creek:** creek valleys including Meadow, Johnson, and Kelly; with meadows along open ridgelines.

Management: Mount Baker–Snoqualmie National Forest
Status: Introduced in both the U.S. House of Representatives and U.S. Senate
Further Information: Washington Wilderness Coalition, 206-633-1992 or www.wawild.org

PROSPECTIVE WILDERNESS AREAS (BY NATIONAL FOREST)

Name: **Colville National Forest**
Location: Northeastern Washington, where the arid lands of central Washington merge with the far western foothills of the Rocky Mountains
Total Acreage: Approximately 1.09 million acres   **Existing Wilderness:** 31,438 acres
Roadless Acreage: 188,631 acres inventoried; 344,167 acres uninventoried
Notes: Colville National Forest has the lowest percentage of congressionally designated wilderness of any national forest in the state. The **Kettle River Range** is one of the main migratory routes for wildlife between the Colville Indian Reservation and Canada. Several other roadless areas are adjacent to the existing Salmo-Priest Wilderness. Important roadless areas include **Abercrombie-Hooknose, Grassy Top Mountain,** and **Quartzite.** Known wildlife includes cougar, lynx, bobcat, black bear, fisher, pine marten, pileated woodpecker, northern goshawk, elk, mule and white-tailed deer, and the only remaining herd of woodland caribou in the lower 48 states.
Status: No current legislative wilderness proposal
Further Information: Kettle Range Conservation Group, 509-775-3454; www.kettlerange.org

Name: **Gifford Pinchot National Forest**
Location: Southwestern Washington, from Mount Rainier National Park in the north to almost the Columbia River in the south
Total Acreage: More than 1.36 million acres   **Existing Wilderness:** 179,194 acres
Roadless Acreage: 212,962 acres inventoried; 209,536 acres uninventoried
Notes: Gifford Pinchot National Forest is one of the most heavily roaded and logged forests in the Pacific Northwest. However, the **Dark Divide Roadless Area** remains intact and is one of the largest unprotected roadless areas in the state. Dark Divide consists of large stretches of unbroken old-growth forests; a high country of impressive crags and old volcanic formations on peaks like Snagtooth, Craggy, Badger, and Shark Rock; and vast, open meadows. Additionally, ecologically critical areas like **Sasquatch Corridor** and **Mount St. Helens** deserve special protective status.
Status: No current legislative wilderness proposal
Further Information: Washington Trails Association, 206-625-1367 or www.wta.org; Sierra Club Northwest Regional Office, 206-378-0114

Appendix B: continued

PROSPECTIVE WILDERNESS AREAS (BY NATIONAL FOREST)

Name: **Mount Baker–Snoqualmie National Forest**

Location: Western Washington, stretching from the Canadian border to the northern edge of Mount Rainier National Park

Total Acreage: More than 1.71 million acres   **Existing Wilderness:** 720,000 acres

Roadless Acreage: 441,813 acres inventoried; 223,706 acres uninventoried

Notes: Mount Baker–Snoqualmie National Forest, which borders five counties that contain more than 50 percent of the state's population, provides a wealth of recreational opportunities that are an important economic force in the region. Wildlands in the Mount Baker area that deserve permanent protection include **Church Mountain, Park Falls, Ruth Creek, Loomis Mountain, Sauk Mountain,** and **Shuksan Lake.** Plant and tree communities in these areas provide a variety of habitat for many species, including the spotted owl, bald eagle, American peregrine falcon, grizzly bear, and gray wolf.

Status: Except the **Wild Sky,** no current legislative wilderness proposal

Further Information: Washington Wilderness Coalition, 206-633-1992 or www.wawild.org

Name: **Okanogan National Forest**

Location: North-central Washington, in the Okanogan and Methow River valleys

Total Acreage: 1.69 million acres   **Existing Wilderness:** More than 627,000 acres

Roadless Acreage: 427,738 acres inventoried; 316,479 acres uninventoried

Notes: Okanogan National Forest manages most of the largest unprotected roadless area in Washington state, the **Sawtooth.** Other special road less areas include **Pasayten Rim, Liberty Mountain, Golden Horn, Jackson Creek, Long Swamp,** and **Tiffany Mountain.** The landscape is varied, with craggy peaks, lush, rolling meadows, and classic groves of old-growth ponderosa pine.

Status: No current legislative wilderness proposal

Further Information: Pacific Biodiversity Institute, 509-996-2490

Name: **Olympic National Forest**

Location: Olympic Peninsula, partially surrounding the Olympic National Park in western Washington

Total Acreage: 628,068 acres   **Existing Wilderness:** 87,218 acres

Roadless Acreage: 87,979 acres inventoried; 63,955 acres uninventoried

Notes: More than 76 percent of Olympic National Forest's ancient forests have been logged, leaving the landscape highly fragmented by roads and clear-cuts. Yet significant ancient forests and roadless areas remain, most being wildland extensions of the national park and wilderness areas that form the core of the Olympic Peninsula. These include **Sleepy Hollow, Dirty Face Ridge, Rugged Ridge,** and **South Quinault Ridge.** South Quinault Ridge has the most impressive ancient rainforest not already protected by wilderness designation in the lower 48 states. Huge Douglas fir and western red cedar trees are numerous, sometimes topping out at 300 feet and supporting diameters of 9 feet or more.

Status: No current legislative wilderness proposal

Further Information: Washington Wilderness Coalition, 206-633-1992 or www.wawild.org

Name: Umatilla National Fores
Location: Southeastern Washington (and northeastern Oregon)
Total Acreage: 310,742 acres   **Existing Wilderness:** 111,167 acres
Roadless Acreage: 85,068 acres inventoried; 48,583 acres uninventoried
Notes: Umatilla National Forest is special on account of its cool, moist forests, which are rare in eastern Washington. The **Wenaha-Tucannon Wilderness additions** support spring Chinook salmon, steelhead, and bull trout, deer, elk, and the only mountain mahogany trees in Washington—some more than 200 years old. The area contains natural springs and some of the largest known basalt flows.
Status: No current legislative wilderness proposal
Further Information: Sierra Club Inland Northwest Office, 509-456-8802

Name: Wenatchee National Forest
Location: Central Washington along the eastern side of the Cascade crest, from upper Lake Chelan in the north to the Yakama Indian Reservation in the south
Total Acreage: More than 2.19 million acres   **Existing Wilderness:** 845,905 acres
Roadless Acreage: 622,960 acres inventoried; 165,695 acres uninventoried
Notes: Wenatchee National Forest is the largest national forest in Washington state. It includes many spectacular, biologically and recreationally important roadless areas like the **Teanaway, Sawtooth** (partial), **Devil's Gulch,** and **Nason Ridge** roadless areas. Vegetation is diverse, ranging from sagebrush and ponderosa pine to higher-elevation alpine fir and huge fields of mountain huckleberry.
Status: No current legislative wilderness proposal
Further Information: Washington Wilderness Coalition, 206-633-1992 or www.wawild.org

WILD WASHINGTON CAMPAIGN

The information in this appendix was provided courtesy of the Wild Washington Campaign (www.wildwashington.org). Washington state wilderness advocates launched the Wild Washington Campaign to permanently protect the state's wilderness heritage. WWC is an alliance of conservation, recreation, angling, and other organizations working together to build the citizens' wilderness movement.

Appendix C: Addresses

The following are useful as contacts for specific and up-to-date information on hiking trails, access, permits, and conditions.

OLYMPIC PENINSULA

Hood Canal RD
PO Box 68, 150 N. Lake Cushman Road
Hoodsport, WA 98548
360-877-5254

Olympic National Park
600 E. Park Avenue
Port Angeles, WA 98362
360-565-3130

Olympic National Park
Mora RD
Forks, WA 98331
360-374-5460 (seasonal)

Quilcene RD
PO Box 280, 295142 Highway 101 South
Quilcene, WA 98376
360-765-2200

Quinault RD
PO Box 9, 353 South Shore Road
Quinault, WA 98575
360-288-2525

Washington Maritime NWR Complex
33 S. Barr Road
Port Angeles, WA 98362
360-457-8451

EASTERN WASHINGTON

BLM Spokane Office
1103 N. Fancher Road
Spokane, WA 99212
509-536-1200

Chelan RD
428 W. Woodin Avenue
Chelan, WA 98816
509-682-2576

Methow Valley RD
24 W. Chewuch Road
Winthrop, WA 98862
509-996-4003

Methow Valley Visitor Center
Building 49, Highway 20
Winthrop, WA 98862
509-996-4000 (seasonal)

Pomeroy RD
Route 1, Box 53F
Pomeroy, WA 99347
509-843-1891

Sullivan Lake RD
12461 Sullivan Lake Road
Metaline, WA 99153
509-446-7500

NORTH CASCADES

Chelan RD
428 W. Woodin Avenue
Chelan, WA 98816
509-682-2576

Glacier Public Service Center
542 Mt. Baker Highway
Glacier, WA 98244
360-599-2714

Methow Valley RD
24 W. Chewuch Road
Winthrop, WA 98862
509-996-4003

Methow Valley Visitor Center
Building 49, Highway 20
Winthrop, WA 98862
509-996-4000 (seasonal)

Mount Baker RD
810 State Highway 20
Sedro-Woolley, WA 98284
360-856-5700

North Cascades National Park
810 State Highway 20
Sedro-Woolley, WA 98284
360-856-5700

North Cascades Visitor Center
502 Newhalem Street
Newhalem, WA 98283-9725
206-386-4495

Tonasket RD
1 W. Winesap
Tonasket, WA 98855
509-486-2186

CENTRAL CASCADES

Chelan RD
428 W. Woodin Avenue
Chelan, WA 98816
509-682-2576

Cle Elum RD
803 W. Second Street
Cle Elum, WA 98922
509-674-4411

Darrington RD
1405 Emmens Street
Darrington, WA 98241
360-436-1155

Entiat RD
PO Box 476, 2108 Entiat Way
Entiat, WA 98822
509-784-1511

Lake Wenatchee RD
22976 State Highway 207
Leavenworth, WA 98826
509-763-3103

Leavenworth RD
600 Sherbourne Street
Leavenworth, WA 98826
509-548-6977

Mount Baker RD
810 State Highway 20
Sedro-Woolley, WA 98284
360-856-5700

North Bend RD
42404 SE North Bend Way
North Bend, WA 98045
425-888-1421

Skykomish RD
74920 NE Stevens Pass Highway
Skykomish, WA 98288
360-677-2414

Verlot Public Service Center
33515 Mountain Loop Highway
Granite Falls, WA 98252
360-691-7791 (weekends)

SOUTH CASCADES

Cowlitz Valley RD
PO Box 670, 10024 US Highway 12
Randle, WA 98377
360-497-1100

Enumclaw RD
450 Roosevelt Avenue East
Enumclaw, WA 98022
360-825-6585

Mount Adams RD
2455 State Highway 141
Trout Lake, WA 98650
509-395-3400

Mount Rainier National Park
Tahoma Woods, Star Route
Ashford, WA 98304-9751
360-569-2211

Mount Rainier National Park
Longmire Wilderness Information Center
360-569-4453 (seasonal)

Mount Rainier National Park
Wilkeson Wilderness Information Center
360-829-5127

Mount St. Helens
National Volcanic Monument
42218 NE Yale Bridge Road
Amboy, WA 98601
360-449-7800

Naches RD
10061 US Highway 12
Naches, WA 98937
509-653-2205

Appendix D: Recommended Reading and Internet Resources

BOOKS

Baker, Victor R. *Paleohydrology and Sedimentology of Lake Missoula Flooding in Eastern Washington*. Boulder, Colo.: Geological Society of America, 1973.

Carpenter, Cecelia Svinth. *Where the Waters Begin: The Traditional Nisqually Indian History of Mount Rainier*. Seattle: Northwest Interpretive Association, 1994.

Darvill, Fred T., Jr., M.D. *Stehekin: A Guide to the Enchanted Valley*. Mount Vernon, Wash.: Darvill Outdoor Publications, 1996.

Douglas, William O. *Go East, Young Man: The Early Years; The Autobiography of William O. Douglas*. New York: Random House, 1974.

————. *My Wilderness: The Pacific West*. Garden City, N.Y.: Doubleday, 1960.

Foxworthy, Bruce L., and Mary Hill. *Volcanic Eruptions of 1980 at Mount St. Helens: The First 100 Days*. U.S. Department of the Interior, Geological Survey. Washington, D.C.: United States Government Printing Office, 1982.

Friedman, Mitch, and Paul J. Lindholdt, eds. *Cascadia Wild: Protecting an International Ecosystem*. Bellingham, Wash.: Greater Ecosystem Alliance, 1993.

Gulick, Bill. *A Traveler's History of Washington: A Roadside Historical Guide*. Caldwell, Idaho: Caxton Printers, 1996.

Hackenmiller, Tom. *Ladies of the Lake*. Manson, Wash.: Point Publishing, 1998.

Hardy, Martha. *Tatoosh*. New York: Macmillan, 1946. Reprint, Seattle: The Mountaineers, 1980.

Hazard, Joseph T. *Snow Sentinels of the Pacific Northwest*. Seattle: Lowman & Hanford, 1932.

Knibb, David. *Backyard Wilderness: The Alpine Lakes Story*. Seattle: The Mountaineers, 1982.

McNulty, Tim. *Olympic National Park: A Natural History Guide*. Boston: Houghton Mifflin, 1996.

McPhee, John. *Encounters with the Archdruid*. New York: Farrar, Strauss and Giroux, 1971.

Mueller, Marge, and Ted Mueller. *Exploring Washington's Wild Areas: A Guide for Hikers, Backpackers, Climbers, X-C Skiers & Paddlers*. Seattle: The Mountaineers, 1994.

Muir, John. *Steep Trails*. 1918. Reprint, with a foreword by Edward Hoagland, San Francisco: Sierra Club Books, 1994.

————. *The Wilderness World of John Muir*. Edited by Edwin Way Teale. Boston: Houghton Mifflin, 1954. Reprint, 1982.

Prochnau, William W., and Richard W. Larsen. *A Certain Democrat: Senator Henry M. Jackson; A Political Biography*. Englewood Cliffs, N.J.: Prentice-Hall, 1972.

Roe, Joann. *Stevens Pass: The Story of Railroading and Recreation in the North Cascades*. Seattle: The Mountaineers, 1995.

Schwartz, Susan H. *Nature in the Northwest: An Introduction to the Natural History and Ecology of the Northwestern United States from the Rockies to the Pacific*. Englewood Cliffs, N.J.: Prentice-Hall, 1983.

Smithson, Michael T., and Pat O'Hara. *Olympic: Ecosystems of the Peninsula*. Helena, Mont.: American and World Geographic Publishing, 1993.

Snyder, Gary. "The Etiquette of Freedom." In *The Gary Snyder Reader: Prose, Poetry, and Translations, 1952-1998*. Washington, D.C.: Counterpoint, 1999.

Tilling, Robert I. *Eruptions of Mount St. Helens: Past, Present, and Future*. U.S. Department of the Interior, Geological Survey. Washington, D.C.: United States Government Printing Office, 1990.

Williams, Chuck. *Mount St. Helens: A Changing Landscape*. Portland, Oreg.: Graphic Arts Center Publishing, 1980.

Wood, Robert L. *Trail Country: Olympic National Park*. Seattle: The Mountaineers, 1968.

Woodhouse, Philip R., with Robert L. Wood. *Monte Cristo*. Seattle: The Mountaineers, 1979.

INTERNET RESOURCES

Green Trails Maps
www.greentrailsmaps.com
Buy online from this Seattle company or view a list of retail outlets that carry these maps.

National Park Service
www.nps.gov/parks.html
Choose Mount Rainier, Olympic, North Cascades, or any other park/area under NPS management about which you'd like to learn more.

National Weather Service
www.nws.noaa.gov
This is the premier site for accessing weather conditions and forecasts.

National Wilderness Preservation System
www.wilderness.net/nwps
Click "Wilderness Maps" to see wilderness areas plotted on an interactive map of the state of Washington, or select specific areas from the national list of all 662 wilderness areas.

Patuxent Wildlife Research Center
www.pwrc.usgs.gov
This site has lots of interesting information on birds including a fairly comprehensive identification page with good photos.

USGS Cascade Range Volcanoes and Volcanics
http://vulcan.wr.usgs.gov/Volcanoes/Cascades
Learn everything you always wanted to know about volcanoes and enjoy great photos.

Wild Washington Campaign
www.wildwashington.org
An alliance of organizations working together to protect wilderness across the state.

Index

Kai Huschke

Kai Huschke has made the Northwest his home for the last 15 years. He has backcountry skied, backpacked, hiked, mountaineered, and rock-climbed in the mountains of British Columbia, Idaho, Montana, Oregon, and Washington. Kai's love of adventure has taken him on a 1,400-mile, solo bicycle trip across the northern United States. He also has worked in the Bering Sea as a commercial crab fisherman and in Montana as a lookout and wildland firefighter. Kai earned an MFA in creative writing from Eastern Washington University. He went through five pairs of shoes to complete this book. He currently lives in Idaho.

Charles Gurche

Charles Gurche is one of the country's foremost nature photographers. His large-format (4x5) images have appeared in such magazines as *Audubon, National Geographic,* and *Smithsonian* and in National Park Service publications. He has received awards from the Roger Tory Peterson Institute of Natural History, the Society of Professional Journalists, and the Nature's Best International Photography Awards. As sole photographer, Gurche has completed 70 calendars and 10 books, including four for Westcliffe Publishers, *Washington's San Juan Islands, Washington Wildflowers, Washington Reflections,* and the forthcoming *Washington's Best Wildflower Hikes.* He lives in Spokane. For print information, please e-mail charlesgurche@msn.com.